WHAT A GREAT IDEA!

2.0

WHAT A GREAT IDEA! 2.0

Unlocking Your Creativity in Business and in Life

2.0

 CHIC THOMPSON

Sterling Publishing Co., Inc
New York

Library of Congress Cataloging-in-Publication Data Available

2   4   6   8   10   9   7   5   3   1

Published by Sterling Publishing Co., Inc.
387 Park Avenue South, New York, NY 10016
© 2007 by Chic Thompson
Distributed in Canada by Sterling Publishing
c/o Canadian Manda Group, 165 Dufferin Street,
Toronto, Ontario, Canada M6K 3H6

Manufactured in the United States of America

Sterling ISBN-13: 978-1-4027-4188-3
ISBN-10: 1-4027-4188-X

For information about custom editions, special sales, premium and
corporate purchases, please contact Sterling Special Sales
Department at 800-805-5489 or specialsales@sterlingpub.com.

DEDICATION

To my first employer, Bill Gore, who challenged me to come up with a new use for Gore-Tex® every week.

To my childhood neighbor, Rube Goldberg, whose cartoons helped me see solutions from a different point of view.

To my younger brother, Larry Thompson, who usually got blamed for my childhood ideas that went wrong.

And, most important, to my parents, Larry and Eleanor Thompson, who supported my every act—creative and otherwise—with unconditional love.

C O N T E N T S

ACKNOWLEDGMENTS

My passion is helping clients, communities, and countries find creative and effective solutions for really tough challenges. I would therefore like to acknowledge our new virtual ideation team, www.impossibleproblems.com, which will take the creativity techniques in *What a Great Idea! 2.0* to new heights and to new audiences, and with new voices: Anna Belyaev, Type A Learning Agency; Kevin Carroll, Katalyst Consultancy; Rob Cross, The Network Roundtable at UVA; Rob Frohwein, Lava Group; Allison Hart, Bank of America; Jim Gilmore, Strategic Horizons; Carol Ann Kobza, Hallmark Cards; Kurt Ling; Craig McAndrews, Innovative Retail Group; Gary Muszynski, One World Music; Susan Patrick, North American Council for Online Learning; Aris Persidis, BioVista; Anil Rathi, IdeaCrossing; Becky Shambaugh, Shaumbaugh Leadership Group; Dr. Barry Silbaugh, American College of Physician Executives; Philippe Sommers, UVA Darden Business School; and Steve Van Valin, QVC.

Writing this book fostered a creative collaboration that I hope expands to many new projects. My editor, Meredith Peters Hale, was the perfect catalyst for this dyslexic writer. She crystallized my thoughts with such kindness. I only wish I had met her when I was struggling in college. Unfortunately, she hadn't been born yet. Copyeditor Diana Drew made many editorial improvements, and I am grateful for her role in this project.

Also a special thank-you to Ron Leishman and Steve Burgess for their excellent cartoons, which generate warm smiles and a few laughs in each chapter.

The Edison of Japan

Dr. Yoshiro NakaMats

Dr. Yoshiro NakaMats holds the record for inventions, according to the Guinness Book of World Records, with over 3,200 to his credit—three times that of his closest rival, Thomas Edison. Dr. NakaMats's inventions include the floppy disk, the CD, the DVD, the digital watch, Cinemascope, and the taxicab meter.

All of these accomplishments inspired me to consider interviewing Dr. NakaMats. However, when I realized that he came up with almost all these brainstorms while swimming underwater, I knew I had to personally meet this man and share our creative secrets.

The NakaMats method of invention involves diving underwater without an oxygen tank or snorkel and staying below the surface for as long as possible until an idea bubbles up. Upon resurfacing, he then writes down the idea on a dripping-wet Plexiglas tablet. When asked if all that underwater breathing was dangerous to his health, he said yes, but that dying was not part of his research.

NakaMats, doesn't mind being called eccentric. He is a graduate of the University of Tokyo and completed a doctorate program in engineering. Now seventy-eight years old, NakaMats refers to himself as a middle-aged man, thanks to his theory of longevity, which emphasizes equal attention to five basic elements: spirituality, food and drink, muscle training, sleep, and sex.

His most creative time is between midnight and 4 a.m., and then he gets four hours' sleep. NakaMats believes that if you sleep more than six hours in any twenty-four-hour period, your brainpower decreases. He eats only one meal a day—at dinner—with a maximum of seven hundred calories. He also photographs every dish he eats to recall the stimulating ones.

NakaMats doesn't drink or smoke, and does daily weight lifting and swimming. He is a big advocate of the twenty-minute power nap in the special Cerebrex chair that he, of course, invented.

He has appeared on American TV shows, such as *Lifestyles of the Rich and Famous* and *Late Night with David Letterman,* and has been given the distinctly American honor of throwing out the first pitch at a major league baseball game (in Pittsburgh).

NakaMats's inventive career started at five years old, when he came up with the idea for a landing stabilizer for his model airplane. A few years later he saw his mother struggling to pour kerosene out of a big container, so he devised an automatic pump. His mother was a schoolteacher and encouraged her son to build models of his inventions and then helped him apply for patents.

His biggest success came in 1950 when, as a student at the University of Tokyo, he manufactured the floppy disk. After six of Japan's leading corporations turned down his request to have them produce the floppy disk, he granted the sales license for the disk to IBM, which now holds the patents for sixteen of his inventions.

While studying or working on his inventions NakaMats usually listened to Beethoven's Fifth Symphony on 78 rpm records. He kept getting distracted by the hissing sounds from dust and popping sounds from scratches on the records. So he realized he had to create a higher quality recording device, and the CD was born.

NakaMats's latest project is a revolutionary house that is energy self-sufficient and has themed rooms that either relax or stimulate his mind. In his home, NakaMats uses three areas to spark his creativity. First, there is a "static room" with a rock garden and running water to provide a serene background for free thinking. Second, there is a "dynamic room" with special audiovisual equipment to play music to refine his ideas. Finally, he spends hours underwater each day in his pool jotting brainstorms down on his Plexiglas writing pad.

Dr. NakaMats's new home is filled with three hundred of his inventions and is dominated by a home-theater system with a two-hundred-inch (508cm) screen. The home also features white NakaMats floor tiles with special energy-regulating properties to keep the room's heating and cooling to a minimum.

Dr. NakaMats is also an idea promoter. He can be seen on Japanese television demonstrating his "Bouncing Shoes" to improve athletic performance or his "Perfect Putter" that is almost guaranteed to hit that little white golf ball into the hole.

There's a "techie" adage in Asia that the nail that stands up in Asia gets hammered down, while the nail that stands up in Silicon Valley drives a Ferrari and has stock options. Having developed a complete ideation process of freedom, expression, creation, and action, Dr. NakaMats is a nail that keeps standing taller with each new invention.

Now here is my interview with Dr. NakaMats, in which he describes his unique theories of creativity and freedom.

The Interview

NAKAMATS: In my country, the drive to succeed—and the competition—is unbelievably intense. From early on, Japanese children are under enormous pressure to learn. I was fortunate that my parents encouraged my natural curiosity, along with my academic learning from the very beginning. They gave me the freedom to create and invent—which I've been doing for as long as I can remember.

CHIC: What are the teaching methods used to prepare Japanese children for the strong competition they face? And how does this affect creativity?

NAKAMATS: One method is memorization. We teach our kids to memorize until the age of twenty, for we have discovered that the human brain needs memorization up to that point. Then young people can begin free-associating, putting everything together. That's how geniuses are formed. If a child doesn't learn how to memorize effectively, he doesn't reach his full potential.

CHIC: So you feel that creativity comes from a balance of regimentation and freedom?

NakaMats: Yes, and freedom is most important of all. Genius lies in developing complete and perfect freedom within a human being. Only then can a person come up with the best ideas.

Chic: We have a difficult time in this country because we don't allow ourselves that kind of freedom. We have what we call the Protestant work ethic that says, "If at first you don't succeed, try, try again." To me, trying too hard stifles creativity.

NakaMats: That's unfortunate. It's crucial to be able to find the time and the freedom to develop your best ideas.

Chic: Then tell me about your routine to spark creativity. I've heard that you come up with ideas underwater!

NakaMats: Yes, that's part of a three-step process. When developing ideas, the first rule is you have to be calm. So I've created what I call my "static" room. It's a place of peace and quiet. In this room, I only have natural things: a rock garden, natural running water, plants, a five-ton boulder from Kyoto. The walls are white. I can look out on the Tokyo skyline, but in the room there is no metal or concrete—only natural things like water, rock, and wood.

Chic: So you go into your "static" room to meditate?

NakaMats: No, just the opposite! I go into the room to free-associate. It's what you must do before meditating, before focusing on one thing. I just throw out ideas—I let my mind wander where it will.

Chic: I call that *naïve incubation*.

NakaMats: Yes, it's my time to let my mind be free. Then I go into my "dynamic" room, which is just the opposite of my "static" room. The "dynamic" room is dark, with black-and-white-striped walls, leather furniture, and special audio and video equipment. I've created speakers with frequencies between 12,000 and 40,000 hertz—which, you can imagine, are quite powerful. I start out listening to jazz, then change to what you call "easy listening," and always end with Beethoven's Fifth Symphony. For me, Beethoven's Fifth is good music for conclusions.

Chic: And finally you go to your swimming pool . . .

NakaMats: Exactly—the final stage. I have a special way of holding my breath and swimming underwater—that's when I come up with my best ideas. I've created a Plexiglas writing pad so that I can stay underwater and record these ideas.

CHIC: That seems to fit very well with the strategy I teach in my creativity workshops: Discover and use your "idea-friendly times."

NAKAMATS: Yes, but in doing this, you must prepare your body. You can only eat the best foods. You cannot drink alcohol.

CHIC: I've heard that you've come up with your own "brain food."

NAKAMATS: Yes, these are snacks I've invented, which I eat during the day. I've marketed them as Yummy Nutri Brain Food. They are very helpful to the brain's thinking process. They are a special mixture of dried shrimp, seaweed, cheese, yogurt, eel, eggs, beef, and chicken livers—all fortified with vitamins.

CHIC: How many people—technicians, researchers, and assistants—do you employ to help with your inventions?

NAKAMATS: In all, I have 110 employees.

CHIC: And what exactly do they do?

NAKAMATS: They work with my ideas, make prototypes, and give other assistance with details.

CHIC: Do you come up with ideas at night?

NAKAMATS: I come up with ideas anytime! I only sleep four hours a night.

CHIC: That's interesting—that's very similar to Thomas Edison. Do you take naps as he did?

NAKAMATS: Yes. Twice a day I take twenty-minute naps in a special chair I've designed—the Cerebrex chair. It improves memory, math skills, and creativity, and it can lower blood pressure, improve eyesight, and cure other ailments.

CHIC: How does the Cerebrex work?

NAKAMATS: Special sound frequencies pulse from footrest to headrest, stimulating blood circulation and increasing synaptic activity in the brain. Twenty minutes in my chair refreshes the brain as much as eight hours of sleep.

CHIC: So, like Edison, you're awake most of the time. Do you agree with Edison's claim that ideas are 1 percent inspiration and 99 percent perspiration?

NAKAMATS: No, now it's just the opposite! Now it's 1 percent perspiration and 99 percent "ikispiration." Now, more than ever, we have to have ikispiration. This means I encourage myself to go through my three elements of creation: *suji*—the theory of knowledge; *pika*—inspiration; and *iki*—practicality, feasibility, and marketability. In order to be successful, you must go through all three stages and make sure that your ideas stand up to all of them, which is *iki*spiration. Also, these days, the computer saves time and cuts out the 99 percent perspiration.

CHIC: Do you find that most research-and-development firms take themselves through your three stages?

NAKAMATS: Most are very thorough with *suji,* or theory, but don't concentrate on the *iki,* marketability. Hardest of all, of course, is *pika,* the creative inspiration. Researchers often have trouble with *pika* because they're too focused on one particular element. A genius must be a well-rounded person, familiar with many things—art, music, science, sports. He or she can't be restricted to only one field of expertise.

CHIC: Well, you certainly appear to practice what you preach. You know so much about music, about art, about sports.

NAKAMATS: That's what genius is, when you're able to discuss, and to be good at, many things. As much as I enjoy hearing about the things you [Chic] have invented during your chemistry career, about your teaching, about your video programs, I'm most fascinated by the fact that a person who can be a chemist and a teacher and a speaker can also be a cartoonist. And at such a young age!

CHIC: Well, people do kid me about looking young, but I could say the same thing about you.

NAKAMATS: That comes from eating the right foods and participating in the right athletics. Certain activities I believe aren't good for creativity. To be creative, you must have perfect freedom. I don't believe sports like jogging, tennis, and golf are conducive to the brain waves for creativity. Swimming is the perfect sport for freedom.

CHIC: Hmm. I know a lot of people who feel they come up with their ideas when they go out jogging. Maybe, for Americans, because we don't allow ourselves to have perfect freedom at work, we can get part of the way there by jogging or golfing—that's the only time we give ourselves permission to be free enough to come up with new ideas.

NAKAMATS: Maybe so, but they won't be your best ideas—you're not at your peak creative performance if you have to use athletics or techniques to get your ideas. It's only when you have perfect freedom that your best ideas come out.

CHIC: I'm very impressed by your openness to discuss this and your willingness to spend so many hours with me. So many people who have one or two good ideas don't share them with anyone. They're afraid that people are going to steal them.

NAKAMATS: My rationale is very simple: We need to open up the world. We need to share and interact. I always tell young inventors to forget about the money and create ideas out of love for benefiting mankind. Love is the mother of invention. And, by inventions, I don't just mean visible inventions. There are invisible inventions, too.

CHIC: Invisible inventions???

NAKAMATS: An invisible invention is something you can't see but you can use. It's a new way of teaching something, a new way to spark creativity in others. *Invisible* inventions are just as powerful and far-reaching—if not more so—than *visible* inventions.

CHIC: How empowering it is to consider a great classroom teacher as an invisible inventor!

Thank you, Dr. NakaMats, for such a wonderful afternoon. My brain is alive with *invisible* ideas and I hope that my sharing this interview will generate the love for mankind that I hear in your voice.

Dr. Yoshiro NakaMats's Web site is www.nakamats.com.

A goal of every living creature is to break out of the box.

Become the change you seek in the world.
—Mahatma Gandhi

INTRODUCTION

Break Out!

Key Steps Creative People Take

How ironic that in a world populated by "knowledge workers," there is virtually no time left to think.

—*Gary Hamel, author of* Leading the Revolution

This morning, while you are lathering up in the shower, sweating on the treadmill, or stuck in traffic, that little voice inside your head throws out a great idea. Your body gets excited and you ask your mind to remember it.

Unfortunately, by the time you get to your desk—poof!—the idea is gone. Then, like magic, your new idea pops back into your consciousness while you're doodling through a boring meeting. You quietly whisper your idea to the guy sitting next to you.

Within eight seconds he tells you what's wrong with it: "It's not in the budget," or "It'll never work," or "We tried that before." Your smile turns to a frown; you slump back in your seat—poof!—your idea is gone again.

Being a "knowledge worker" in today's environment requires persistence. Your day consists of multitasking your way through endless e-mails, instant messages, text messages, phone calls, voice mails, letters, interoffice memos, Post-it™ notes, and express mails. You spend twenty minutes looking for a phone number to place a two-minute call. Your intuitive thoughts happen a moment too late, instead of just in time. Sooner, rather than later, you're going to find your arms crossed, your teeth clenched, and your eyes staring blankly. Nothing works. Life seems unfair and your stomach is tightening its knot. Face it . . . you're "stuck."

On the other hand, you just think you are stuck. You are in a state that is not creative, and you are not readily able to find new alternatives or directions. You are probably trying too hard to get where you want to go. The good news is that you actually have several choices:

1. Do nothing and wait for the storm to pass.

2. Try even harder to break through the walls.

3. Step out of your own way to find a solution.

What's your choice?

1. Waiting is the most common decision. Are you waiting for things to slow down? Sorry. This seldom happens.

2. Conventional wisdom says, "If at first you don't succeed, try, try, try again." And with each try your voice gets louder and your patience gets shorter.

3. Stepping out of your own way is the easiest and most fun way to unstick yourself. Think of stepping out as a short sabbatical or detour rather than procrastination.

If you choose #3, this book is right for you. It is laid out as a four-step strategy to step out of your own way, to set goals and generate new ideas, and then to focus your resources to make the idea happen.

The new questions you'll learn to ask will help you reveal the answers you have been looking for. Simply put, in the mind-set of innovation, the question is the answer. It's the answer to entering a world of new ideas and breakthrough solutions.

The First Step: Freedom

The first step creative people take, whether or not they do it consciously, is to gain the inner freedom to consider new ideas and new possibilities.

The Second Step: Expression

One step beyond the freedom to consider new possibilities is the ability to give voice to the problems and questions that the new ideas will address.

The Third Step: Creation

Freedom and expression take you to the point of creation itself. Here's the heart of generating great ideas, here are the techniques, and here's much of the fun.

The Fourth Step: Action

Action is the most challenging step in the creative process. It's where our new idea meets the real world. It's where we need to believe enough in our idea and in ourself that a rejection or a suggested improvement doesn't short-circuit our energy.

We need to bring fresh and bold new thinking to all four steps of the innovation mind-set to give our ideas a chance to thrive in this competitive, attention-deficient environment.

The World Is Round . . . No, Flat . . .

Thomas Friedman wrote *The World Is Flat: A Brief History of the Twenty-first Century* so we would understand how today's world differs from that of our childhood. Our parents used to say, "Finish your dinner because people in India and China are starving." Now Friedman tells his daughters, "Finish your homework because people in India and China are starving for your jobs and in a flat world, the job is going to go to the most efficient, smartest, most effective person who can do that job."

Friedman describes the technological and social shifts that have leveled the economic world, and "created a flat world: a global, Web-enabled platform for multiple forms of sharing knowledge and work, irrespective of time, distance, geography, and, increasingly, language." He then points out that "on a flat earth, the most important attribute you can have is a creative imagination."

Indeed, to stay competitive today's companies and individuals will need to harness their creativity to come up with innovative ways to solve problems and create the products that will become the must-haves in tomorrow's marketplace. Outside the business world, everyone—authors, artists, students, inventors, designers—will also benefit from learning how to access and use the creative imagination Friedman describes.

Based on my own experiences, I see a greater emphasis being placed on creativity all over the "flat world." I receive almost as many requests to teach creativity workshops in Asia as I do in the United States. Around the world, people are recognizing the benefits of infusing technical know-how with imagination and vision.

A Creative Progression

As a teacher of creativity for more than twenty-five years, I have had the wonderful opportunity to teach, interview, and survey more than 500,000 executives in private and public organizations. My work has consisted largely of helping creative people learn universal ways of discovering and developing new ideas.

In my first book, the original edition of *What a Great Idea!,* published in 1991, I provided proven, yet flexible, techniques that can help any organization generate ideas immediately. *What a Great Idea!* went through twenty-one printings and was translated into six languages. In 2001, Harvard Business School released a case study on my speaking career with the same title: "What a Great Idea!"

Now, as a fellow at the University of Virginia's Darden Business School and an adjunct faculty member at the American College of Physician Executives, the YPO University (Young Presidents' Organization), and the Brookings Institution, my scope has broadened. These days I focus on designing creative strategies to reduce medical error–related deaths, fight terrorism, and reform our public school systems.

The call to update *What a Great Idea!* came from people attending my lectures and workshops, who were looking for ways to tap their creativity in the new millennium. So I went back to the *What a Great Idea!* manuscript and expanded on every chapter and, most important, added many new creative voices. New features include:

- An illustrated guide to fighting back against Killer Phrases to overcome the "Yes, *but* . . ."s in your life.

- Additional Great Idea Action Sheets to steer you through the idea-generation process.

- Fresh examples of innovation in the marketplace.

- New creative techniques to tap into your imagination and keep your brain alive and engaged.

- A nine-step Creative Action Plan to help solve any problem.

The Final Exam

Studying in school always led up to a final exam—and we all now know why it was called the "final exam." Because that was the last time that you would remember the answers to the test. We hadn't learned the lessons; we had just memorized the facts.

In *What a Great Idea! 2.0* there is no final exam. Instead, there are Great Idea Action Sheets, designed to encourage you to practice the idea-generating techniques and gain self-sufficiency in exploring the mind-set of innovation.

As you read through this book, I hope you become even more empowered to make creativity a conscious and powerful part of your life and work. By cultivating our creative freedom, we can all join more fully in the underlying innovation movement of this decade. We begin, as we will end, with recognition of the free human spirit, one of the greatest of the world's truly great ideas.

Enjoy the journey.

Smiling,

Chic Thompson

Charles Chic Thompson
Charlottesville, VA
chicthompson@whatagreatidea.com

FREEDOM

Between stimulus and response there is a space. In that space lies our freedom and power to choose our response. In our response lies our growth and our freedom.

—Deepak Chopra

Whether you put a pencil to paper, draw a brush across canvas, or bring a new idea to fruition, you demonstrate your creative capacity to express your freedom. Creativity is a feeling, a mental state. Freedom is a feeling as well.

Most of us have physical freedom, but achieving mental freedom takes personal responsibility. Achieving mental freedom is much more important than acquiring power, because, while power gives you a measure of control, freedom allows you to unleash power in unexpected ways.

The first step creative people take, whether or not they do it consciously, is to gain the inner freedom to consider new ideas and new possibilities. This step is rarely as easy as it sounds.

Embedded within many of us are obstacles to considering new horizons, particularly when these new vistas involve our own thoughts, our own dreams—our own potentially great ideas. Most of us need help to break the bonds we've placed around our own creativity.

Do It for Mickey!

As you start reading *What a Great Idea! 2.0*, I want you to break a long-ingrained pattern and move your watch from the wrist where you normally wear it to the other one. If you don't wear a watch, just move your cell phone or BlackBerry to the other hip.

Then every time you look at your wrong arm to tell the time, I want you to put a really big smile on your face. This will literally open up your mind to the creative strategies that I'm about to lay out for you.

I recommend that you do this switch every time you pick up this book, because your brain is looking forward to the mental exercise and the smiles. If you are now saying, "I'm not going to move my watch; it's fine just where it is," you are going to have a tougher time making the most of the strategies that I suggest here. I'll be patient if you'll be open-minded.

When I was with Disney and we wanted visitors to the theme park to do something they didn't want to do, we would say, "Do it for Mickey."

Please move your watch . . . for Mickey.

CHAPTER 1

The Second Right Answer

Unlearning the Rules of School

We entered school as question marks, but graduated as periods.
—Dr. John Holt, educator

We all started out creative. Remember the sandbox, with your bare toes and your plastic bucket?

Ask children in kindergarten if they like to sing, dance, or draw. All the hands go up. Ask a group of adults and only about 15 percent of the hands go up. Then someone will ask, "What kind of dancing?" or "Can I have two beers first?"

What happened in twenty-five years?

Most of us started school with a full box of sixty-four brightly colored crayons. The really lucky ones had the tin box of 128 colors with a sharpener on the side. But if we lived in a world of purple tree trunks and orange skies for too long, we probably began to hide our creativity.

Why? Because every year more of the colors and colorful wall hangings were taken out of the classroom. We graduated not with sixty-four colors but with two colors—black or blue inside a disposable Bic pen. We

3

hated the color red because when we saw it in writing, it meant we were wrong.

George Ainsworth Land, author of *Grow or Die,* gave five-year-olds a creativity test used by NASA to select innovative engineers. Ninety-eight percent of the children scored in the "highly creative" range. When these same children were retested at ten years old, only 30 percent were still rated "highly creative." By the age of fifteen, just 12 percent of them were ranked "highly creative."

What about the average adult population? Only 2 percent of the adults who took the NASA tests were rated as "highly creative."

Therefore, our lifetime creativity, measured in terms of our ability to generate a number of new ideas, is at its highest point at five years old and lowest around forty-four years old. It seems that creativity is not just learned, but *un*learned as we advance through life.

Your creativity does, however, start to rebound upon retirement. So what am I going to teach you in this book? *How to retire!* You'll learn how to retire from your challenges so that you can look at them with fresh, creative eyes. You'll learn how to unlearn those nagging, ingrained, judgmental rules from elementary school.

Asking "Why?"

Referring to George Land's study, at age five, we asked sixty-five questions a day; this number drops to a mere six questions a day at forty-four. And, as those of us with children know, a five-year-old's questions all start with *why*.

As children, we ask exploratory *whys*. As adults, when we ask *why*, it usually is framed in an accusatory tone, like "Why did you do that?" We spend most of our adult life just giving answers, with a few questions thrown in to sound as if we were listening.

Our lifetime responses can almost be stratified into three ages:

1. The age of "Why?"   Birth–5 years old

2. The age of "Why not?"   5–12 years old

3. The age of "Because!"   12–Retirement

Retirement, however, brings us full circle, giving us a chance to reexperience the joys of childhood, including indulging our creative impulses.

Based on work by the oncologist Dr. Carl Simonton, who introduced the concept that our state of mind could influence our health, our laughter level follows the same curve, dropping from 113 times a day as a child to eleven times a day as a "terminally serious" adult. Some of you are thinking, "Eleven times—*that's a lot*." Many of us know people in the negative numbers on laughter.

In figure 1-1 you'll see a chart I created that shows the relationship between age and the various aspects of creativity we're discussing. As you can see, our creativity bottoms out at age forty-four, right when our decision-making skills are being tested on a daily basis.

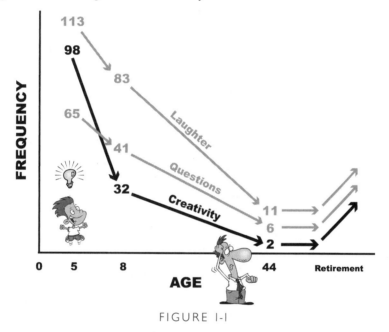

FIGURE 1-1

One of the reasons for these declines is that the experiences children seek out are the ones that we as adults avoid. Remember the old playground teeter-totter? If today's bureaucratic organizations took the form of a teeter-totter, they'd brace it on both ends to create a level playing field.

How boring. The reason you got on the teeter-totter was to experience the ups and downs.

Unlearning the Rules

Okay, we know that we all need to be more creative. We think that means devising new "creative solutions" for the challenges we face. However, Dr.

Jonas Salk, who developed the polio vaccine and helped rid the world of this blight, states:

> **The answer to any problem preexists. We need to ask**
> **the right question to reveal that answer.**

What an important insight. We don't find, create, or invent creative solutions; we reveal them. Therefore, our creative charge is to ask more creative questions that will uncover second and third right answers.

We also need to forget the obsolete answers. Your creative success will be determined by what you know *and* by what you can forget. "Unlearning" those school rules we grew up with may be the quickest way to a breakthrough idea. Here are some "rules of school" that may be holding you back:

1. There is only one right answer.

2. The teacher is always right.

3. The right answer is in the back of the Teacher's Edition.

4. Don't pass notes.

5. The answer is not on the ceiling.

If you were to take a person from one hundred years ago and put him on a street corner, he'd be blown away. But if you were to take that same person and put him in a classroom, within five minutes he would know exactly what's going on. That's because in many schools, it's the same chalkboard; it's the same book-based learning; it's the same directive to sit at your desk in a row and write down what the teacher is saying in the front of the room. In third grade, many of us dreamed of magically finding a copy of the Teacher's Edition so that we would have all the right answers.

These rules worked well in the industrial age, before the advent of information technology, when companies mined the land for their assets. Today, successful organizations mine our minds to extract the precious gems called *ideas*. To create an environment for idea harvesting, the rules definitely have changed:

1. Look for second and third right answers.

2. Challenge management and look for answers from all levels.

3. Constantly revise policy manuals.

4. Pass notes, collaborate, and appreciate diversity.

5. The answers still aren't on the ceiling, but if you look with creative eyes, the questions might be.

Finding the Second Right Answer

Einstein was once asked what the difference was between him and the average person. He said that if you asked the average person to find a needle in a haystack, she would stop when she found a needle. He, on the other hand, would tear through the entire haystack looking for all possible needles.

When we are confronted with a problem, we feel strong internal pressure to find a solution. When we are encouraged to find a second solution, the second answer is invariably more creative.

Einstein handed out his final exam to a second-year physics class and one student raised his hand and said, "This is the same exam you gave us last year." Einstein replied, "You are very observant, but the answers are different this year."

Plato said, "It is better to answer one question eight different ways than eight different questions one way." Leonardo da Vinci believed that the first way he looked at a problem was too biased toward his usual way of seeing things.

The challenges facing you on your desk and at home probably do not call for true-or-false answers. Let looking for second and third right answers become part of your job description and your family activities.

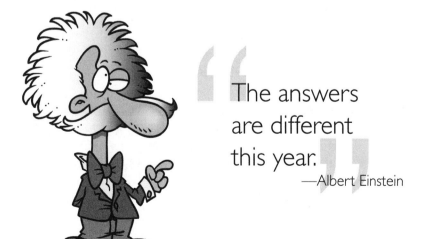

"The answers
are different
this year."
—Albert Einstein

THE SECOND RIGHT ANSWER

This exercise demonstrates the benefits of revisiting your challenges and looking for additional answers.

Count the number of squares you see in this graphic.

Your first answer: _____

Now, look for more: _____

Look one more time: _____

Your FINAL Answer: _____

Exercise Answer on Next Page (Please Don't Peek)

During a middle school talk using a laptop computer and PowerPoint slides, a nine-year-old student challenged me. He politely said that there are more than thirty squares, since the graphic is being viewed on a computer screen. Luckily, I asked the child what he saw, and he said he saw the square pixels that compose all the objects on the LCD screen. So based on your computer screen's resolution, the lines making up the graphic comprise millions of square pixels.

Curiosity in the Classroom

Remember how we used to learn vocabulary words? We memorized the spelling and then we had to write the word in a sentence. Two days after the test, we forgot the spelling because we had only memorized it.

I still remember the first time I was sent out of class into the hall. I couldn't spell *succinct,* much less use it in a sentence. So I went for cleverness and wrote, "The ship se-sinked in the se-sea." My buddies liked it. I also met the other "clever" kids out in the hall; sometimes I would act up just to visit them.

To my distinct pleasure, I recently watched a progressive fifth-grade teacher teach her class the word *curiosity*. The teacher asked the students to find as many words of two or more letters in the word *curiosity* as they could in three minutes. They could rearrange the letters and even spell words in foreign languages. The only rules were that spelling counts and you could not use a letter more than once except for the two "i's." They were to strive for quantity over quality.

> Class, *curiosity* is a big word with nine letters, and we are going to learn how to spell it and then define it.
> —Fifth-grade teacher

Now it's your turn. Grab a blank piece of paper and *go!*

The class came up with forty-three words. Then they were asked to create their own definition for *curiosity* by only using the words they came up with. They could use nothing else—just those words. The task sounds impossible—

Exercise Answer
Most see the sixteen individual squares first. Then they see the big outside 4 x 4 square. Then they see nine more 2 x 2 squares. Finally they see the four 3 x 3 squares for a total of thirty squares. The formula is $4^2 + 3^2 + 2^2 + 1^2 = 30$.

or at least like a waste of time—because there are few prepositions with which to make a meaningful sentence.

All the class teams then presented their lists of words and their sentence definitions. Here's my favorite definition for *curiosity* (and imagine it being sung as a rap song):

> *Yo . . . your story is crusty.*
> *Yo . . . your toy is rusty.*
> *So . . . stir your rut.*
> *So . . . tour your city.*
> *Rio is rosy.*

As I was applauding, I wondered if I could use this exercise to help my adult clients define an organizational culture of innovation. So I said to my next group:

> *Class, "leadership" is a big word with ten letters and I*
> *bet there are numerous words that can be made from*
> *those ten letters to help define leadership.*

The class found forty-seven words within the word *leadership* and my favorite definition, using only those words, was this: "Leaders help peers see ripe ideas." Needless to say, the class was jazzed and their brains were alive with curiosity and new insights into the ten-letter word *leadership*.

So the next time you need to define *communications* or *innovation* or *customer service* with your department, you'll know how to start the discussion!

Where Did the Smiles Go?

All the world loves babies—especially when they smile. According to one doctor I spoke to, babies, on average, smile seventy-five times a day. Where do the smiles go, as we grow older?

Just think! No matter where you go on this planet, your smile is your passport to the best of all human-to-human interactions. We're all different in so many ways: language, education, culture, and customs. But the one thing we do the same the world over is smile.

> " A smile is the shortest distance between two people. "
> —Victor Borge, entertainer

This is a good thing, because smiling does more for us than just push our cheeks out and show our teeth. A smile is a welcome. It's a reassurance. It's a flirtation. It's a job offer. It's acceptance. It's appeasement. It's an apology. It's the bridge from one soul to another.

Behavioral and physiological research has shown us for years that the smile is one of the most important tools in our personal success and survival kits. A smile can boost our self-confidence, help us achieve a state of serene creativity, nurture important relationships, enhance concentration, and combat those blue funks that periodically threaten to drag us down.

A full-face smile also integrates both hemispheres of our brain, which in turn increases our receptivity to new ideas. Next time you are stuck for an idea, try unfolding your arms and turning your "serious" face into a smiling face. You'll be amazed at how much more receptive conscious smiling makes you to the ideas of others and to your own musings.

Mother Teresa showed us a path to open up our acceptance to new ideas when she stated:

> *The smile is the beginning of love. If you can begin to smile naturally upon one another, you will begin to love one another naturally.*

The smile is the first step toward reaching out beyond ourselves and into the hearts of humanity. We all have the will and the ability to smile. And, in an instant, the decision to smile can transform our perceptions and our emotions. The emotions we select for ourselves can change our world in a heartbeat.

 **GREAT IDEA ACTIONS**

1. Before starting a brainstorming session, ask your participants, "What do we have to *un*learn to be truly successful at brainstorming today?"

2. Pick a problem that you have solved successfully. Then brainstorm a second and third solution to your solved problem. Compare all three solutions in terms of creativity, effectiveness, and ease of implementation.

3. The next time you are feeling a little blue, try smiling every thirty seconds, five times in a row. It works!

C H A P T E R 2

A Teaspoon of Baking Soda

The Nature of Creativity

Add one teaspoon of baking soda for each batch of two dozen cookies ...

One teaspoon, for heaven's sake. For two dozen cookies. Not a cup. Not half a cup. Not even a tablespoon. What a business to be in! Selling baking soda by the teaspoon. Not much future there. The box would just sit around on the shelf, next to the spices, until it . . . until it . . . until it began to smell like oregano?

Hey, the stuff absorbs odors!

And where in our lives could we use a little of this odor-absorbing ability of baking soda?

Car ashtrays . . .

Running shoes . . .

The cat's litter box . . .

Underarms . . .

The refrigerator . . .

The refrigerator! Baking soda in a refrigerator. The whole box, folks. Not just one measly teaspoon. Imagine what that great idea did for the sales of baking soda at Arm & Hammer!

From one teaspoon to the whole box. No, make that two boxes. One for the veggies and one for the ice cream. How about a box in my golf locker . . . We're on a roll.

We've just witnessed one of the most vital principles of creativity at work: The best way to get great ideas is to get *lots* of ideas. You can then toss the ones that miss the mark into an idea file waiting for a new problem to solve.

What is creativity? How do we come up with our ideas? What is the magic that can alter the way we use baking soda or revolutionize the way we communicate or transform our view of the world?

Creativity and the Idea Person

Although creativity is difficult to define, for our purposes let's put it this way:

> *Creativity is the ability to look at the same thing as everyone else but to see something different.*

Innovation is then turning those ideas into action. Here's a story of life-saving creativity and innovation.

Twenty-nine-year-old graphic designer Deborah Adler was having dinner with her parents and they were discussing how her grandmother had taken the wrong prescription medicine and been rushed to the hospital. She had taken the wrong medicine because her pill bottle and labeling looked just like her husband's pill bottle.

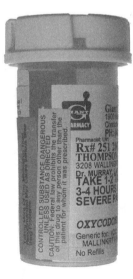

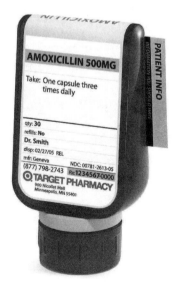

Deborah asked, "Why can't we create a safe pill bottle with large, easy-to-read labeling?" She created the prototype for the new Target pharmacy ClearRx pill bottle. As you can see on the previous page, the new bottles are "upside down," with the labeling flat and wrapped over the top so that there's more space for large type. The coolest feature is the color-coded ring at the base that acts like the color ring on an electric toothbrush designating the user. The new ClearRx has been a real success, and it's probably already saved lives. According to the Institute of Medicine, at least 1.5 million Americans are sickened, injured, or killed each year by errors in prescribing, dispensing, and taking medications.

So the Big Question is this: Why didn't this new design come from a pharmacist or a health care worker?

1. Are they too close to the situation, focusing exclusively on putting the right pills in the right bottle with the right label?

2. Had they suggested changes to the pill bottle in the past, only to have management tell them, "Yes, but we have 100,000 of these round pill bottles in stock?"

3. With the rising popularity of mail-order delivery of medications, have pharmacists stopped communicating with customers and learning about their problems?

There is probably some truth behind all these reasons.

So now, here's another Big Question: Is it because Idea People are just born that way?

Fortunately, that's a myth.

Creativity is not the exclusive domain of a few fortunate souls. Every person is creative, because creativity is one trait that makes us human. To be creative is to be able to perceive and recognize the world around us, to understand what we need or wish to do in response to it, and to set about changing it. To be creative is to find a way, a thought, an expression, a human manifestation no one else has found and to make newly discovered possibilities reality.

The Creative Process

How do we change the world? Just by coming up with great ideas? No, creativity is more than idea generation. The greatest idea on earth is worthless unless someone acts on it. Someone must evaluate the quality of the idea. Someone must take the idea and run with it. Someone must develop the necessary systems of people, machinery, finances, packaging, distribution, service, and marketing. Those systems need ongoing management. Idea People alone are not enough.

Creativity isn't so much a personality trait or a talent as it is a process, a continuum. From the beginning of an idea to its ultimate fruition, all along this line, a variety of people with different abilities and traits play vital roles. The Idea Generators give birth to the idea. The Idea Promoters see an array of applications of the idea and sets in motion the forces to try out the more promising ones. The Idea Systems Designer creates the organizations of people, machines, space, and money, and gets them rolling toward the goal. The Idea Implementers establish the routine tasks necessary for reaching that goal. And all along the way Idea Evaluators constantly question the quality and effectiveness of the way things work—and don't work.

Contemplate the process and you'll see yourself somewhere along this line:

Generation ➔ Promotion ➔ Design ➔ Implementation ➔ Evaluation.

You might excel in several of these areas. Or perhaps you primarily do your best work in just one. You might even shy away from some of the other functions. If you're an Idea Implementer, and particularly if you don't understand how your own creativity dovetails with the others, you might resent the Evaluator, envy the Generator, and barely tolerate the Promoter. If you're an Idea Generator, you'd probably rather run naked through the snow than implement the nitty-gritty details of your own idea.

So the Idea Generator is the one most of us call *creative*. The Idea Generator just has that knack of coming up with great ideas. But what about the Idea Promoter? The Designer? The Implementer? The Evaluator? Don't they have to be creative as well?

Indeed, won't each participant in this creative process be more creative by developing the characteristics of others in the process? Certainly, the Implementer who takes on the characteristics of the Generator will come up with some great ideas for the implementation process. And the Generator who understands the ins and outs of implementation will generate better, more workable ideas—ideas that are likely to be more efficient and more realistic.

I believe that people behind the most successful creative endeavors:

1. Recognize that all these types of people are necessary for successful creativity.

2. See themselves as they are and as other people most likely see them.

3. Try other creative styles on for size.

As you develop and mature, you need to see those areas in the creative process that naturally attract you and then try out skills needed in the other areas. You can flex and stretch your unused creative muscles. Once you do, you'll never be the same again. In the words of Oliver Wendell Holmes:

> *The human mind once stretched to a new idea never goes back to its original dimensions.*

Stretch the Balloon

To understand the words of Oliver Wendell Holmes, think back to the first time you tried to blow up a balloon. How old were you? Three, four, maybe five years old? You didn't have very good lung capacity at that age, so you couldn't get it started.

But then you intuitively stretched out the balloon with your hands. You tried blowing into the balloon again and finally had success. You ran around the room all excited until the balloon got away from you and flew across the room. You picked up the wet balloon and (without washing it off) put it right back in your mouth and blew it up again.

It was actually easier to blow it up this time, and it just kept getting easier each successive time you blew it up and it flew around the room. The question then is this: Why did it get easier? Here are a few explanations:

1. You built up confidence.

2. You stretched out the latex.

3. The latex stayed stretched after every flight.

For a balloon, being malleable is called having plasticity. Similarly, the term *neuroplasticity* is used to describe the effects of learning on the human brain. Because, just like the balloon, when our mind stretches to a new thought it never goes back to its original dimensions. Unfortunately, both the balloon and your brain will "snap back" to some extent after being stretched. So the key measure of how far your mind stretches is how strong a memory you retain about the experience.

Fifteen Minutes Ahead

This book will help you do some mind stretching to come up with great ideas. Ideas that are light-years ahead of their time? No. To borrow from Woody Allen, the best idea is fifteen minutes ahead of its time. Those that are light-years ahead often are ignored and certainly get delayed.

The copy machine was "light-years" ahead when Chester Carlson invented it in 1929 and Xerox introduced it in 1948. It took twenty more years, until 1968, to become essential to our offices. The office fax machine was "fifteen minutes" ahead and became a standard office fixture within two years.

CREATIVE FLUENCY

Let's play the game of creativity and measure your "baking soda creative fluency." This is your ability to come up with multiple uses for baking soda over a measured period of time. Take three minutes to write down as many uses as you can for baking soda. Let your mind blast away in divergent directions. This will boost your creative fluency potential—and you just might find a new use for that old box in your refrigerator. Remember: Quantity, not quality, wins.

Ready, set, go! (You've got three minutes.)

1.	11.	21.
2.	12.	22.
3.	13.	23.
4.	14.	24.
5.	15.	25.
6.	16.	26.
7.	17.	27.
8.	18.	28.
9.	19.	29.
10.	20.	30.

How'd you do: 9, 13, 21?

The individual record from my sessions is 107. The adult group record is 83 uses, held by a Hewlett-Packard sales force of seventy-four members. The school group record is 147 uses, held by a fifth-grade class of nineteen students in San Diego.

My favorite creative use for baking soda was submitted by a ten-year-old boy:

Mix the baking soda with vinegar. Gargle with it and pretend you have rabies on Halloween.

This child's response represents true creativity: It's a unique combination, it stretches our imagination, and, if this child goes into new product development, he just might invent the next breakthrough toothpaste or mouthwash.

"Google Brain"

I was invited to present a lesson for a fifth-grade class and all the students were wired with Apple laptops and wi-fi access. I decided to try an experiment. I divided the class into five teams of five students each. I gave all of them the baking soda exercise above as a team brainstorm and allowed them also to use their Internet searching skills to find uses for baking soda. They still had to abide by the three-minute time frame in coming up with a list of uses. I wanted to see if the Internet helped or hindered the normal dynamics in a team brainstorm.

The winning team found 541 uses because they found a book online called *Baking Soda: Over 500 Fabulous, Fun, and Frugal Uses.* They printed out the index, which listed all the uses. Other members of their team were concurrently brainstorming their own ideas. They were thrilled to come up with uses that even the authors hadn't thought of.

I offer one word of caution in using "Google brain": Don't rely exclusively on the Internet and neglect to consider your own knowledge and experiences. The Internet is meant to complement the workings of the 2½-pound computer between our ears.

How to Think Dyslexic

Recently, I was teaching a two-day "Creativity in Medical Management" course for the American College of Physician Executives. Midway through the course, after the discussion on using "opposite thinking" to come up with creative solutions (which we'll discuss later in this book), a doctor approached me and said, "You are teaching us how to think dyslexic."

I loved his insight and found out that, like me, he, too, was dyslexic. All my life, I've had this ability to see things differently—very differently. I read words in a different way. I see numbers in a different way. For that reason, I shied away from the written word in school and gravitated toward the spoken word. I couldn't deal very effectively with written words, so I became rather good at giving speeches. In grade school, for example, I ran for class president; when I gave my first campaign speech, my opponent bowed out of the race.

Because of this "handicap," I also gravitated toward pictorial depictions of situations, problems, and solutions to problems. I developed my artistic ability and became fairly adept at cartooning. At one time, I even worked for Walt Disney Productions. Mr. Disney was fond of saying: "It's always fun to do the impossible." I was fond of adding: "Because that's where there's less competition."

I had a falling-out with the powers at Disney in 1976 when I suggested that they consider putting some of their educational cartoons on videotape for sale and rental to schools and libraries. What a great idea that was! But the president of Disney at that time said, "We will never release our cartoon films on videotape. There's too great a danger of illegal copying." That same year, Disney sued Sony over the introduction of the Betamax videocassette recorder.

So I took my "impossible" idea and started my own firm, Creative Cartoon Company. That company developed some rather successful cartoon videos in the health field. My firm, for example, was the first on the market with a video about the dangers of AIDS. My first client was an innovative thoracic surgeon from Cincinnati named Dr. Henry Heimlich.

On reading about our success in the *Wall Street Journal,* the president of Encyclopedia Britannica Films asked me to put together a workshop for his staff on how we came up with the ideas for our videos and how we developed ideas to market them. Halfway into my presentation to the Britannica executives, one of the vice presidents shouted out, "We've just come up with more ideas to solve this problem than we've had in the last three months of endless meetings."

On the flight home, I realized that the creativity techniques that came so easily to me could be taught to others and, more important, *needed* to be taught to others. So I looked carefully at the ways creative people come up with ideas and began to compare them with my own techniques of idea generation. Slowly, over time, I began to develop a series of lectures on the nature of creativity itself, and found my services in demand for training programs at Du Pont, NASA, the Federal Executive Institute, the FBI Training Academy, General Electric, and a host of other companies and government agencies.

Now, after twenty years of teaching, over three thousand presentations, and teaming up with talent ranging from Tony Robbins and Stephen Covey to Cirque du Soleil and Second City, I can confidently say that great ideas don't belong just to creative giants; we all live in the forest of creativity, where great ideas are as natural and accessible as the sun. We just need to look around us and grab the great ideas that thrive in our midst.

 GREAT IDEA ACTIONS

1. Think of the new ClearRx pill bottle and the lives it is saving. What other products or services are in need of an extreme makeover? How can I help the world see them from a "fresh" perspective?

2. Where do you fall on the Generation ➔ Promotion ➔ Design ➔ Implementation ➔ Evaluation continuum? What are your strongest traits when it comes to creativity, and what are your weakest? How can you best help your team be successful?

3. Go find a balloon, stretch it out, blow it up, and let it fly. As you retrieve the balloon after every crash and burn, notice the "stretch." Then think back through your memory banks and list some major and minor setbacks you've experienced in your life. Consider the new knowledge or "stretch" that came from each setback and the behaviors that you subsequently changed. List them below:

CRASH & BURNS	NEW LEARNING	DISCONTINUED BEHAVIOR
1.	1.	1.
2.	2.	2.
3.	3.	3.

CHAPTER 3

Ready, Fire . . . Aim!

The Origin of Ideas

One of the most commonly asked questions in my seminars is "Where do ideas come from?" In an academic text, I'd be tempted to say that ideas come from "divergent thinking." But because I'm not writing an academic text, I prefer to say that great ideas come from:

"Ready, Fire . . . Aim!" Thinking

Traditionally, many people would say that ideas come from brainstorming. But successful brainstorming often involves much more than our typical image of the process assumes. "Ready, Fire . . . Aim!" brainstorming follows a one-two-three process—and can follow these steps on at least three different levels. The steps:

1. Define your problem [READY].

2. Come up with as many ideas as you can as fast as you can without criticizing or editing them [FIRE].

3. Sift, synthesize, and choose [AIM].

Creativity consists of coming up with many ideas, not just that one great idea. These ideas typically are not focused at the time you conceive them. They are not anticipated. They are not, in a word, "aimed." They don't come with teeth-clenched concentration. They don't require "effort" in their creation. Idea making, then, requires you, the Idea Person, to get ready, fire away, wait for the smoke to clear, and then look around to see if you hit anything worthwhile. Look at all the ideas lying around and see whether any of them seem promising. If none are any good, get ready, fire again, blast away, and then . . . aim. Maybe this time you'll hit something.

This approach is a hybrid of "divergent" and "convergent" thinking. A convergent thinker focuses on the problem as stated and tries to synthesize information and knowledge to devise a solution. By contrast, instead of concentrating inwardly on a problem or goal, the divergent thinker looks elsewhere for solutions: up, down, under, over, far away, backward, inside out, outside in, in the clouds, in myths, in dreams. The divergent thinker tries to envision the problem solved. The divergent thinker plays strange mental games and may imagine a refrigerator in dire need of two boxes of baking soda—one for the crisper and one for the freezer!

> "The problem with brainstorming is that everyone thinks they already do it. But brainstorming is like playing the piano: It takes practice, and the better you get, the more rewarding it can be."
>
> —Tom Kelley, general manager, IDEO
> *The Art of Innovation*

Three Levels of Brainstorming

I've noticed that brainstorming often occurs on three levels, each more sophisticated than the last, and that these tend to move from convergent to divergent in approach.

Level 1 brainstorming seems to be a sharing of facts and experiences. Here, "Ready, Fire . . . Aim!" doesn't yet involve throwing out ideas that strike the people offering them as great "Aha!" discoveries. But this level is what I think most people mean by brainstorming. It could be called "convergent firing"—narrowly aimed, like the shot from a .22 rifle.

On **Level 2,** we look around and realize that even though we've thrown out everything we knew, we need to come up with something new and different. That's when we're inspired to fire away in the unpredictable, divergent pattern I've described, like the shot from a shotgun. The first level is based on what we know and isn't really original, but on the second level we don't know where the process is going or what it might yield. To succeed, the process has to create a universal "aha"; the answer typically will be new, original, and unexpected, even to the person who comes up with it.

Level 3 is a wild one, where we not only don't know where the process is going, we don't know where the reframing or main idea came from. These are the kinds of flashes that happen while you are commuting or taking a shower—what I call higher-level self-brainstorming. It doesn't happen very often in groups; it's what artists, writers, and musicians tend to experience in the flow state of acute awareness and focus.

The following chart summarizes how the three levels of brainstorming work:

	LEVEL I	LEVEL 2	LEVEL 3
Time	fast	takes a while	needs to germinate
Depth	known	unknown	surprise yourself
Solution	expected	unexpected	challenges organization
Risk	none	a little	a lot
Reward	a little	a little	a lot

Many people using only Level 1 brainstorming just look at what's wrong with their situation, their environment, their company, their boss, their organization, their spouse. By focusing on the current state of affairs, they tend to limit their view of the possibilities. By trying so hard to come up with a single solution, they often actively stand in the way of the multiple solutions they need to envision. By using only analytical and deductive reasoning, they force themselves down the rigid path of linear reasoning. The perils of this path were summed up by philosopher Emile Chartier:

> *Nothing is more dangerous than an idea when it's the only one you have.*

We've all known monomaniacs, people hell-bent on one way of doing something. Monomaniacs are quite likely to have that one great scheme that's so good they won't breathe a word about it unless you sign some sort of nondisclosure form. By contrast, think back to Dr. NakaMats and his openness to new ideas and his willingness to share his own.

When Hanley Norins, formerly a creative director at the Young & Rubicam advertising agency, asked other successful advertising people how they came up with ideas, almost all of them said, "through free association." This is Level 2 and 3 brainstorming, and the importance of free association lies in the word *free*. In Harley Norins's *The Young & Rubicam Traveling Creative Workshop,* one creative director compared the creative process to a sponge soaking up information, which is followed by "the squeeze part: when you wring out the sponge and scribble down the most promising splashes and driblets."

The motivational author and speaker Tony Robbins teaches in his RPM (Rapid Planning Method) a similar "Ready, Fire . . . Aim!" approach for personal problem solving called "What . . . Why . . . How." He asks:

1. "What is the result that you want to achieve (and be specific with your expectations)?" [Ready]

2. "Why do you want to achieve this (and be passionate with your thoughts)?" [Fire]

3. "How are you going to achieve this result (and be bold with your actions)?" [Aim]

"Ready, Fire . . . Aim!" allows you to be open to many ideas while at the same time defining your challenge and later arranging your actions in order of priority. And it helps make the idea-creating process a way of life. It emphasizes the joy of idea making, rather than the misery that comes from trying to figure out that one idea that will somehow change everything. Creators derive their satisfactions from diving into the river of creativity and swimming—from the creative life itself.

Creating an Idea-Friendly Environment

Highly creative people are quite attuned to those times and places in which they come up with their best ideas. Dr. NakaMats, for example, travels from his "static" room to his "dynamic" room and finally to his "wet" room—all in his daily pursuit of a new idea for another patentable invention.

Other great thinkers, writers, and inventors have had their own times and places for their best creating. Hemingway wrote in cafés during the early morning. Duke Ellington wrote his music on trains. René Descartes worked in bed. Thomas Edison slept in his lab so he could write down ideas when they came to him, even in the dead of night. Beethoven carried a notebook around with him to write down ideas for compositions.

Others come on their ideas by surprise and are simply ready to recognize the moment when a great idea shows up. They prepare the ground for innovation; they create an idea-friendly environment. In 1890, Friedrich von Kekule, a professor of chemistry, had been attempting to determine the structure of the benzene molecule. He fell asleep in a chair and dreamed of a serpent eating its own tail. That dream revealed to him the structure he had been searching for—the closed carbon ring structure that revolutionized organic chemistry.

Artists commonly recognize the value of "accidents" in their work, and, of course, a multitude of inventions have been discovered "by accident," while the inventor was trying to produce something else. Professor Robert Austin tells in a *Harvard Business Review* article, "The Accidental Innovator" (July 5, 2006), how Jacques Mande Daguerre invented photography. Daguerre put an exposed photographic plate into a cabinet with a broken mercury thermometer. By accident, the mercury vapors from the broken thermometer developed the photographic image. Austin mentions other examples of creative accidents, including anesthesia, cellophane, cholesterol-lowering drugs, cornflakes, dynamite, the ice cream soda, Ivory soap, NutraSweet, nylon, penicillin, rayon, PVC, smallpox vaccine, stainless steel, and Teflon.

Even those of us who are not in the same league with the great thinkers of Western civilization know that certain times and certain places are more conducive to creating than others. When you're driving down the road, suddenly something strikes you and, in a fraction of a moment, you solve that problem that's been nagging at you all day. Or you're taking a shower, and, almost without knowing it, you come up with a brilliant plan. Creativity just seems to thrive in particular times or places.

And even though we might not rank with the world's great thinkers, we can benefit by following their example and establishing idea-friendly times and places.

Where Do YOU Come up with Ideas?

In my creativity workshops, I've conducted informal surveys of the most idea-friendly times. Counting down, the top ten are:

10. While performing manual labor.

9. While listening to a sermon.

8. On waking up in the middle of the night.

7. While exercising.

6. During leisure reading.

5. During a boring meeting.

4. While falling asleep or waking up.

3. While sitting on the toilet.

2. While commuting to work.

1. While showering or taking a bath.

Discovering that the bathroom was a fertile place for ideas didn't surprise me. According to a recent *USA Today* poll, during our lifetime we spend three years in the bathroom. While in the bathroom:

53% of us are reading

47% of us are thinking

33% of us are on the telephone

> My best thinking about the future of the economy occurs while I'm soaking in the bathtub.
>
> —Alan Greenspan, former Federal Reserve chairman

Maybe water is the secret to sparking new ideas. I bet all of us who've ever taken a shower or soaked in a hot bath have had an idea originate there at some time in our lives. Now think for a moment: How many times have you said that you would write down this shower-inspired idea as soon as you got to your desk? But, by the time you got there, the idea was gone, never to be found again.

Ideas come from the stimuli of your setting. The loss of ideas may occur because, as you start to dry off, you are changing this stimuli. This effect is similar to opening your eyes after dreaming. In an instant burst of light, the dreams are either gone or only vaguely remembered. So here are my three solutions for grabbing hold of your shower ideas: (1) Invest in bathtub crayons, (2) keep an idea pad by your sink, or (3) turn your shower idea into a pneumonic song lyric or poem. As Albert Einstein once said:

> ‘I spend so much time thinking in the shower that my employees jokingly measure the complexity of my ideas in ‘‘shower units.’’
>
> —Ray Ozzie, creator of Lotus Notes

Make friends with your shower. If inspired to sing,
maybe the song has an idea in it for you.

You, of course, should search your own habits and identify those times when you tend to come up with the best ideas. Chances are that your idea-friendliest time won't be while sitting at your desk straining to come up with something clever. Then, when you need some great ideas, maximize your chances by seeking out those idea-friendly times.

Dream with Your Eyes Open

The software in your 2½-pound brain spends twenty-four hours a day producing and processing ideas. According to one study, our best ideas come at the following times:

6 a.m.–noon:	30%
Noon–6 p.m.:	14%
6 p.m.–midnight:	33%
Midnight–6 a.m.:	23%

When your brain is in sleep mode, we call the idea production you're doing *dreaming*. When you are awake and looking out the window, we call it *daydreaming*. When you are awake and focused on a task, we call it *thinking*.

In school we were told, "Don't stare off into space—pay attention!" So we learned not to daydream but to just sit, think, and recite. Yet, daydreaming is

> **"**All men dream but not equally. Those who dream by night in the dusty recesses of their minds wake in the day to find that it was vanity, but the dreamers of the day are dangerous men, for they may act on their dreams with open eyes to make it possible.**"**
>
> —T. E. Lawrence, *The Seven Pillars of Wisdom*

vital to our success because the future is the only area we can do anything about. The past is finished and it's too late to change the present. As Walt Disney said,

Impossible dreams don't know they're impossible.

Creative daydreaming requires you to assume that the future already exists within the present. It just hasn't grown to full size yet. Your task is to find and cultivate the seeds of the future, because the kernel of each seed is an idea waiting to grow.

TAKE FIVE

Gary Hamel says in Leading the Revolution *that, to be an effective leader, you need to spend 20 percent of your day thinking about the future. His survey of corporate leaders showed that the majority only spent 1 to 2 percent of their time daydreaming.*

Calculate how much time you spend daydreaming to create the future:

1. What percentage of your day do you spend daydreaming?

_____

2. What percentage of your daydreaming is about the future?_____

3. What percentage of this daydreaming do you share? _____

To me, the most important question is how many of your daydreams do you actually share with your colleagues. Therefore, I recommend a prescriptive "Take Five" approach to inspiring future-oriented thinking:

1. Daydream for five minutes every day.

2. Center your daydreams on things one to five years in the future.

3. Share your thoughts with five friends.

Creating an Idea-Friendly Time

Creating an idea-friendly time for yourself can be as simple as taking a break: Get up from your desk, get a cup of coffee, walk to another department, or stay at your desk and do something simple on your to-do list, glance at a magazine, or look out the window. "I'll just start typing random thoughts," an ad agency creative director says in *The Young & Rubican Traveling Creative Workshop*. "The act of typing . . . helps me get loose, the way a runner warms up before a race."

Nancy Badore, a former director of Ford Motor Company's Executive Development Center, uses her commute time to recharge her creative batteries. As recounted in *The Female Advantage: Women's Ways of Leadership* by Sally Helgesen, Badore says that she is "very conscious of letting my brain wander and float while I'm driving. I don't turn the radio on, I don't concentrate on tasks I have to do. The day's so fast-paced, it's hard to find time to totally tune out; I do that in the car, and find I have some of my most creative moments while driving on the highway."

Paul MacCready, the creator of the award-winning flying machine, the Gossamer Condor, credits daydreaming for his inspiration. He cites a month-long, seven-thousand-mile driving vacation and endless hours of watching red-tailed hawks as primary factors leading to his design of the Gossamer Condor, which now hangs in the Smithsonian next to the Wright brothers' first airplane.

Creating an Idea-Friendly Office

Of course, when it's time to create, you can't always take a shower, run to the john, or commute to work. At least not without creating quite a stir in the office. So you must pay attention to your surroundings, to the place where you hang your hat most of the day or night, and see whether it promotes or inhibits the creative process. Of immediate concern, and the place over which you exert considerable control, is, most likely, your office.

Take a look around. Is your office a friend or foe to the creative process?

Think of all the stimuli that you had around the classroom to help pique your curiosity and make you want to learn. You had maps, globes, paints, pictures, and the alphabet going around the room on the wall. You even ate soup with floating letters. Learning was fun, and you saw success all around you.

Now think about your conference room. It probably has drab, beige walls and not one picture of your customers or of the activities that made your organization successful. IBM used to have a rule that only two signs were allowed to be left on a conference room wall. One said, "Think!," which was the company's mantra at the time, and the other said, "Clean up when you're done." It's hard to imagine slogans more conducive to in-the-box thinking.

The least likely place to come up with a new idea is at your desk at work. Look around your desk. Where are the stimuli to spark ideas? Are your visitor's chairs filled with old newspapers, discouraging people from coming in, having a seat, and chewing the fat (an often fertile source of great ideas)? Is your office a trophy case, adorned with awards, degrees, and other testimonials to your past performance? Does it contain any monuments to your future? Do the diplomas on your wall really impress your visitors? Perhaps they are necessary displays of knowledge and competence to reassure a paying client, but if no paying clients visit your office, it's more likely that your degrees intimidate and thwart those who do stop by. Most of all, perhaps they dull your own sense of the possibilities the present and the future hold.

If you agree that you need to be more innovative in your thinking, it's time to change the rules and put some creative stimuli back into your life. Einstein kept a portrait of Sir Isaac Newton above his bed. What portraits do you have in your office or home?

Conduct a stimulus audit of your office. Rank items as inspiring, perspiring, or neutral.

INSPIRING	PERSPIRING	NEUTRAL
1.	1.	1.
2.	2.	2.
3.	3.	3.
4.	4.	4.
5.	5.	5.

To help you make your office a place that invites the creative process, here are some suggestions, all borrowed from participants in my creativity workshops.

1. Put your baby picture on your desk. Not your baby's picture, but your own baby picture. That's right. A picture of you when you were young and innocent and oh-so-creative! This friendly touch will open up you and your staff and some will realize for the first time that you weren't forty-five years old on the day you were born!

2. Put a marker board or flip chart in your office so you can easily initiate "Ready, Fire . . . Aim!" sessions when a colleague or employee brings in a problem.

3. Spend $25 for something on your desk to represent your vision. I've used this device in my creativity workshops. Here are some items purchased by workshop participants: a toy fire hydrant ("I put out fires!"), a jar full of cat's-eye marbles ("I'm keeping an eye on the future!"), a picture of Mickey Mouse ("To remind me of the incredible customer service at Walt Disney World!").

4. Find and hang a picture of your vision on your wall. NASA has lots of pictures of space stations and the moon. Bob Stripling, now city manager of Staunton, Virginia, who wanted a new downtown parking garage, hung pictures of award-winning parking garages in his office as a reminder of his vision and as a prompter of ideas necessary to reach that vision.

5. Put some toys on your desk—Legos, a box of Crayola crayons, and other childlike toys to remind you of the innocence and simplicity of creativity. You'll be amazed at how many of your visitors pick them up and play with them.

6. No office is complete without a cartoon book on the same table as your issues of *Harvard Business Review*. You never know, it might be a cartoon, rather than an article, that generates the next great idea for you or your office guest!

Putting Faces on Innovation

As a leading design firm, IDEO creates innovative products, services, and experiences for Fortune 1000 companies and employs designers, engineers, human factors experts, and business strategists.

To foster a culture of innovation in its offices, Tom Kelley, the IDEO general manager, has identified the ten human faces that fuel the company's innovation. The following list is summarized from his new book, *The Ten Faces of Innovation:*

1. The Anthropologist observes how people interact with products and services to come up with new ideas.

2. The Experimenter keeps testing possible scenarios to make ideas tangible.

3. The Cross-Pollinator finds connections between unrelated ideas to create fresh new ones.

4. The Hurdler enjoys jumping over barriers to innovation to create something new.

5. The Collaborator values multidisciplinary team dynamics over individual input to generate broad-reaching ideas.

6. The Director sees the bigger picture while taking the pulse of the current organization.

7. The Experience Architect focuses on turning ordinary experiences into remarkable ones.

8. The Set Designer promotes an idea-friendly culture by designing work environments that stimulate creativity.

9. The Storyteller inspires us with narratives of how innovation will lead the organization into the future.

10. The Caregiver understands and empathizes with the customer and creates a dynamic relationship of sharing and trust.

Do you see yourself in the IDEO list? Think about the faces of innovation in your organization—what faces are missing, what faces are dominant? Giving a face to our differing, yet synergistic, roles in the innovation process is a wonderful way to visually lead our people toward the future.

Eliminating "Junk Work"

Management expert Peter Drucker said right before his death at ninety-five years of age that "abandoning the obsolete, the irrelevant, or the program with promise that never materialized is the key to innovation."

If you're inundated by pointless reports, endless meetings, and redundant approvals, you're not alone. In one poll, 74 percent of executives said they were mired in outdated, counterproductive methods of doing business, bogged down by pointless meetings, and smothered by yet another report that probably belongs in the trash can.

Ford Chairman and CEO Bill Ford Jr. recently stated, "Meetings that are held for the infamous 'management entertainment,' attended out of fear of not being seen, or scheduled simply because 'that's the way we've always done it' need to go." He added, "Meetings worth our time are those that help us move quicker, break through bureaucracy, and drive decision making to the appropriate levels throughout the organization."

According to Jack Welch, former CEO of General Electric, "For a large organization to be competitive, it must have Speed, Simplicity, and Self-Confidence." Today's global organization has to be able to deliver services anytime, anywhere, to anyone, no matter what. That's customer satisfaction.

Speed, however, is not necessarily "stepping on the gas," doing everything the same way, only faster. In fact, speed can involve slowing down, taking an in-depth look at the way your organization is doing things, and asking, "How can we do this in half the time?"

Speed comes from streamlining the organization as a whole and streamlining the work of each employee. Jack Welch asked executives to compile a list of the twenty things they're doing that make them work seventy hours each week. "I bet five of them are 'junk work' and can be eliminated," he said. This reaffirms the quote by the great cartoonist Rube Goldberg:

> **Man will always find a complicated means to perform a simple task.**

True or False: Time Pressure Fuels Creativity

In an interview with *Fast Company,* titled "The Six Myths of Creativity," Teresa Amabile, who heads the Entrepreneurial Management Department at Harvard Business School, described her recent creativity research. Amabile collected nearly 12,000 daily journal entries from 238 people "working on creative projects in seven companies in the consumer products, high-tech, and chemical industries."

She dispelled the myth that time pressure fuels creativity:

> *In our diary study, people often thought they were most creative when they were working under severe deadline pressure. But the 12,000 aggregate days that we studied showed just the opposite: People were the least creative when they were fighting the clock. In fact, we found a kind of time-pressure hangover—when people were working under great pressure, their creativity went down not only on that day but the next two days as well. Time pressure stifles creativity because people can't deeply engage with the problem. Creativity requires an incubation period; people need time to soak in a problem and let the ideas bubble up.*

Amabile also found that, when facing an imminent deadline, distractions can get in the way of creativity:

> *In fact, it's not so much the deadline that's the problem; it's the distractions that rob people of the time to make that creative breakthrough. People can certainly be creative when they're under the gun, but only when they're able to focus on the work. They must be protected from distractions, and they must know that the work is important and that everyone is committed to it. In too many organizations, people don't understand the reason for the urgency, other than the fact that somebody somewhere needs it done today.*

Amabile's research dovetails with Peter Drucker's thought that innovation requires us to jettison obsolete or irrelevant projects.

So look around you. Challenge everything you do, every report you write (or read), your well-worn way of getting through the day. What in your routine aids the creative process? More important, what hinders the free flow of great ideas? What do you do during the day that slows you down? What gets in your way? Lost phone numbers? Forgotten messages? Misfiled reports? Junk work?

What if, the next time you ask a department to create a scenario for cutting their budget by 10 percent, you also ask them to cut the number of reports, approvals, and meetings they require by 10 percent? Removing hindrances and junk work promotes the creative process. These steps signal that an organization's priority is innovation, not defensiveness. Creating an idea-friendly office can be a good first step in stripping away obstacles to performance and barriers to great ideas.

Creating an Idea-Friendly Office Meeting

You're probably not surprised that meetings—other than boring meetings—did not make the Top 10 Idea-Friendly Times list. And chances are that even if you did generate a great idea in a boring meeting, you'd likely keep it to yourself. It takes courage to break into the drone of a typical meeting to insert your passion for a new direction. For some people, the political risk of stepping out of line can be daunting, and for others, it's downright terrifying or demoralizing.

You can make your meetings energizing, engaging, fun, productive, creative, collaborative—a breath of fresh air. Believe me, you don't have much competition in this area, and you can quickly build a fantastic reputation for leadership by seizing the opportunity to run great meetings. Here's an important truth to keep in mind: If you're the leader, people will shadow your emotions. They will rarely be more energized, humorous, candid, and open-minded than you are. You set the tone and people will follow, for better or worse.

Absolutely begin with rapport in your meetings. Connect with people by offering appreciation with warmth and sincerity. Here are some things to focus on as you enter your meetings:

1. What have people been working hard on?

2. What can you say that "catches" them doing things right?

3. What else is going on that is positive about the people in the room?

4. Who is getting married, just had a baby, or has a milestone anniversary at work?

If you're still stumped, how about something positive that's happening in the company, in pop culture, or in sports? Do your homework and know your team. In return, they will trust you and follow you.

Never underestimate the value of building rapport as a way to enhance collaboration. Don't be tempted to sacrifice it because the agenda is too long and time is too short. Get people talking and smiling, and the great ideas will follow—whether you're brainstorming or not.

Consider smashing one of the all-time meeting paradigms. Switch from "tell" mode to "ask" mode. Let the team build the agenda. You'll discover what's really on their minds. Don't panic; you can always add your hot items to the list. Instead of dominating the airtime, weave your items into the flow of the meeting to create an inclusive dynamic.

Make team expectations clear by the tone of your meetings. So many meetings get bogged down in the blame game, as people castigate other departments, company leadership, vendors, even the customers, for an array of failings. Victims love to vent and will suck the life and creative juices right out of meeting participants. You'll need to act quickly and consistently in these circumstances. Revert to "ask" mode again by asking powerful questions:

1. "What can we do to solve this problem?"

2. "What can we do to move this issue forward?"

3. "How can I help you make it happen?"

All these tactics empower people by making them accountable and sparking their creativity.

Recording Your Ideas

As you focus on your idea-friendly times, places, and meetings, be ready to write your ideas down. Otherwise, if you're like many creative people, you'll forget your ideas before you have a chance to act on them.

Here are some of the methods I've used to record my ideas:

1. Put a pad of paper and a pencil or pen by your bed or in your kitchen.

2. Keep a grease pencil in your shower. It comes off with any liquid cleaner.

3. Drive with a tape recorder in your glove compartment.

4. Carry 3" x 5" cards in your pocket or carry a small notebook.

5. Call your answering service or your answering machine and leave a message.

6. Write it on your wrist.

7. If you don't have a pen or pencil, be creative and use dust on your dashboard, steam on your bathroom mirror, or sand on the beach.

Creating an Idea Bank

The Idea Note shown here is the size of a dollar bill, for saved ideas are like money in the bank. They will gain interest—your interest—as you look through them to spark even more new ideas. Print up pads of these Idea Notes and give them to your colleagues or employees. Carry some around in your wallet for those flashes of insight and then file them away in a card box labeled "Idea Bank."

A Climate for Creativity

Creativity, then, comes from a process, a way of thinking about and looking at the world, a way of approaching problems. Creativity arises from the unexpected: from a clash of opposites, from metaphors, from dreams about the future. A creative office environment recognizes these ways of creative thinking and tries to encourage them through design and decor. If your "busy executives" say they can't afford to leave their desks, you might remind them about idea-friendly times or you might challenge that assumption and say that "busy execs can't afford *not* to leave their desks." You might indeed try to design an environment that nudges people away from their desks and into more idea-friendly times and places.

Leaders at Steelcase, Inc., the large office furniture company, saw that as a maker of "office environments," the company had to come up with a creative environment of its own for its new corporate development center in Grand Rapids, Michigan. Company leaders engaged top organizational psychologists and charged them with designing a physical layout that would encourage formal and informal interactions between people, as a way to generate ideas, and foster both planned and spontaneous communication and team building.

The innovative interior design of Steelcase's $111 million, pyramid-shaped Corporate Development Center features break areas, "neighborhoods," and an executive cluster. The break areas—informal gathering spots that foster impromptu meetings—are strategically positioned between neighborhoods throughout the building. All break areas are equipped with marker boards, coffeemakers, and soft drinks. The company even coined the term *functional inconvenience* to describe the effect of requiring people from different departments and disciplines to intermingle.

 GREAT IDEA ACTIONS

1. Elevate your brainstorming from Level 1 to Level 2 and enjoy the free association, the unknown, the unexpected, and the big ideas.

2. Figure out your idea-friendly times and places, and learn to take a break when your mind is "stuck" but your brain wants you to keep staring at the computer.

3. Change your offices around, create spaces where people congregate, and allow them to interact. Rename your meeting or break areas to fit your vision. Apple Computer named its meeting rooms *Dorothy* and *Toto* to let everybody know that a wizard dwells within each person.

4. Eliminate one piece of "Junk Work" this week to experience the satisfaction of Speed, Simplicity, and Self-Confidence.

C H A P T E R   4

Killer Phrases

The Enemies of Ideas

*The innovator has for enemies all who have done well
under the old, and lukewarm defenders in those who may
do well under the new.*

—Machiavelli, The Prince, 1513

You know that no idea is any good until someone does something with it or to it. Someone has to accept it, adopt it, run with it, put it into action. That someone, of course, is often someone other than you. Implementing great ideas requires a team effort.

So you must tell somebody about your idea. And if you've ever tried to bring up new ideas to other people, you know that, while your idea could be met with thunderous applause, it may just as easily elicit derisive laughter, or perhaps just a nonchalant, concept-killing shrug.

What determines the success or failure of your idea? Two things—the quality of the idea and the quality of its promotion. If the idea turns out to be unworkable, then you want it to fail—and fast. If it doesn't fail fast, count on it eating up precious time and resources. But assuming that your idea is a good one, what is it out there that just might make it fail anyway and shoot it down before it has the slightest chance to spread its wings?

In fact, what do you *know* will happen to your great idea as soon as you suggest it to your boss, colleague, spouse, or other important person in your life? Somebody, somewhere, at some time, will come up, gun loaded, aim, and say . . .

"It's not in the budget."

"We don't do it that way."

"We've tried that before."

Bang! Bang! Bang!

Somebody shoots down your great idea with a Killer Phrase. Killer Phrases just might do in your great idea before it even gets on track.

> **Killer Phrase (kil´ r fraz): n. 1. a knee-jerk response that squelches new ideas; most commonly uttered by bosses, parents, and government officials. 2. a threat to innovation.**

We are bombarded by Killer Phrases every day. They stifle our ideas, short-circuit creative thinking, and undermine the very notion of innovation. Even worse, they talk us out of our hopes and dreams.

The negative voice of "It'll never work" has been around a long time. In 1899, the director of the U.S. Patent Office, Charles Duell, declared, "Everything that can be invented, has been invented." Persuaded that there was nothing worthwhile left to invent, he tried to close the office down. Now, eight million patents later, that negative voice is still stifling employees' suggestions. Look at the good old reliables, such as "It'll never fly." Check out today's hottest topics and you'll find today's latest Killer Phrases—for instance: "Yes, but it's not scalable."

Of course, we need warnings. I'd be grateful to have anyone shout, "No, don't do that!" right before I step into the path of a moving train. And when I'm trying out a new idea, I certainly appreciate constructive feedback. However, Killer Phrases are different, arising from our natural resistance to change. They are those uniquely negative statements that make us think, "Gee, I wish I'd never said that" and think twice before we offer the next suggestion. The result, according to a report from the Employee Involvement Association: The average worker now only submits one written suggestion every ten years.

But now, more than ever, we need great ideas. We need them to revive our economy, to restore our family, to empower our employees, and to reinvent our schools. So, to give new ideas a chance, we need to understand the root cause of Killer Phrases and evolve past them.

> "All new and truly important ideas must pass through three stages:
> 1. *first dismissed as nonsense,*
> 2. *then rejected as against religion,*
> 3. *and finally acknowledged as true, with the proviso from initial opponents that they knew it all along.*"
>
> —Karl Ernst von Baer, biologist and father of embryology

Idea Generators must get a handle on Killer Phrases, for they are as inevitable in the innovation process as ideas themselves. Successful Idea Generators must learn what these phrases are, where they come from, when they are likely to rear their ugly heads, and how they might best be overcome. Psychologists have said that the human reaction to a new idea unfolds something like this, which we could call the Five Stages of Idea Acceptance:

1. It's irrelevant to this situation.

2. It's relevant, but it's unproven.

3. It's proven, but it's dangerous.

4. It's safe, but it's not saleable.

5. It'll sell, what a great idea!

From conception to fruition, successful ideas tend to follow a path of ultimate but grudging acceptance. All along the way, Killer Phrases dive in from all angles, seeking to obstruct, demean, diminish, counteract, undermine.

A Killer Phrase was hurled at those considering business relationships with the former Soviet Union:

Their currency isn't convertible!

PepsiCo and Ben & Jerry's ice cream didn't let that stop them. They overcame the convertibility problem by devising unique systems of barter:

> *One bottle of Pepsi = three-quarters of an ounce of*
> *Stolichnaya vodka*
> *One ice cream cone = one-hundredth of a Matroiska*
> *nesting doll (plus some walnuts and honey thrown in*
> *for good measure)*

Killer Phrases are part of our culture, part of our upbringing. One study showed that negative *no-can-do* statements are all around us, outweighing positive *can-do* statements by substantial margins. At home, parents average eighteen negative statements for every one positive statement they utter, usually to a naturally inquisitive child trying to find out how something works. The average is 432 negative statements a day! "Don't touch. Don't play with that." The same study showed that teachers utter twelve negative statements for each positive one, damping down the enthusiasm of students eager to answer or ask a question. "Be still. Don't talk. Don't do that."

Resist Being "Critical First . . ."

When children think up or hear a new idea, their initial thoughts are all about the possibilities . . . and the fun they could have. But mature, educated minds usually see first what is wrong with a new idea. "Yes, but it's too costly . . . ," goes the voice in their head. Then to compound the negativity, many times their inner voice puts them down for even thinking up the idea.

> "Son, you tried your hardest and failed miserably. The lesson is: Never try."
>
> —Homer J. Simpson

"Yes-butters" are geniuses at devising excuses for inaction. Within seconds of hearing a new idea, they voice their criticism. This allows excuses rather than possibilities to drive the conversation.

Are excuses driving your organization's innovation process?

Several studies have shown that up to 83 percent of our self-talk is negative. As Dr. Phil points out in his book, *Self Matters*:

1. Your internal dialogue is constant.

2. It happens in real time.

3. It drowns out any other conversation.

4. It becomes the loudest when you need it the least.

5. When you have a negative conversation with yourself, it can cut your functional, or task-related, IQ in half.

Therefore, if you allow yourself to be critical first about new ideas, you are only operating at half your potential . . . YIKES.

Stage Fright

You are getting ready to deliver the biggest speech of your life. All of a sudden your inner voice starts saying, "I won't remember the data to go with these charts." You are now multitasking two speeches—one to your audience and one to yourself. Your IQ for the big talk has just dropped from 120 to 60.

So how do we challenge this knee-jerk, self-defeating self-talk?

By thinking like a one-year-old toddler trying to walk for the first time. The child doesn't say:

1. "This walking thing is too hard" or

2. "I look stupid down here" or

3. "Does my butt look big in this diaper?"

Of course not. The child recognizes that this thing called *walking* is a difficult skill that will help her get what she wants in life, and she'll keep trying to do it right until she succeeds. And when she falls, she falls with a smile on her face.

So your stage fright strategy is this:

1. To smile because it will loosen up your face and your voice.

2. To practice and practice so if you slip up you can recover gracefully.

3. To recognize that the audience wants you to succeed.

After your talk, you'll be back in the audience, hopefully encouraging the next speaker.

Killer Phrases: The Top 40

"The Top 40" is a list of Killer Phrases I've collected in my creativity workshops. The last five in the list are *unspoken* killer phrases—many times these are the most deadly.

1. "Yes, but . . ."

2. "We tried that before."

3. "That's irrelevant."

4. "We haven't got the manpower."

5. "Obviously, you misread my request."

6. "Don't rock the boat!"

7. "The boss [or the competition] will eat you alive."

8. "Don't waste time thinking."

9. "I'm the one who gets paid to think."

10. "Great idea, but not for us."

11. "It'll never fly."

12. "Don't be ridiculous."

13. "People don't want change."

14. "It's not in the budget."

15. "Put it in writing."

16. "It will be more trouble than it's worth."

17. "It isn't your responsibility."

18. "That's not in your job description."

19. "You can't teach an old dog new tricks."

20. "Let's stick with what works."

21. "We've done all right so far."

22. "The boss will never go for it."

23. "It's too far ahead of the times."

24. "Don't fight city hall!"

25. "What will people say?"

26. "Get a committee to look into that."

27. "If it ain't broke, don't fix it."

28. "You've got to be kidding."

29. "No!"

30. "We've always done it this way."

31. "It's all right in theory, but . . ."

32. "Be practical!"

33. "Do you realize the paperwork it will create?"

34. "Because I said so."

35. "I'll get back to you."

Nonverbal Killer Phrases:

36. . . . silence . . .

37. . . . laughter . . .

38. . . . suppressed laughter . . .

39. . . . condescending grins . . .

40. . . . dirty looks . . .

When I hear managers flinging a lot of Killer Phrases, I'm often reminded of seagulls. I think of Seagull Management—the act of swooping in on unsuspecting office staff, dumping unpleasant information on them, and then flying away. There's also the Seagull Consultant, who sails in, eats your food, dumps on you, and then flies off without a care in the world.

The Culture of "No"

In his book *Who Says Elephants Can't Dance?* IBM CEO Lou Gerstner describes the 1993 challenge when smaller companies that could make the same products better, faster, and cheaper were beating IBM in the marketplace. Analysts on Wall Street called for IBM to be broken up into small, independent business units, but Gerstner wanted to keep the company together, change the way it did business, and teach the corporate elephant how to dance.

Gerstner describes IBM's dysfunctional culture as one in which no one would say yes, but everyone could say no. The long-held value of "respect for the individual" had morphed into an institutional system of nonaction, with long delays in reaching decisions and projects that took weeks of work terminated by lone dissenters.

This is the perfect example of a culture stuck in the "critical first . . ." response to ideas. As a result, the curiosity, creativity, and confidence of IBM employees atrophied, allowing the smaller competitors to rule the fast-changing marketplace.

The dance steps that Gerstner taught the elephant—Win, Execute, Team—will help anyone become more nimble on the dance floor:

1. **Win:** *The marketplace is the driving force behind everything we do.*

2. **Execute:** *Speed and discipline must supersede the obsessive perfectionism that caused IBM to miss market opportunities.*

3. **Team:** *Everyone must commit to acting as one IBM.*

On top of these guidelines Gerstner added one more: "If it's broken, fix it. If it's not broken, fix it anyway."

Being "Curious First . . ."

Have you ever painfully sat through a series of presenters being "evaluated" by their peers? As soon as a speaker has finished, she is immediately critiqued by her colleagues. Then the speaker, now sitting in the audience, prepares her attack on the next presenter. All everyone sees are the pitfalls of the newly presented ideas. Just think: If humankind looked at every pitfall before leaping, we'd still be crouching in caves sketching animal pictures on walls.

> "A successful "Imaginer" has the imagination of a five-year-old with the wisdom of a grandparent.
>
> —Walt Disney

Creative leaders are different. They want to sketch a vision of possibilities. Being curious first allows them to find out what is *right* with an idea. They see a "six-month competitive advantage" in the new idea rather than the knee-jerk response of "We don't have the resources" to do that.

If you are "curious first" you have the vision of possibilities still dancing in your head when you're passing judgment. Even if the idea is an abysmal failure, you are aware of the idea's potential and can apply its strengths to another challenge that you are facing.

The following slide from my workshop shows the three stages that the creative facilitator goes through during a successful brainstorm.

Positive	**Negative**	**Opportunity**

Step 1: List what's positive about the idea.

Step 2: List what's negative.

Step 3: Ask if any negatives can be turned into an opportunity? If so, add to positive list.

Improv genius Drew Carey, star of *Whose Line Is It Anyway?*, gives us great advice on how to be curious first. According to Drew:

> ***In improv, it doesn't matter what the question is, the answer is always "Yes, and . . ."***

The creative person knows when to respond with "yes, and . . ." as opposed to the deadly "yes, but . . ." The former is curious first and allows for a dialogue. The latter is critical first and offers an excuse for ending a conversation or brainstorm.

You could call the "yes, and . . ." strategy a solution in search of a problem. It works magically in new product development when you want to conceive products that the consumer hasn't anticipated. It's also effective when you are trying to offset a budget cut by looking for new ways to increase revenue. It even unsticks you when you have writer's block and need to complete a report.

Being curious first also works wonders at home, communicating with your spouse. As Dr. Phil states:

> *How you interact during the first four minutes, not the first ten, dictates how your relationship is going to go the rest of the day.*

Being Terminally Serious

Albert Einstein once said, "I have no special gift, I am just passionately curious." He later said, "People who live their lives without being curious have made up their minds about everything." These people are not creative leaders—they are the terminally serious bosses that appear in Dilbert cartoons.

As we discussed in chapter 1, at five years of age, most people score higher on creativity tests than at any other time in their life. At age forty-four, they score the lowest. Fortunately, there's a magic day in your life when you start scoring higher again.

It's called retirement.

Why do we have to retire to become creative? I believe that the constant Killer Phrases we encounter in our work life—"Because I said so!" or "You've got to be kidding!"—make us all a bit terminally serious. Once we see only a serious world, devoid of curiosity, we lose hope, health, and happiness.

How many times have you laughed today? Remember: You laughed approximately 113 times a day as a young child, and you get down to only eleven times a day during middle age. Upon retirement—you guessed it—the laughter level goes up again. Laughter, joy, and strategic optimism are all vital to "playing with" and revealing new ideas that will achieve new solutions. Niels Bohr, the Nobel Prize–winning physicist, said that you hear laughter in the world's greatest laboratories before you hear the word *eureka*.

Imagine what might happen to your joy of cooking if your dinner guests immediately graded the cuisine you prepared upon each serving. "Your fish is only about a B minus." This would give you heartburn and probably be your last dinner party. Let the pungent aroma of new ideas suspend your judgment for those all-important first few minutes of the next presentation, meeting, or brainstorming session you attend—long enough to see at least one possibility and watch your personal creativity and your organization's innovation soar.

GREAT IDEA ACTIONS

To help you become curious, rather than critical, first, here are some simple phrases that will foster a dialogue of possibilities:

1. Rather than "Yes, but . . . ," which gives an excuse for inaction, say, "Yes, and . . . ," which encourages a dialogue.

2. Rather than cast blame with "Why did we . . . ?" ask, "How can we . . . ?" and discuss ways to move the idea-generating session forward.

3. Rather than respond with "We tried that before," focus on what's different about the idea or the environment this time.

4. Rather than reflexively saying, "Get a committee to look into this," say, "Tell me more . . ." so you can find the right people to evaluate the idea.

Now sell your idea with passion, because the life of your idea depends on it.

Fight Back

Your Winning Strategy

The most dangerous person in corporate America is the highly enthusiastic incompetent. He's running faster in the wrong direction, doing horribly counterproductive things with winning enthusiasm.

—Jay Kurtz, management consultant

It's time to fight back against counterproductive Killer Phrases and the naysayers themselves. You just learned about Killer Phrases in the last chapter. Now it's time to rehearse strategies to "defuse" these negative phrases so that you can turn potential roadblocks into expected hurdles and foster conversations about innovations that are not only possible, but possibly great.

Think about the most powerful Killer Phrases in your life, ones that strike fear and terror in your new idea's heart. I've got great news. One strategy effectively fights most Killer Phrases— even the most vicious ones.

Step 1: Identify the Killer Phrase

This step is short, yet awareness is the most important step you can take to overcome Killer Phrases. They are like overdue bills. Ignoring them won't make them go away. The instant you hear or anticipate a Killer Phrase, your inner voice should kick in with "Hey, that's a Killer Phrase!" and begin to deal with it.

Step 2: Determine the Root Cause

When you detect a Killer Phrase, your mission is to determine why someone is flinging a Killer Phrase at you, so you know what to do to overcome it.

To get you started, I've organized the top Killer Phrases into seven initial categories, based on the reasons they're hurled your way. They are based on cognitive psychology, a discipline devoted to moving beyond self-defeating, negative thought patterns.

CATEGORY	WHEN PEOPLE SAY	WHAT THEY REALLY MEAN
Overgeneralization	It'll never work!	In a win-lose world, your idea loses.
Put-downs	Don't waste time thinking.	Your idea [and you] are threatening to the status quo.
Selective Editing	Great idea, but not for us.	Your idea isn't worthy of our consideration.
Stalls	Put it in writing.	Your idea is too much, too fast.
Comparative Thinking	We've always done it this way.	The status quo looks better than your idea.
Catastrophizing	Do you realize the paperwork . . . ?	Your idea is a huge problem.
Zero Defects	It doesn't meet our standards.	Your idea isn't perfect right out of the box.

Also examine the Killer Phrase and see whether or not the person is simply asking a question. For example, "It's not in the budget" might be the disguised question "How much will it cost?" "We've tried that before" might be the disguised question "What's new and different about your approach?" If the Killer Phrase is really a question, the strategy is simple: Answer it.

Step 3: Explore Your Options

Your basic approach is always to respond to the real issue. So for:

1. **Comparative Thinking/Selective Editing:** Help the naysayer shift to a new perspective to create an accurate comparison. We'll explore how to do this in detail on pages 61 and 65.

2. **Catastrophizing/Overgeneralization/Zero Defects:** Help the naysayer put your idea into a larger context, creating some room to maneuver and making it safe to take a manageable risk. We'll discuss these strategies on pages 58, 67, and 69.

3. **Put-downs/Stalls:** Get some grassroots support for your idea before the meeting where it will be discussed. See pages 59 and 63 for more information on marshaling on that kind of support.

Step 4: Act

Realize that to act on your idea, you need to sell your idea. This requires a boundaryless promotional campaign that works in, out, up, and down.

Sell yourself so that your vision becomes a fire *in* your belly—then radiate that energy out to others. When it's time to influence a wider audience, sell *out*side by telling family and friends, and publicizing your idea in the media. Think like your boss' boss to help your idea take wings and fly *up* the organization. Change shoes with employees two levels *down* to identify the best ways to encourage active involvement and buy-in to your idea.

Broadening Your Political Base

Figure out whether the person flinging the Killer Phrase at you has *more* decision-making power than you do. If he is your boss or occupies a higher position in the organization than you do, his beliefs and power to make decisions can squelch your bright idea. Indeed, those higher up in the organization are paid to be skeptical. They are looking for good ideas—that's for sure. But they also want to unmask bad ideas to see that they fail, and fail fast. Assuming that your idea is a good one, your strategy becomes: Sell upward.

To sell upward, first and foremost, you've got to broaden your political base. One way is to identify the person who's likely to mount the strongest opposition, in an attempt to defuse anticipated Killer Phrases before they arise. Approach an associate of this potential foe, show the associate the merit of the idea, and try to win the associate over to your point of view. If you do, then approach the likely foe with your idea *before* you float the idea in front of the organization as a whole.

Selling upward requires you to marshal your political forces, to capture their imagination, to seek the input and assistance of others, and to anticipate their concerns and potential objections.

Another strategy in dealing with Killer Phrases hurled from above might be one of defiance. David Packard, cofounder of Hewlett-Packard (HP), talks about the HP Medal of Defiance in his book, *The HP Way*. In the late 1960s, an engineer at HP was developing a computer graphics display system. Top management felt the system had limited sales potential, so on an annual lab inspection tour, they told the young engineer, "We don't want to see any signs of this project on our next lab visit." The engineer decided to interpret this Killer Phrase to mean: "Hurry up, produce it, and get it out of the development stage." Chuck House did just that, and eventually his graphics display system was repositioned as a computer display monitor. HP sold more than 17,000 monitors representing $35 million in sales revenue. David Packard states, "Some years later, at a gathering of HP engineers, I presented Chuck House with a medal for 'extraordinary contempt and defiance beyond the normal call of engineering duty.'"

Companies that truly encourage their people to buck the system are still in the minority. Leadership expert Warren Bennis maintains that at least seven out of ten employees in companies keep quiet when their opinions are at odds with those of their superiors. Systems for rewarding those who dare to stand up and say, "I've got a better way" still make news today. However, as more walls come down and competition keeps increasing, finding a better way will be incorporated into everyone's job description.

Mobilizing the Troops

It's also important to figure out whether the person hurling the Killer Phrase at you has *less* decision-making power than you do. You must be ready to defuse Killer Phrases coming from your employees, your subordinates, or others lower on the organization chart. An idea requiring team effort that is opposed by members of the team is doomed to failure. The strategy in that case: Sell downward. People in lower positions fear change because:

1. They might not have the skills for a faster-paced operation.

2. Their job might be eliminated.

3. They might be near retirement and worry that a change would jeopardize their pension.

4. They think this change is only a temporary whim—just another management consultant's "idea of the week."

To buy in, they must see direction from above, support for possible failure, a tie-in with the mission of the company, and rewards for their successful implementation of this idea.

Both selling upward and selling downward call on you to present your idea in a positive light, encourage the participation of others, and demonstrate that everybody wins. We'll discuss selling up and down—as well as selling in and out—further in chapter 14, "Visible Ideas."

Illustrated Killer Phrase Playbook

Now that you understand the creative strategy of defusing Killer Phrases, the following playbook will help you with any Killer Phrases that are sent your way.

Overgeneralization

Groups with guitars are on their way out.
    —Decca Records, turning down the Beatles, 1962

There is no reason for any individual to have a computer in his home.
    —Ken Olsen, president of Digital Equipment, 1977

Yes/no. Good/bad. Always/never. Overgeneralizers are binary. Overgeneralizers save time. Overgeneralizers have already decided key issues *before* they hear your new idea. Extreme? Possibly. Efficient? Probably. Idea-deadly? Definitely.

True, educated opinions are based on a collection of past experiences. But most of the ideas and inventions we take for granted wouldn't exist if Overgeneralizers throughout history had had their way.

The chink in the always/never armor is the exception to the rule. Turn *never* into *ever, can't* into *can*—and your idea into reality.

Killer Phrase: "It'll Never Work!"

A door-slamming, ego-deflating idea-squasher suitable for business, home-repair projects, or play. Also known as:

> **It'll never fly.**
> **It'll never sell.**
> **It'll never win approval.**

Defusing Strategy

There are several ways to fight back against overgeneralizations, such as "It'll never work":

1. Open doors and minds to a new way of doing things by creating a "working" definition. Often the core issue is reconciling different definitions of the verb *to work*. Here's a quiz. Does *to work* mean:

   - 100% perfection?

   - Zero defects?

   - Leaping tall buildings in a single bound?

   - Producing a desired result?

2. Does the naysayer's definition match yours? If not, establish criteria for success. Ask how well the initial idea has to work to be considered successful.

3. Change the rules. Ask, "What exactly do you mean by 'never work'?" Often, the only thing not working is our old way of viewing the problem.

4. Replace "It'll never work" in your own conversations with:

   - Can we do a test first to see the results?

   - Where do you think this will work best?

   - What will it take to make this work?

Put-downs

What use could the company make of an electric toy?
  —*Western Union, rejecting rights to Alexander Graham Bell's telephone, 1878*

What? You would make a ship sail against the wind by lighting a bonfire under her decks? I have no time to listen to such nonsense!
  —*Napoleon I of France, dismissing Robert Fulton's steam engine*

Zing! Pow! Fwap. Smash. Meet the Put-downs, those pseudo-powerful Killer Phrases designed to keep your new idea "in its place."

Yes, efficiency and stability often depend on some type of pecking order. But Put-downs are the trademark, automatic response of any dysfunctional hierarchy—from executives to managers to staff, or from parents to teenagers to children. Put-downs run rampant down the ranks of unhealthy organizations, those branded "learning disabled" by MIT's Peter Senge. Look behind the manager who utters a Put-down and you'll likely find an executive who said it first.

Like other addictive behaviors, Put-downs benefit from intervention. This section can help you stop putting up with Put-downs.

Killer Phrase: "You're kidding, right?" (Laughter)

A favorite axiom among creative thinkers is this: "If everyone says you're wrong, you're one step ahead. If everyone laughs at you, you're two steps ahead." Therefore, if your great idea is met with chuckling, you might just be proposing something so innovative, no one has ever considered anything like it before!

Other forms of Put-downs include:

> *. . . a fake smile.*
> *. . . rolled eyes.*
> *You've got to be joking.*

Accept the laughter and run with it. You have a head start. Make laughter the best medicine for your new idea with one of these healthy prescriptions.

1. You're in good company. Recall other laughable ideas that are now success stories. The adhesive that didn't stick is a must-have when combined with yellow paper squares to make the Post-it note. So, agree that your idea is way out there, then ground it with a statement of benefits.

2. Times change. In the '50s, the United States laughed at what it perceived to be the low quality of Japanese products. Now we have Sony, Nintendo, Lexus, extended warranties. . . . Who's laughing now?

> If an idea does not appear bizarre, there is no hope for it.
>
> —Niels Bohr, physicist

3. Smile back. Sound simple? Yes, and effective. Returning a smile builds rapport, sets a tone of equality, and encourages conversation. It makes you feel better, too.

Selective Editing

Sensible and responsible women do not want the right to vote.
—Grover Cleveland, president of the United States, 1905

The world capacity for computers is five.
—Thomas Watson Sr., founder of IBM, 1943

Each of us takes in new information through a unique set of filters. At its worst, this filtering process causes us to hear only what we wish to hear, see only what we wish to see. Selective Editors wear Killer Phrase–colored glasses, causing them to see each new idea from the same, shortsighted viewpoint.

But from women in politics to computers in virtually every business and home, we are surrounded by proof that people can and do change their perspective. Business as usual now means boundaryless environments and the death of parochialism.

This section helps you expand tunnel vision and break through "not invented here" mind-sets to give ideas the filter change they deserve.

Killer Phrase: "It's NOT in the Budget!"

This is a favorite response, especially by accountants, who cannot evaluate an idea outside the context of profit-and-loss statements. This Killer Phrase puts formal, bureaucratic muscle behind anything having to do with dollars and cents—or dollars and sense.

This familiar phrase also goes by these variants:

There's no such thing as a free lunch.
Do you think money grows on trees?
Just wait 'til they run the numbers.

Defusing Strategy

Move beyond funding issues to fundamental changes with one of these bottom-line approaches:

1. Think like an entrepreneur. If this were your company, how would you fund your great idea? Would you spend X% of your own money to put this idea into practice?

2. Know thy budget. Be prepared to sell your idea and separate realistic budgetary concerns from Killer Phrases. When your department is experiencing a significant revenue shortfall, it's realistic to expect to hear, "It's not in the budget." However, consider responding like this:

   - Can we fund a prototype or a test?

   - Can we borrow the money from other sources or pool budgets?

   - How can we enact our plan for free or on a shoestring budget?

   These questions raise cost-conscious possibilities, rather than concede defeat.

3. Journey to the future. Work with colleagues to visualize the future by showing what will happen if you *do* implement the idea—and what will happen if you don't.

Stalls

People see what is wrong with a new thing, not what is right. To verify this, . . . submit a new idea to a committee.
—Charles Kettering, engineer and inventor

Who the hell wants to hear actors talk?
—Harry Warner, president of Warner Brothers, 1927

Sometime. Next time. Soon. Later. Sooner or later, your great ideas will encounter the Staller—the naysayer with an iron will and a Jell-O spine. Sure, new ideas benefit from additional input. But the Staller is an expert in the art of energetic nonaction.

"Putting it through channels" spells defeat in today's market. To survive, organizations must advance with straightforward speed and simplicity—what GE calls "getting that small-company soul inside a big-company body."

Although we tend to envision stalls as stone walls of resistance, the best Stallers devise mudholes and quagmires. The Staller's uniquely circular goal is to slow you down, to buy time, to keep your idea in limbo until it no longer poses a threat.

Your mission is to uncover the perceived threat—and get your idea back on solid ground.

Killer Phrase: "Put It in Writing."

This is the first date of Killer Phrases. You have to show your stuff and then wait by the phone until "they" condescend to call. This gives you plenty of time to think the worst, especially if they forget. . . .

This phrase also goes by:

> **Put it through channels.**
> **Fill out this form.**
> **Let's refer it to a committee for further consideration.**

Defusing Strategy

Sending your new idea off by itself can leave you feeling exposed and helpless. Besides packing your idea a nice lunch, here are some things you can do to give it a reasonable chance of winning over doubters:

1. Get on the same wavelength. Schedule a ten-minute idea briefing session with your boss before you write anything. Define mutual criteria for the success of your idea.

2. Make it reader-friendly. Double spacing with wide margins leaves room for editorial comments and buy-in. Include a cover note offering to discuss any questions or concerns.

3. Clarify the next steps. If you haven't heard by the agreed-upon response date, what can you do to close the deal?

4. Show that "Put it in writing" does not spell Killer Phrase in your organization. Set clear guidelines for submitting ideas, formally and informally. Focus on rapid turnaround and specific feedback.

5. Join industry leaders like Toyota, whose Creative Idea Suggestion System has generated over twenty million ideas in forty years, with more than 90 percent accepted. Toyota's GI (Good Idea) Club helps orient new hires to the system, while managers assist, as needed, with anything from a feasibility test to writing tips.

Comparative Thinking

Wellington is a bad general; the English are bad soldiers.
We will settle this matter by lunchtime.
—Napoleon I of France, at Waterloo, 1815

No mere machine will replace a reliable and honest clerk.
—president of Remington Arms Company, rejecting patent
rights for the typewriter, 1897

My dog's bigger than your dog. Our firm won the contract over yours. He's younger. She's prettier. We all use benchmarking—measuring products, services, and practices against the toughest competitors—to place ourselves in context within the world. That's fine—up to a point.

Shakespeare may have been talking about Killer Phrases when he remarked that comparisons are odious. The Killer Phrases in this section represent benchmarking's evil twin. They compare apples to oranges, fact to fiction, new challenges to glorified history. All with a single goal: to justify keeping innovation at bay.

You can help Comparative Thinkers reframe their reality to ensure a fair comparison—and a fair chance for your idea.

Killer Phrase: "We've Always Done it THIS Way."

Ye Olde Killer Phrase. You may also hear it in this form:

> **Let's stick with what works.**
> **It's change for the sake of change.**
> **We've done all right so far.**

Defusing Strategy

Tradition is admirable, but smart organizations know that complacency can lead to collapse. Break this endless loop with one or more of the following strategies:

1. Put "it" in perspective. Think together for a moment. Is there anything in life that hasn't evolved? Recall examples by saying, "At one time we believed that [so-and-so] would never work and it has been a surprising success."

2. Don't argue apples and oranges. Agree that the old way was good for its time. Show how things have changed, and how new ideas lead to new successes. Support your idea with concrete examples. New times demand new thinking.

3. Identify the core issue. What stated or implied belief does the existing method support? Is that still valid? Maybe it's time for spring cleaning.

4. Remember the questions you asked as a new hire:

   - Why do we have to fill out that form?

   - Who's in charge of this?

   - What if . . . ?

Most of these questions come up during a person's first three months at a new company or in a new position. After that, employees adapt to company policy and stop asking. Keep the questions alive by spending 10 percent of each staff meeting challenging a different ingrained assumption.

Catastrophizing

> *The sky is falling.*
> *—Chicken Little*

> *My figures coincide in setting 1950 as the year that the world must go smash.*
> *—Henry Adams, historian, 1903*

> *Good God! I can't publish this. We'd both be in jail.*
> *—publisher, rejecting William Faulkner's Sanctuary*

Uh-oh. Ghoulies and ghosties. Nightmares. Paranoia. Panic in the streets. Catastrophizers assume the worst, then build a case to match. Result: They are never unpleasantly surprised—or *pleasantly* surprised.

Granted, we need to consider potential risks and dangers. But these quintessential pessimists rush immediately to the dark side of every new idea—and stay there. Blessed are they who have low expectations, for they shall not be disappointed.

The key to brightening the Catastrophizer's view is to provide a little contrast. You can add a few shades of gray to the Catastrophizer's palette, thus shedding some light on your great idea.

DAVID VS. GOLIATH REVISITED

Killer Phrase: "The Competition Will EAT You Alive."

This super-efficient Killer Phrase chews up your idea and spits it out before the competition ever has a chance. With naysayers like these, who needs enemies?

Such naysayers may also warn you:

> *They'll clean your clock.*
> *They'll eat you for lunch.*
> *They'll make mincemeat out of you.*

Defusing Strategy

If the naysayers in your organization are fixated on your competitors, try these tips to transform your "dangerous" suggestion into the New Idea du Jour.

1. Examine the worst-case scenario. How badly will the competition trounce us? What's the best-case scenario? Could we eat *them* alive? What happens in between? If we succeed, maybe all the competition will be eating is our dust.

2. Examine the past and look to the future. The naysayer has sacrificed personal opinion in favor of appeasing a more powerful group. Why? Has the dire prediction been true in the past? What's different about this time?

3. Don't accept personal attacks, which make you the target. Shift the attention back to your idea. Look for ways to neutralize resistance and gain support.

4. Toss out a few crumbs of your idea first to find out exactly how hungry "they" are. What will it take to pacify your competition long enough to give your idea a chance?

5. Automakers and computer manufacturers are discovering what field mice have always known: Stationary targets are easy prey. So learn from nature—keep evolving, keep moving, and survive. If you can't beat 'em, join the steady migration from "Never trust the competition" to "Let's form a partnership."

Zero Defects

Do it right the first time.
—Quality department slogan

Perfect skin. Perfect relationship. Perfect world. *Zero Defects* makes an admirable goal but a rotten motivational slogan. We need standards, but Zero Defects naysayers want to begin at the end. Truth is, it's a dead end, generating more problems than it solves. The demand for instant perfection creates play-it-safe environments where no one expects serendipity and people hide their mistakes, only compounding them.

Face it: We humans don't always get it right the first time. But give us the freedom to fail and learn, and hang on to your hat. As Steve Jobs, inventor of Apple computers, said in *Fortune* magazine, "You never heard of the Apple I."

The flaw in the Zero Defects veneer is that *perfectionism* and *quality* are not interchangeable terms. Open up a new dialogue—one of continuous improvement. You can redesign the work environment to shorten development cycles, and establish a collaborative climate for your idea. But most important is to anticipate and learn from failures, so when you fail you "fail fast" and correct what's wrong immediately.

Killer Phrase: "If It Ain't BROKE, Don't Fix It."

Or, as they say in New York City, "If it ain't broke, it's unbreakable!"

Also be prepared to run into these obstacles to innovation:

> *You can't argue with success.*
> *Leave well enough alone.*
> *If it's still working okay, why change it?*

Defusing Strategy

Break the impasse with one of the following strategies. Because if it ain't broke today, it might be tomorrow.

1. Preventive maintenance. Before presenting your idea, identify its benefits, such as new products or a chance to acquire new market share. Then, work with the naysayer to brainstorm advantages of breaking "it"—before your competition does. See chapter 9 for the theory of creative destruction.

2. Streamline your thinking. How can you achieve it in half the time or at half the cost? What are the best and worst potential outcomes? How can you shift the odds of success in your favor?

3. Show and tell. Provide a quick history of new products improving things that weren't broken, such as express delivery, compact discs, and microwave dinners. Reynolds Metals invented flip-top cans when most of us were satisfied with using can openers.

Putting the Classroom Rules Behind You

How often does voicing a new idea at work recall the uncomfortable experience of being in school—raising your hand out of turn, challenging the teacher, or asking a dumb question? I believe the rules of school still plague us deep in our subconscious.

1. "The boss will never go for it" sounds a lot like "The teacher is always right."

2. "That isn't your responsibility" is just the grown-up version of "Keep your eyes on your own paper."

3. And my favorite, "Be realistic," reminds me of my English teacher saying, "No daydreaming."

School rarely allowed for collaboration. It's no wonder that today's self-directed teams struggle to accomplish their goals. Working in teams, we want to be able to borrow, we want to pass notes, we want to share early in the process. But that's not how work teams are set up much of the time. Corporate teams often resemble relay teams, passing the baton from one department to another. We want to act more like a jazz group, continually improvising.

So what can we do? In your next staff meeting, ask everyone to write down the rules of school that they remember. Then ask if any of those rules stifle creative thinking in your group. If so, challenge the offending rules and create new guidelines for your discussions.

OLD RULES OF SCHOOL	GUIDELINES FOR CREATIVITY AND INNOVATION
The teacher is always right.	Solicit opinions from those doing the work.
There's one right answer.	There are several right answers.
Keep your eyes on your own paper.	Collaborate and share ideas.

Raise your hand.	Ask introverts, "What do you think?"
Grade by report cards.	Don't measure everything.
Stay on the subject.	Allow for divergent thinking.
Work alone.	Form self-directed teams.
Stop daydreaming.	Envision problems as solved and work backward.
No spitballs.	Throw foam balls at naysayers.

Five More Ways to Overcome Killer Phrases

My workshop participants have devised unique approaches to turn attitudes away from "why we can't" to "why we can."

1. Institutionalize the Term Killer Phrase

You must first get everyone around you accustomed to the term *Killer Phrase,* which should be as recognizable as the phrases themselves. Only when people recognize such phrases will they be able to overcome them and prevent the destructive effects they can have on an organization's creative energy.

I recommend sending out a memo declaring war on Killer Phrases. Below is a sample memo for you to put into your own words and send out to those people whose aid you want to enlist.

To:
From:
Re: Killer Phrases

Every organization develops ingrained responses to new ideas and new ways of doing things. Typically, these responses are negative and try to shoot down ideas before they have a chance to prove themselves as good ideas or even as great ideas.

I've recently been reading a book called *What a Great Idea! 2.0.* It reports that all organizations have these institutionalized, negative ways of reacting to new ideas.

The author calls them *Killer Phrases.* The name is apt, I believe.

I think we have similar phrases in our office, and I'd like your help in identifying the most popular Killer Phrases we use. By knowing what these are and why people reflexively fling them around, we can begin to anticipate them and perhaps reduce the harmful effects they often have.

I've started a list of Killer Phrases on the next page. Please add to the list those you hear or those you use. I'll collate the results and send out a list of the most frequently listed Killer Phrases to everyone in the company.

Many thanks for your help.

2. The Killer Phrase Response Outline

At your next meeting, after gathering the most common Killer Phrases in your office or organization, you might want to explore ways to overcome them. At the meeting, you should pass out the Killer Phrase Response Outline Action Sheet (see pages 75–76), a systematic approach to analyzing Killer Phrases, identifying their sources, determining their legitimacy, and overcoming those that threaten creativity and innovation. Ask everyone to submit their most effective Response Outline and present a "Comeback of the Month" award.

3. The Foam Ball

At your next meeting, hand out a supply of red foam balls. Instruct everyone to throw a foam ball at anyone who utters a Killer Phrase during the meeting. Some people will start to catch themselves in the middle of saying a Killer Phrase—instruct them to throw the ball at themselves. You'll run a meeting you'll never forget!

Advanced ESP Version: Throw foam balls *before* you actually hear the Killer Phrase—because you just *knew* that person was thinking it!

An Opposite Version: Whenever you want a person or a team to come up with a new idea, throw a yellow foam ball their way. By tossing the ball back and forth, you'll produce a remarkably effective idea-generation session.

4. The Criminal Penalty

At your next meeting, announce a fine of 25 cents for each Killer Phrase uttered by any member of the group. Enforce the fines, save the money, and buy your team a gift with the proceeds—a motivational tape, refreshments for the next meeting, or a popcorn popper for the coffee room.

5. The Billboard

Make sure your meeting room has a flip chart or marker board. Ask group members to list on it the ten most frequently uttered Killer Phrases. Making the Killer Phrases known in advance typically will reduce their use during the meeting. Some managers in my creativity workshops have produced Killer Phrase posters for their meeting rooms. You can download several of these posters from my Web site: www.whatagreatidea.com.

Just for Fun, Some More Killer Phrases . . .

Are you putting me on? . . . Because might makes right . . . Business is business . . . But with the economy the way it is . . . CYA . . . Don't get me wrong . . . Don't give up your day job . . . Don't overload your plate . . . Do you think we're made of money? . . . Go soak your head . . . Have you lost your marbles? . . . I couldn't care less . . . I don't want to hurt your feelings, but . . . If it doesn't work, I won't back you up . . . If you weren't so lazy, you wouldn't be thinking of an easier way . . . Is it supported by research? . . . It costs too much . . . I think you've got a screw loose . . . It's my way or the highway . . . It's not a high priority . . . It's too blue sky . . . It's too late . . . Let's not go off on a tangent . . . Nobody makes a product like that . . . Oh, yeah, I had that idea a long time ago . . . Our place is too small for it . . . Sounds half-baked to me . . . Sure it will . . . That's pie in the sky . . . That's too hard . . . That will screw up the works . . . The idea has to get instant results . . . The old-timers won't use it . . . The only problem with that is . . . There's no community support . . . There you go, sticking your neck out . . . Too academic . . . What a harebrained idea . . . What you are really saying is . . . What's behind that suggestion? . . . When pigs fly . . . Who cares? . . . Who do you think you are? . . . Why start anything now? . . . You can't make a silk purse out of a sow's ear . . . You can't save everyone . . . You don't know what you're talking about . . . You don't understand our problem . . . You're setting yourself up for failure . . .

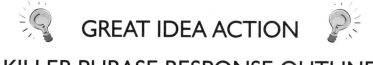

GREAT IDEA ACTION

KILLER PHRASE RESPONSE OUTLINE

Write down ideas for effective responses to anticipated Killer Phrases.

Step 1 Identify the Killer Phrase

Identify and jot down three anticipated Killer Phrases:

1.

2.

3.

Who will utter these Killer Phrases?

1.

2.

3.

Step 2 Determine the Root Cause

Identify a reason why the person might fling each of the above Killer Phrases at you.

1.

2.

3.

Step 3 Explore Your Options

Is the Killer Phrase really a disguised question? If so, jot down the real question.

1.

2.

3.

Write down short answers to the above disguised questions.

1.

2.

3.

Step 4 Act

Refer to the illustrated Killer Phrase Playbook earlier in this chapter to find similar situations. Then jot down a suggested response or defusing strategy to overcome the anticipated Killer Phrases.

1.

2.

3.

After completing the above mental exercise, take ten deep breaths, proceed with your idea, and be ready to jump over the Killer Phrase hurdles on your way to the finish line.

Conclusion

The essence of creative *freedom* is the ability to gather a quantity of ideas; the rest of the creative process flows from this all-important accumulation of ideas. To generate a multitude, a kaleidoscope, of ideas requires the ability to identify and overcome those deadly assumptions we've called Killer Phrases. We've discussed a number of ways you can "fire" off ideas and fight Killer Phrases; it might be helpful to supplement these methods with some thoughts about how to generate ideas and hold your own in everyday, moment-by-moment situations. In other words, how do you integrate freedom so that you have it in all kinds of circumstances, including those where you don't have the luxury of thinking through these steps or philosophizing about creativity?

Corresponding to every formal method written in this book, there are the quick, informal, intuitive, unwritten ways people have of being creative. These are very personal; I can only give guidelines and examples that will help you recognize those ways that might be yours.

To be "ready," in the process of "Ready, Fire . . . Aim!" involves most of all a willingness to direct our attention away from what we assume and accept and to refocus our thinking in a new way. In day-to-day situations, this means being willing to give up the safety of straight-line thinking in order to hear yourself think

or say the unexpected, the "maybe-this-is-crazy-but-it-just-occurred-to-me" hunch. And, indeed, it *may* strike everyone else as crazy—that's the risk we all take in the name of great ideas, human progress, and personal gratification!

Refocusing often means opening a side door or a back entrance in your mind, so that daydreaming and doodling, for example—or walking or playing music—have a chance to enrich your work. The process of free association requires first *un*association, then *re*association, letting yourself drift away or detach from those things "we all know" so that maybe you can find something none of us ever thought of. In conversations, conferences, or meetings, it means going with your gut, whatever that means to you. And even though that can also require gutting it out against Killer Phrases, you don't necessarily have to remember a battery of techniques for overcoming them. Your fundamental ally, which can sooner or later overcome any set of killer assumptions, is your faith in your own creative process. In yourself.

EXPRESSION

One step beyond the freedom to consider new possibilities is the ability to give voice to the problems and questions that the new ideas will address. At the beginning of the idea-generating process, you must feel free to say what's wrong or what's needed, what's going on and what has to be done to correct that. You must appeal for help by asking questions.

In the following chapters you'll find ways to make certain that your real questions get asked. Question asking, you'll discover, is an art form, with specific techniques required of the truly creative person. The correct ways of expressing those questions are all-important, for on the questions hinge the answers.

It has been said that the number-one performance fear is speaking in front of others. Fear of speaking our ideas aloud has stifled even our most brilliant thinkers. According to historians, Thomas Jefferson was terrified of speaking publicly. In his later years he said that he was hurt deeply by the Continental Congress' drastic revisions to his personal masterpiece, the Declaration of Independence. Unfortunately, he was too afraid to defend his work in the public arena.

Why do we fear expressing ourselves and our true thoughts? One answer is that we need to defend our egos, our need to be right. We've learned that being called on to give an answer is only fun if we know the *right* answer. Otherwise, we are faced with an instant—and often traumatic—learning experience.

It's true that knowing the right answers helps us keep up with the competition. But to get *ahead* of the competition, we need to ask the right questions. In this step, called Expression, you'll learn to articulate new questions and, without noticing it, you'll begin to live with new answers.

Think Outside the Lines

Idea Mapping the Problem

As the artist creates the work, the work creates the artist.
—*Eric Maisel, author of Artists Speak*

As young students sitting alphabetically in rows, our teachers said the lines on our paper were our "friends." As we progressed from staying within the lines for coloring, to writing on the lines for penmanship, to linear outlining for book reports, rules were established.

1. Start at the top of the page.

2. Put your name in the upper right-hand corner.

3. Arrange your thoughts in descending order (I., II., A., B., 1., 2., a., b., etc.).

4. Use parallel sentence structure.

5. Create the outline before writing the paper.

Unfortunately, following these rules didn't always lead to success. Think back: Did you ever write the paper first and then create the linear outline? Did doing the outline first ever give you a mental block?

Let the Blank Page Be Your Friend

Thankfully, today's progressive teachers are demonstrating a new outlining technique called Idea Mapping. With this technique you:

1. Start in the center of your paper with your topic heading.

2. Rapidly fill up the page with your thoughts.

3. Swap your paper with the student sitting near you.

4. Don't worry about proper spelling.

The goal is to fill up the page with thoughts, ideas, pictures, and inspiration. (One child told me the secret to filling up your page: Write BIG!)

Problem Articulation

Before you can come up with ideas to solve a problem, you must know what your problem is. Sure, that's obvious, but you'd be surprised at how many people have trouble articulating what the problem is. And, of course, not everyone views a given situation in the same way. Some might look at a situation and not see any problems at all.

The first requirement, then, is problem articulation. As in any other phase of the creative process, there are creative ways to do this.

In my workshops, participants try a relatively simple step-by-step process to formulate problems. The process relies on "Ready, Fire . . . Aim!" thinking to state what the problem is. It also seeks new perspectives by having you look at the problem from the viewpoints of other people affected by it.

To assist you in articulating problems, I've prepared the Problem Articulation Action Sheet on page 87. People in business or government can use it as the broad outline of a report or plan; students may find the approach helpful as they prepare to write a paper or dissertation.

Before you start using this Action Sheet, you need to know a little more about Idea Mapping. Idea Mapping is a fast, five-minute exercise in word and idea association. It relies on keywords, colors, and graphics to form a non-linear network of potential ideas and observations, which leads to spontaneous idea generation and a vast amount of visible information. To show you what an Idea Map looks like, I've prepared an Idea Map on—why not?—the potential uses of Idea Maps (Figure 6-1).

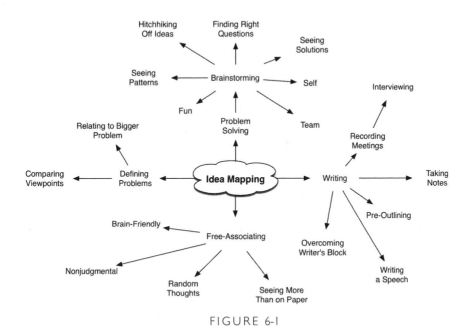

FIGURE 6-1

To create an Idea Map, I follow these steps:

Step 1

State the problem [Ready].

Step 2

Write in the center of your sheet a word or phrase that describes the essence of your problem and put a circle around it. Let's call that word the Trigger Word [Ready].

Step 3

Now, without judging, fire away for two minutes and write down around this Trigger Word as many aspects of your problem as you can think of. Do not evaluate the quality of your ideas at this point—just keep firing [Fire].

Step 4

See if any of the words are related to any of the others. If so, draw arrows between them, connecting your key thoughts. Build up as many associations as you like. Add more words as necessary [Fire].

Step 5

Step back and look at your entire map to find three or four main concepts or recurring themes. Assign a geometric symbol to each of those main concepts and put that symbol around each of the words in the map that would be grouped under that concept. This process is called "clustering" [Aim] (see Figure 6-2).

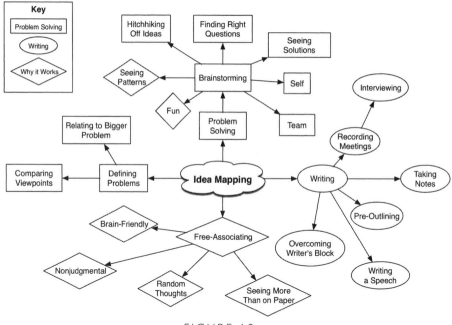

FIGURE 6-2

Step 6

Now create a cluster outline. Put the three or four geometric symbols with main concepts written inside at the top of another sheet of paper. Then list the related words from the map below each symbol. Rank them in an order that seems logical to you [Aim]. A cluster outline for our Idea Map is shown as in Figure 6-3.

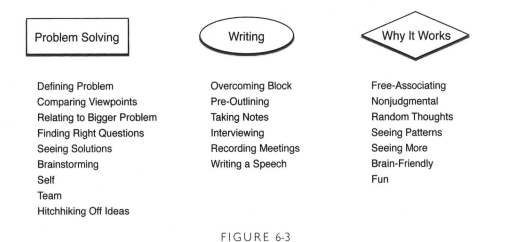

Problem Solving	Writing	Why It Works
Defining Problem	Overcoming Block	Free-Associating
Comparing Viewpoints	Pre-Outlining	Nonjudgmental
Relating to Bigger Problem	Taking Notes	Random Thoughts
Finding Right Questions	Interviewing	Seeing Patterns
Seeing Solutions	Recording Meetings	Seeing More
Brainstorming	Writing a Speech	Brain-Friendly
Self		Fun
Team		
Hitchhiking Off Ideas		

FIGURE 6-3

Step 7

If you prefer a linear outline, transcribe your Idea Map into an outline by using the main concept words for "Roman-numeral" entries and the other words for "A, B, C," "1, 2, 3," and so on [Aim].

The resulting linear outline of Idea Mapping looks like this:

I. Problem Solving
   A. Defining the Problem
      1. Comparing different viewpoints
      2. Relating to the bigger problem
      3. Finding the right questions to ask
   B. Seeing Solutions
      1. Brainstorming
         a. Self
         b. Team
      2. Hitchhiking from other solutions

II. Writing
   A. Overcoming Writer's Block
      1. Report writing
      2. Writing a speech
   B. Pre-outline Techniques

1. Taking notes

2. Recording lectures

3. Interviewing

III. Why It Works
   A. Free Association

     1. Suspends judgment

     2. Disjointed thoughts, then arranged

     3. See more than is written down
   B. Brain-Friendly
   C. Fun

Step 8

Referring to your outline, write out suggested solutions to your stated problem or question [Aim].

For example, based on the entry for Roman numeral I, subentry A, you might write:

Idea Maps facilitate problem solving by helping to define the problem. They place different viewpoints about the problem side by side in a graphic relationship, which helps us see the questions we need to ask.

Discovering the Target

To borrow from our discussion of "Ready, Fire . . . Aim!" in chapter 3, you can see that you're firing off as many words as you can, hoping you'll hit something. *After* firing, look at your Idea Map to see whether you scored any worthwhile relationships between words. The relational patterns and concepts will jump out at you, prompting you to come up with new ideas.

PROBLEM ARTICULATION ACTION SHEET

On another sheet of paper, answer the questions and complete the exercises below.

1. **Write a tentative problem statement.** Without thinking in detail about the problem, record your initial impressions. Focus on central issues; don't worry about causes or cures at this point.

2. **Explore your problem with an Idea Map.** Write a Trigger Word (or phrase) describing the essence of your problem in a center circle. Then write down as quickly as you can words associated with your Trigger Word; put these words all around the center circle. Look for new associations. Draw arrows from one word to another, connecting your key thoughts. Add more words as necessary.

3. **Look for the main concepts and patterns in your Idea Map.** Assign geometric symbols to your main concepts and "cluster" your words by putting the respective symbol around each related word.

4. **Create an outline.** Now transcribe your Idea Map into either a cluster or a Roman-numeral outline.

5. **Further clarify the problem.** This exercise will help you clarify the views of those people most concerned with how the problem is solved, that is, the "stakeholders" in the problem. The key question to ask is this: "Do the other major stakeholders in this problem have different points of view and, if so, why?"

STAKEHOLDER	POINT OF VIEW	WHY?
_____	_____	_____
_____	_____	_____
_____	_____	_____

6. **Restate your problem.** Looking carefully at your problem outline and incorporating different points of view, now write a carefully worded description of the precise problem needing great ideas for its solution.

Idea Mapping for Solutions

According to Yoshiro NakaMats, one way to facilitate the creation of ideas is to allow your thoughts about a problem to flow freely before you begin to do research or talk about it to others, and to record those thoughts as they bubble to the surface. By allowing your thoughts to wander in any direction, you build a foundation of how you feel about the problem, you stay close to your original vision or impulse, and you get a record of it. This is contrary to how many of us were taught to approach problem solving, which was to plunge into research or interview experts before we even formed our own opinion about the subject at hand.

Idea Mapping is an excellent tool for downloading these original thoughts. Just before brainstorming in a meeting, I recommend that everyone do an individual Idea Map about the problem we're going to discuss; this way their own thoughts are recorded and not lost among the group's brainstorming. The individual maps also provide an excellent warm-up for the brainstorming session.

Let's see how Idea Maps work in a real situation. As an example, suppose your company or division suffers from poor morale. Everybody's down in the dumps; no one seems energized or inspired; malaise suffuses every project you undertake.

You decide to use an Idea Map to pinpoint as many aspects of the current situation as possible. Figure 6-4 shows what your Idea Map might look like, based on the Trigger Words *Poor Morale*:

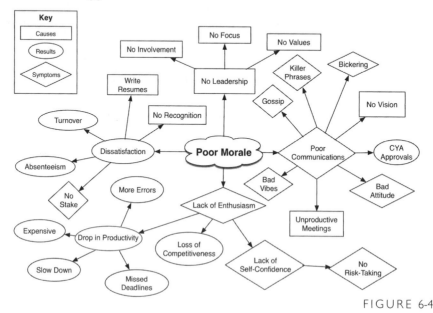

FIGURE 6-4

That's Just the Beginning

The example of "Ready, Fire . . . Aim!" Idea Mapping that we've just done could help us produce a number of good ideas. However, let's assume that you're not sure how the various elements are linked to one another. What may seem to be a cause might really be a symptom of the problem, forcing you to look more deeply for the root cause.

To reach a more refined understanding of your problems and opportunities, try varying your Trigger Word to produce new Idea Maps until you can see your priorities clearly. I recommend changing the Trigger Word in five ways, all of which we will discuss shortly:

1. Trigger Word *When Solved* . . . (a future-state Trigger Word that represents a desired outcome)

2. Trigger Word *Comes from* . . . (a past-state Trigger Word that examines the roots of the problem)

3. A metaphorical Trigger Word

4. An opposite Trigger Word

5. A random Trigger Word

Trigger Word When Solved . . .

Here we use a problem-solving approach discussed in detail in chapter 8, "Self-Fulfilling Prophecies." We envision the desired situation—*high morale*—as if it were accomplished and we were there right now. What's our company or unit like with high morale? What does that tell us—what can we infer from this picture—about the steps that got us there?

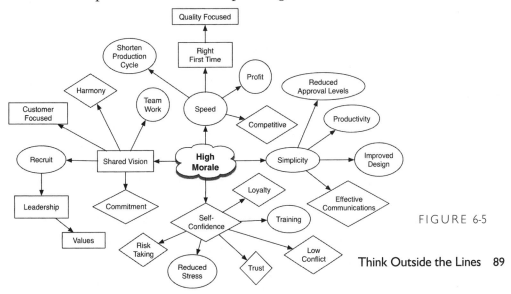

FIGURE 6-5

Think Outside the Lines 89

Looking at the Idea Map sparked by the Trigger Word *High Morale* (see Figure 6-5) could very well give you all the ideas you need. But let's save those for our final outline and build an even greater store of ideas by moving on to:

Trigger Word Comes from . . .

Get to the problem's roots by adding *comes from* after your Trigger Word. Using *Poor Morale* again, we produce the Idea Map shown in Figure 6-6.

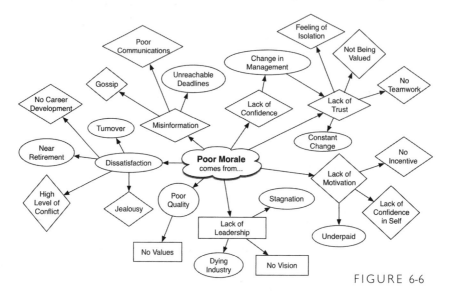

FIGURE 6-6

By now you can see that your company's outcomes follow from the identified symptoms, which are the result of underlying causes. These insights could lead you to some great-idea leaps. However, you may not have as many ideas as you'd like to address the problem in a creative way. That's why I make several maps that reframe the problem. The following three maps do just that.

Metaphorical Trigger Word

To gain a different perspective on your problem, couch it in metaphorical terms. By framing the problem in terms of metaphors or similes, you can often come up with ingenious solutions.

Let's try this technique out. Poor morale in an organization is like . . . a rainy day! (See Figure 6-7 on the next page.) It's a drip undermining your culture. The mud from poor morale gets tracked all over the office and makes a mess until it gets cleaned up. These figurative thoughts would not have come from just brainstorming about *poor morale*!

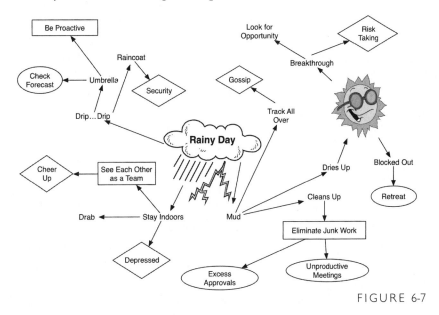

FIGURE 6-7

Opposite Trigger Word

You can often figure out what something *is* by exploring what it *is not.* Instead of putting your problem in the Idea Map as the Trigger Word, write down its exact opposite. The opposite of *poor morale,* of course, is *enthusiasm* (see the Idea Map in Figure 6-8).

In the example of using an opposite Trigger Word, the opposite was similar to the *when solved* Trigger Word; however, it nicely generated new insights for the hoped-for future state.

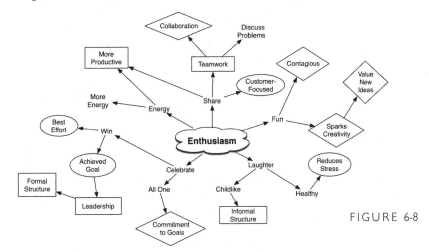

FIGURE 6-8

Finally, to give you yet another perspective on your problem, use an absolutely random Trigger Word in your Idea Map. Use anything at all. Go to the dictionary, turn to a page at random, and blindly point to a word on the page. Use that word as a Trigger Word. If a dictionary isn't handy or if you need to ruminate on a problem, take a hike. Literally. Go for a walk around the block or a stroll through the park. The first thing that catches your eye—use that as a Trigger Word.

If you need encouragement, consider the experience of Knute Rockne, the famous Notre Dame football coach. "I got my idea for my 'four horsemen backfield shift,'" he said, "while watching a burlesque chorus routine."

Let's see this in action. As I'm writing this book I am now turning away from my computer keyboard toward my telephone. I'm picking up my copy of the yellow pages and wondering whether readers will really believe that the word I pick was chosen completely by chance. Whatever the word is, I hope it doesn't look too easy. Okay, I'm turning to a page at random, and, let's see, pointing to the word . . . *tours.* Tours?

Tours. So let's use *tours* as the Trigger Word in our final Idea Map (Figure 6-9) on the problem of poor morale.

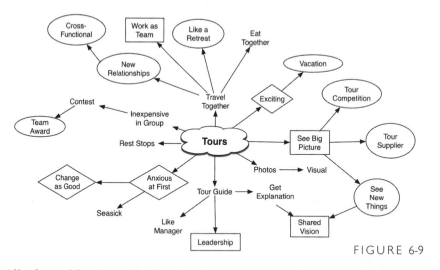

FIGURE 6-9

All of a sudden I see that leadership in an organization with poor morale requires a tour guide to help everyone see the big picture. The journey of change also requires numerous rest stops along the way. And photographing accomplishments serves as a reminder of the poor morale that we are—happily—leaving behind.

Comparing Your Idea Maps

In addressing the issue of *Poor Morale,* we've generated key concepts related to everything from "Where it comes from" to "What it is not." To synthesize your Idea Maps, you can put them side by side on a table or tape them to a wall. Then step back and see if you notice any connections or overlaps from one map to another.

For the collected Idea Maps on poor morale, we next make an outline of all the thoughts and associations we've come up with. This outline can be organized by immediacy of action or just by definition of the problem from general to specific.

The following outline is my analysis of the problem of poor morale, as taken from the five Idea Maps.

I. Factors Affecting Organizational Morale
   A. Causes
   B. Symptoms
   C. Results

II. Variables
   A. Causal variables
      1. Lack of leadership
      2. Values not followed
      3. No shared vision
      4. No focus on customer
      5. Constant change
      6. Don't see organization as a whole
   B. Intervening variables
      1. Weak commitment to organization
      2. No risk taking
      3. Poor communications
      4. High level of conflict
      5. Gossip
      6. Lack of confidence
      7. No teamwork

8. Lack of trust

9. No incentive

C. Outcome Variables

1. Poor quality

2. Customer complaints

3. Decreasing productivity

a. Slowdown

b. More errors

4. Lack of competitiveness

5. Missed goals and deadlines

6. Falling profit and ROI

7. Job dissatisfaction

a. Turnover

b. Absenteeism

c. Underpaid

8. Too many CYA approvals

9. Constant management changes

10. Act like dying organization

III. Action Recommendations

A. Create a vision

1. Make it understandable

2. Make it inspiring

3. Include performance appraisals

B. Encourage collaboration

1. Set up project work teams

2. Knock down hierarchical and divisional walls

3. Foster an environment for creativity and risk taking

4. Measure and reward team efforts

5. Hold off-site retreats

6. Initiate cross-functional training

C. Take a customer-focused orientation

1. Understand external customer

2. Understand internal customer (coworkers or departments that depend on us to provide products or services)

3. Identify customer needs

4. Measure and reward customer satisfaction

D. Initiate a continuous improvement process

  1. Eliminate unnecessary junk work

    a. Reports

    b. Approvals

    c. Meetings

    d. Measurements

    e. Policies

  2. Work as cross-functional teams to find better ways to do things

  3. Include customers and suppliers in process

You can also convert the outline back into a graphic representation to specify important relationships—as shown in Figure 6-10.

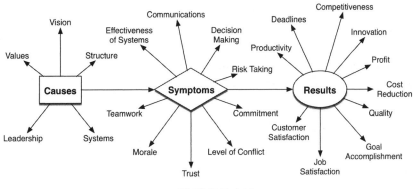

FIGURE 6-10

IDEA MAPPING FOR THE FAMILY

Create an Idea Map for picking your next vacation spot.

1. Put the word *vacation* in the center and write your ideas all over the page.

2. Try an advanced technique: Locate a large piece of paper, put it on the wall, and include pictures of vacation ideas along with the words.

Create an Idea Map of the earliest childhood neighborhood you can remember.

1. Start drawing in the streets that surrounded your home.

2. Label the street names and write down where you played and where you rode your bike.

3. Fill in the names of your neighbors and show where you went to school.

4. Where were your secret places?

5. What was off-limits?

Did this map open up your memory? Now use this map to give a five-minute talk or to write a short essay on where you grew up.

Uses of Idea Maps

You can expand the uses of Idea Mapping to cover a host of situations and to serve as a catalyst for positive organizational change. Consider the following variations of Idea Mapping.

Idea Maps and Report Writing

Idea Maps are ideal exercises for preparing written analyses of problems, strategies, plans, programs, and policies. The key lies in the notion of *synthesis*. Idea Maps produce a flood of words—unrelated words, concrete words, words that seemingly bear little relation to one another.

But when the Idea Mapping process is over, you can look at the words you've produced and synthesize them into larger conceptual groupings. And when you're looking at a series of Idea Maps, the larger conceptual groupings might merge into even larger groupings. These larger groupings, when appropriately labeled, then serve as the "organizational milestones" for a written report.

A colleague of mine teaches persuasive writing at law firms, government agencies, and corporations. Recently, he began to teach Idea Mapping as a device for organizing and brainstorming topics for written papers. At one recent course, a student raised her hand and said, "This Idea Mapping is similar to the 'front cover/back cover' approach to exam taking we used at Harvard. When I was a freshman, a professor told me to brainstorm on the inside front cover of the exam blue book and to outline on the inside back cover of the blue book. That way, professors could see that I'd covered the main topics even if I ran out of time on the exam!"

Indeed, the approach is similar. The front-cover brainstorming is the Idea Mapping. The back-cover outlining is identical to the synthesis you use to organize your thoughts.

Comparison Mapping

If your task is to synergize the views of various stakeholders, you can create a multi-centered Idea Map with one Trigger Word or phrase, say, *Slow Delivery*, and position other centered Trigger Words derived from different stakeholders. It might look like the one in Figure 6-11.

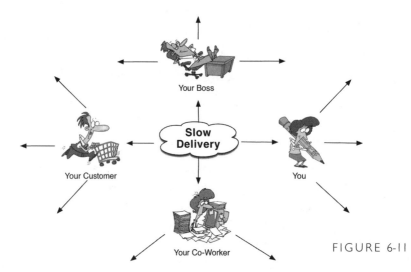

FIGURE 6-11

Then fire away with words from each new stakeholder's perspective. Look for interrelationships, draw connecting arrows, and put geometric symbols around any common elements you spot.

Team Mapping

Use large Idea Maps on the wall as a means of eliciting ideas from a group in a meeting and engendering true collaboration in the organization. My favorite technique is to put different Trigger Words on paper on all four walls of a conference room. Then I encourage the participants to fill up the walls with their responses. They can later transcribe the wall comments onto flipcharts or into their laptops.

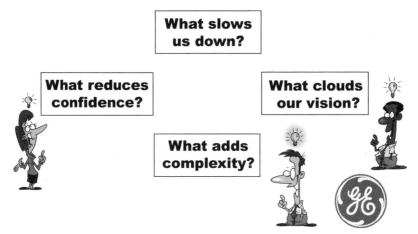

Four-wall brainstorming for GE's Work Out continuous improvement process.

Vision Mapping

On a large marker board, put your goal as the Trigger Word in the center of an Idea Map, surround it with empty circles, hang it up for all to see, and challenge your colleagues or subordinates to fill up the circles with actions that will have to take place to achieve the goal.

The Living Map

Create an ongoing Idea Map to elicit suggestions from staff or department heads. Position the Living Idea Map in high-traffic areas, such as by water coolers, in cafeterias, and in exercise rooms. Alternate by department the responsibility of writing down the Trigger Word of the Month.

The Graphics Map

Create a colorful Idea Map, using graphics, cartoons, symbols, and very few words. I almost always use colors in my Idea Maps. Using colored markers or crayons; I start with one color for the Trigger Word, another color for the words around it, another color for the arrows between them, and additional colors for the geometric symbols. Using different colors helps you to see new patterns; in fact, research by Tony Buzan, the inventor of idea mapping, shows that colors help students recall the Idea Map in their minds when they are taking a test.

Incidentally, since people like to be free and spontaneous—and fast—in their Idea Mapping, I often suggest that they do it in their native language, even if I'm working in the United States or another country where most of the participants speak English. After one session in the United States, a woman came up to me and said, "You know, as soon as you asked us to Idea Map, I started writing down all my words in German—and I haven't written in German in fifteen years!" The process itself brought out her most natural response.

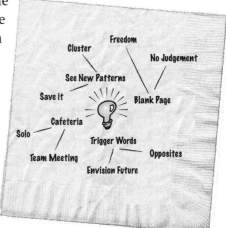

People often ask me why I recommend that they place words all over the page and attempt to link words that are out at the edges of the paper, seemingly scattered and unrelated. I recently reread the book *Chaos,* by James Gleick, which sums it up rather nicely: "At the boundary, life blossoms."

A Final Thought . . .

Idea Maps are excellent tools for quick, unstructured self-brainstorming sessions in everyday situations. Make use of whatever tools you have on hand: Use a legal pad, for example, turned sideways so that it functions as an artist's sketchpad. Or make a map on a napkin or a placemat at a restaurant or cafeteria. Instead of making your usual, linear to-do list, Idea Map it—think outside the lines and your ideas will jump off the page.

There are now excellent software packages that allow you to create Idea Maps. Here are my favorites:

1. **"Inspiration"** by Inspiration Software (www.inspiration.com) is visual thinking software for K–12 education and perfect for family brainstorms.

2. **"MindManager"** by MindJet (www.mindjet.com) is productivity software for visualizing and managing information, allowing individuals and teams to think, plan, and work together more effectively.

3. **"Curio"** by Zengobi (www.zengobi.com) promotes visual thinking in gathering your ideas, while managing all the notes and documents associated with your project.

GREAT IDEA ACTIONS

IDEA MAPPING GUIDE

Take out several sheets of paper—one for stating your problem and recording selected ideas, and the others for Idea Mapping. Make sure to have the Idea Mapping sheets turned sideways so that you don't work from the top down.

Step 1   State your problem on the first sheet of paper.

Step 2   Choose a Trigger Word.   _____

Then choose:

        a Metaphorical Word   _____

        an Opposite Word   _____

        a Random Word   _____

Step 3   Idea Map your trigger words.
Write the Metaphorical, Opposite, or Random Trigger Word in the center circle. Then write down as quickly as you can words associated with that Trigger Word; put these words all around the center circle. Look for new associations. Draw arrows from one word to another, connecting your key thoughts; add more words as necessary. Repeat this process for the other Trigger Words listed above.

Step 4   Look for the main concepts and patterns in your Idea Maps.
For each idea map, assign geometric symbols to your main concepts and "cluster" your words by putting the respective symbol around each related word.

Step 5   Create an Idea Outline on the back of the first sheet of paper.
Now compare your various Idea Maps. Transcribe your maps into either a "cluster" or a Roman-numeral outline.

Step 6   Record your ideas.
Select four ideas that can help you solve the problem.

C H A P T E R   7

Smart Questions

Forerunners to Innovation

> *Most successful organizations that now need help*
> *remember the answers but forget the questions.*
> —Peter Drucker, management consultant
> and best-selling author

Questions invite innovation. A question posed to the right person on the right topic at the right time can yield a wealth of information and ideas.

Questions call for dialogue. Statements, by contrast, require passive listening and often give rise to defensive responses. The creative manager wouldn't approach a division chief and make a statement like this one: "This department is failing." Rather, she would *pose the question:* "If you were me, what would you do to change things around here?"

To Find the Answer, Ask the Question

If you're seeking great ideas, the first step is often to ask smart questions, because the way you look at a problem dictates how you go about solving it. Thomas MacAvoy, former president and chief operating officer of Corning Glass Works, for example, relates the most creative question ever asked in his professional life.

One day, while MacAvoy was a senior chemist in a lab at Corning, Corning's president said to the head of research, "Glass breaks. Why don't you do something about that?" The directive to the lab then became: "We're going to prevent glass from breaking." The lab came up with twenty-five different ways of preventing glass from breaking; eighteen of them worked, and five made money.

The most interesting aspect of this exchange is not what the president asked but what he did *not* ask. He did not ask, "Why does glass break?" That question might have produced months of exhaustive research, resulting in some highly scientific reports, which would have collected dust on a shelf and done no one any good. Instead, the boss went straight for the desired solution: How can we make glass that doesn't break? The end result was the now-famous Corelle line of dinnerware.

Sometimes the smart question has to challenge conventional wisdom to help address complex and long-standing challenges. Dr. David C. Goodman, a professor of pediatrics and family medicine at Dartmouth Medical School, wrote an op-ed piece in the *New York Times* (July 10, 2006), titled "Too Many Doctors in the House?" Dr. Goodman asks:

> *Can we cure our ailing health care system by sending in more doctors? That is the treatment prescribed by the Association of American Medical Colleges, which has recommended increasing the number of doctors they train by 30 percent, in large part to keep up with the growing number of elderly patients. But the most serious problems facing our health care system—accelerating costs, poor quality of care and the rising ranks of the uninsured—cannot be solved by more doctors.*
>
> *In fact, that approach, like prescribing more drugs for an already overmedicated patient, may only make things worse. By training more doctors than we need, we will continue to fill more hospital beds, order more diagnostic tests—in short, spend more money. But our resources would be better directed toward improving efforts to prevent illness and manage chronic ailments like diabetes and heart disease.*

The answers revealed by Dr. Goodman's question show health care moving toward a prevention model with more emphasis on health communicators and nurse-practitioners. The hoped-for result: highly trained doctors with more time to treat the really sick patients.

Smart Questions

A few years ago I was having dinner with the motivational speaker and life coach, Tony Robbins. He is known for coining clever phrases and, before we were done with our salads, he said, "Successful people just ask better questions, and as a result, they get better answers."

So we discussed what constitutes "better" questions. Here are the ones I now use to prepare my mind for solving the toughest challenges.

Ask, "What Can I Be More Open-Minded About?"

Every morning with my cup of green tea, I ask, "What can I be more open-minded about today to be a better teacher?" It could be about something on the news or an issue that I'm facing on the home front. I then jot down my thoughts in my day planner and hope that each day will provide new insights. These notes have made for a wonderful diary.

When conducting a group brainstorm, ask what the group needs to be more open-minded about regarding the challenge to encourage a creative exchange of ideas. This usually leads to participants challenging outdated, unpopular, or institutionalized policies and practices.

Additional questions that will open up your way of thinking about a particular challenge include:

1. How many different ways can we look at the challenge?

2. How can I rethink the way I see it?

3. How many different ways can we solve it?

4. How would someone else try to solve this situation?

A toilet paper manufacturer received a shipment of paper that was too thick and heavy to be made into tissue. The company was unable to return it but remained open-minded to possible uses for thick tissue.

Voilà! Paper towels were born.

An open mind is a glorious thing—it allows us to see things we never would otherwise.

Ask, "What's Unique about This Challenge?"

When you attempt to do something and fail, you literally end up doing something else. That is the first principle of creative accidents.

But the creative accident itself provokes a totally unique question: "What have you done?" The "right people," according to Niels Bohr, answer this question in a novel, unexpected way, and this is the essence of creativity. So when you look at a new challenge, ask, "What's unique about this challenge?" Whatever the apparent similarities, each challenge is unique and requires an approach that focuses on its own particular needs. Looking for the distinctive aspect of a challenge can lead you to a solution that will add lasting value—rather than an easy-way-out solution, which often leads you back to the very problem you started with.

> Innovation comes when the wrong things are used in the wrong way at the wrong time but by the right people.
>
> —Niels Bohr, Nobel Prize–winning physicist

Ask, "What Is This Like?"

According to Gerald Zaltman in *How Customers Think: Essential Insights into the Mind of the Market,* on average, we use six metaphors per minute of speech. Our thoughts are more figurative than they are literal. Entrepreneur George Thomas was searching for a more effective way to apply deodorant. He asked, "What is this problem like?" and realized that the pen he was writing with provided an answer. The concept of the roll-on deodorant was created through the metaphor of a ballpoint pen.

> It is from metaphor that we can best get hold of something fresh.
>
> —Aristotle

Recently I was asked to brainstorm new programs the Automobile Association of America (AAA—Mid Atlantic Division) could offer its current and potential customers. To think about new roadside service and trip-planning offerings, I set up two brainstorming sessions based on two analogies.

What if AAA roadside service were like a NASCAR pit crew?

What if AAA trip planning were like the Starbucks experience?

I selected NASCAR and Starbucks because, as Gary Hamel writes in *The Why, What and How of Management Innovation,* "To achieve 'management innovation' you need to find analogies from an atypical organization that redefine what's possible."

For the morning NASCAR brainstorm, I showed NASCAR video clips of pit crews in action and had model cars and logos scattered on the tables. Just think about the possibilities—a colorfully attired AAA pit crew arrives in record time and stages an exciting repair experience. They already know what's wrong with your car because the AAA logo on your bumper has sent a radio signal alerting them to the car's malfunction and your location. The crew gives out toy cars or racing video games to the kids and your name is entered into a lottery to win tickets to an upcoming NASCAR race. While you're on vacation, your kids would actually be hoping your car broke down—just for the "pit crew" experience! How much more will this cost, you ask? No more than usual, because all the AAA/NASCAR extras are offset by the branded advertising on the repair trucks and uniforms.

For the afternoon Starbucks brainstorm, I had various coffees brewing, music playing, and comfortable, no-hassle seating configurations—a real multisensory experience, just like Starbucks. I encouraged the attendees to envision their AAA trip planning like a visit to Starbucks—complete with free wi-fi with their AAA memberships and maps identifying the locations of the more than 6,000 Starbucks around America. By thinking metaphorically, participants were able to identify new ways to approach brand partnerships and generate new ideas for customer-focused products.

The next week I was giving a talk at St. Barnabas Medical Center in Livingston, New Jersey, about creative problem solving in medical management. I again used the NASCAR pit crew example, but this time the goal was to spark ideas for streamlining the operation of the hospital's Emergency Department. The ideas that surfaced regarding creative new methods of medical triage were amazing and energizing for the participants. The operating values of the pit crew—safety, speed, simplicity, self-confidence, and shared vision—transfer perfectly to health care, whether in the context of emergency services or operating room procedures.

As a frequent flier, I am pleased to see that United Airlines is now sending twelve hundred employees to NASCAR Pit Crew Camp. Their goal is to shave five minutes off the time each plane sits on the ground. If it works, United could add more than one hundred flights a day without having to add any more planes. What if you sent your employees to NASCAR camp? What could your organization learn from an atypical analogy that redefines what is possible?

For more on metaphors and idea generation, see chapter 10, "A Curveball."

Ask "Dumb Questions"

In *Thriving on Chaos: Handbook for a Management Revolution,* management guru Tom Peters emphasizes the power of the dumb question. In his words:

> *Mostly, it's the dumb, elementary questions followed up by a dozen even more elementary questions that yield the pay dirt. Experts are those who don't need to bother with elementary questions anymore—thus they fail to bother with the true sources of bottlenecks buried deep in habitual routines of the firm labeled "We've always done it that way."*

Jimmy Blanchard, CEO of Synovus Financial Corporation, hosts a quarterly meeting with top leaders throughout the Synovus system. The purpose of the meeting is summarized as follows: "Let's talk about the dumb things we do around here so we don't do them anymore."

What if, at your next quarterly meeting you took the first fifteen minutes and asked, "What are the five dumbest things we do around here?" Then you assigned each "dumb thing" to one attendee, and charged that person with digging deeply into the reasoning behind that action and reporting back at the next meeting.

Suggested Dumb Questions

1. Why have we always done it that way?

2. Does anyone actually look at this form?

3. Why do we need a committee to look into this?

4. What's a _____? [fill in the blank with acronym or high-tech term]

Asking dumb or "innocent" questions shows that you have the courage to be naïve, to ask a question even when the answer may be obvious to everyone else, to ask it simply because it puzzles you. Such questions are vital steps, because only when you feel free to voice queries from your own perspective are you ready for the next phase of the idea-generating process, which involves deliberately altering and expanding that perspective.

Ask, "Why?" Five Times

In the early '90s, I spent time with Dr. Edmonds Deming, the father of the Quality Movement, applying his principles to the U.S. public education system. My favorite quote from Dr. Deming was this: "To find the root cause of your problem, ask why the problem occurs—and after every answer, dig deeper by asking why *that* situation occurs. Only after asking *why* five times will you reach the root cause of your challenge."

A book on the Toyota production system, *40 years, 20 Million Ideas* by Yuzo Yasuda, tells how Toyota workers are trained to do just that—generate millions of ideas—when they confront a problem. For example:

1. Why has the machine stopped?
    A fuse blew because of an overload.

2. Why was there an overload?

There wasn't enough lubrication for the bearings.

3. Why wasn't there enough lubrication?

The pump wasn't pumping enough.

4. Why wasn't enough lubricant being pumped?

The pump shaft was vibrating as a result of abrasion.

5. Why was there abrasion?

There was no filter, which allowed chips of material to get into the pump.

Installing a filter solves the problem.

Unfortunately, most of us ask *why* only once, and, consequently, we never break the surface of our problem. We spin from one ineffective solution to the next because we are only addressing the symptoms rather than the causes.

One manager with whom I worked never had enough time to finish her to-do list. Here's how we applied this technique to her problem:

1. Why?—

There are too many unexpected interruptions in my day.

2. Why?—

I have an open-door policy.

3. Why?—

I want my staff to have my input when they have a crisis.

4. Why?—

We work as a team and I can offer many years of experience.

5. Why?—

Teamwork and sharing make our company productive.

By asking *why* five times, she found that her interruptions were necessary to make the company and staff productive. She needs to factor interruptions into her to-do list and time management, and recognize that it's valuable for the organization that members of her team solicit her opinion.

This executive could have gone on indefinitely feeling self-critical and frustrated. If we don't get to the root of the problem it will grow back, just as dandelions do when you only cut off the yellow head.

As discussed, ever since we started school, we've been trained to look for "the right answer." Breaking that habit isn't easy, so I recommend staying away from "We've got to find *the* solution" and instead easing into a new frame of mind by saying, "We need to look at some possible solutions to this problem." Although the difference might seem like mere wordplay, it's really about developing a new perspective—an inquisitive perspective that seeks an array of ideas by asking an array of questions in search of an array of potential solutions.

To that end, I often advise participants in problem-solving workshops and meetings to think of two words when formulating their questions: *flexible* and *focused*. Make your question flexible so that it's open to other people's interpretations and the views of other stakeholders in the organization—and make it focused, so you'll know when the responses you get answer your question.

Here are some excellent flexible and focused questions shared with me by Steve Van Valin, a creativity coach at the leading electronic retailer QVC.

- How can we build our brand image through our upcoming fourth-quarter direct-mail campaign?

- How can we attract new customers during the Spring Fling event?

- How can we partner with our distribution organization to increase the quality of our customer service?

- What new products can we offer that will create a positive public relations story this Christmas?

These questions will generate numerous possibilities for QVC and, with spirited debate and focused facilitation, can be turned into several "right" answers.

Creating a Team-Focused Question

What if you have a clear-cut and predetermined goal, such as "Increase sales in the first and second quarters by 25 percent," but you're not sure what questions to ask that will produce great ideas to help you reach this goal? Just turning the goal statement into a question might not make it specific enough to build momentum in a group brainstorm. For example, "What can we do to increase sales in the first and second quarters?" is probably too broad and unfocused.

Here is a great team technique Steve Van Valin at QVC has used. Along with communicating the goal of increasing sales, Van Valin painted a picture of the emotional benefits of reaching the goal, such as customer satisfaction, employee pride, and overall excitement. He then asked the group to generate a list of questions, which, if answered, would help nail the goal. Here are some of the questions generated by the QVC team:

- What other markets can we tap into in time for first and second quarters?

- How can e-mail marketing help us?

- How can we reactivate our inactive accounts?

- What other events are happening in the first and second quarters that we can piggyback onto?

- What can we put on sale to spike sales activity?

- What have we done in the past that was successful?

- What would our most ferocious competitor do in the first and second quarters?

- What special packaging can we come up with to make our offers especially appealing to high-end customers?

Once completed, Van Valin collected the lists from each team, clarifying any questions that seemed unclear, and then hung the questions on the wall. Each person was given five dot stickers and instructed to vote for the questions whose potential answers would have the greatest impact on achieving the goal.

This highly visible exercise will provide you with a powerful list of focused questions, in order of priority. Then you are ready to start brainstorming answers to your team-focused questions.

Creating a "Stretch Goal" Question

As a consultant commissioned to train General Electric personnel in the "Work-Out!" mind-set—to instill speed, simplicity, and self-confidence in the workplace—I was challenged to come up with the right questions for workshop participants.

"Work-Out!" was designed to speed up GE operations, but instead of asking, "How can you speed up your operations?" I asked, "How can you accomplish your work in half the time?" This "stretches" everyone to search for new ways to do specific tasks and not merely step on the gas in an effort to do the same old things faster.

My favorite idea generated from this question was to cut the number of hiring authorization approvals from thirteen to six. Within two weeks, GE cut this unnecessary bureaucracy and, hopefully, they are still looking at new ways to streamline the process.

Creating a Universal Set of Questions

Idea Generators should be aware of a simple universal truth: There are only six questions that one human can ask another: What? Where? When? How? Why? Who?

As an innovator and Idea Generator, you can constantly ask the Six Universal Questions as sparks for ideas and solutions to problems. You can even use the Six Universal Questions as a way to tear a problem apart or to organize how you present a particular problem. Take each question separately and seek as many answers as you can possibly find. Use questions to lead to other productive questions.

As an exercise, we can use the Six Universal Questions approach to create some really great questions, to unravel a problem to see its many facets, and to frame our problem so that workable solutions emerge. In the Six Universal Questions Action Sheet at the end of the chapter I've posed six questions about your problem.

Idea Mapping Your Questions

The question-asking process is especially powerful when joined to Idea Mapping—because every question can be expanded and answered with the help of an Idea Map, and the answer can then be explored and expanded with another Idea Map. Through Idea Mapping—or any other form of free-associating ideas—question asking translates into positive expression.

On the personal level, remember that Idea Mapping can be informal and quick and can work anywhere—five minutes of drawing on a paper napkin. It's a way for questions to lead to unforced, unexpected, multiple answers.

GREAT IDEA ACTIONS
SIX UNIVERSAL QUESTIONS

This sheet poses the Six Universal Questions about a problem you're having. Answer the questions as freely as you can and then combine your thoughts into two Great Questions to help you solve your problem.

Description of problem:

1. What is it?

2. Where does it happen?

3. When does it happen?

4. How does it happen?

5. Why does it happen?

6. Who causes it to happen? / To whom does it happen?

Now, combine your responses above into two Great Questions.

1.

2.

THE SECOND STEP

Conclusion

Once I was asked whether I thought it was possible to "institutional-ize" the question-asking process so that people could use it on a regular basis in their personal and organizational lives. "Or," my friend asked, "is that a self-defeating concept?"

Any organization can incorporate the basics of expression and question asking, even if you can't plot or predict what the questions will be or where they will lead. This process is never self-defeating; any method that an organization chooses to encourage questioning or free expression will tend to lead to progressive change.

Therefore, it's a fine idea for organizations and groups to incorporate the Six Universal Questions, for example, in a formal way, putting them on display, reminding decision makers to take them into account when consid-ering a problem or goal. A checklist of question-asking procedures, which

must be covered in coming to a decision, could save both large organizations and small groups grief and lead to unexpected new approaches for viewing or solv-ing the problem. New ideas then lead to new questions— and more new ideas.

CREATION

*I encourage the executives "to squint a little" to ignore the
surface detail and just look at the overall shape of the idea.*
—Tom Kelley, general manager, IDEO
The Ten Faces of Innovation

F *reedom* and *expression,* our first two steps, take you to the point of creation itself. Here's the heart of generating great ideas, and here's much of the fun. The most interesting thing about this process of creation, I believe, is how much fun it really is—how positive and effort-free it is, when you understand how it works.

For creating great new ideas is not a process of making something out of nothing—it's not a heroic effort to concentrate one's genius on a problem and somehow conquer it through sheer brilliance. If that's the way problem solving seems to you, you're probably working much too hard—and working against yourself.

Creation is fun because it's play. It involves, most of all, playing with the elements we're given. Rather than making something out of nothing—diamond icicles out of thin air—we're always making something new out of something given. The play is in taking the ingredients of this world and *re*-creating them—toying with them, imagining new combinations, new forms, new applications. The more fun it becomes for you, the more you're pursuing the most productive form of creativity.

Highly creative people see things differently; their perspective on problems is different from that of most other people. Why? Because they have cultivated the habit of imaginatively *un*-creating the world and putting it back together in new ways. But if we look at the way we think when we're at our most creative, then we can begin to change our own perspectives and see more things in a new light more of the time. And see solutions previously hidden from view.

C H A P T E R   8

Self-Fulfilling Prophecies

Envisioning the Future

I was playing golf one afternoon with Bob Rotella. A colleague of mine, Bob has made quite a name for himself in sports psychology, coaching some of the world's top professional golfers. I captured many of Bob's ideas in a highly successful audiocassette program, "Golfing Out of Your Mind." Since that time, *Golf Digest* has retained him to write a regular column on the relationship between the mind and success on the fairway, in bunkers, or on the greens.

On this particular afternoon, I'd become very tentative in my putting, invariably failing to reach the hole. After three-putting a hole, I asked for advice.

Bob shared with me a thought he'd used with various PGA champions. "Don't putt until you know you can make it."

"But, Bob," I said, "I'll be here all day waiting for that moment."

He laughed. "Just picture yourself as making the putt. You're picturing yourself *missing* the putt. *Make* the putt. Make the putt in your *mind*."

Of course, I didn't, and still don't, make every putt I attempt. But using Bob's method has helped me recover from a bad hole and par the next one.

What does the average golfer see when he plays this "water hole"?

Of course he sees the water—the hazard, the worst that can happen. So he switches his $3 golf ball to an old ball or to the one he stole from the driving range.

By visualizing failure, where do the golf balls go? Right into the water.

By contrast, Bob Rotella advises you to visualize your ball going right into the hole and to keep that vision in the forefront of your mind. Then let your body swing through the golf ball without saying to yourself, "Don't hit it in the water."

Executives are finding that the same thing works to help solve problems in business and industry. Envisioning a successful future can be one of the most effective sources of ideas. In a time of rapid change, our problems are becoming more vision-driven; when we focus only on present resources, it very much restricts the range of possible outcomes. We need to balance our "thriving on analysis" method of problem solving—where we quantify our results over the last five years and extrapolate to the future—with the information we can gain from "be curious first" visionary techniques.

From Vision to Reality

Whatever your problem or goal, picture it already solved or achieved. What does your future world look like? What does the future business or work environment look like? What does the solution look like? What are its features or contours? How did it come into being? What had to take place for the problem to be solved, the goal to be reached?

William McDonough—internationally renowned designer, sustainability architect, and author of *Cradle to Cradle: Remaking the Way We Make Things*—envisions the world of tomorrow by creating the cities of today. McDonough has been charged with building seven entirely new cities in China. In coming up with his design sketches he has considered society's future ecological and lifestyle needs. The city soil will be moved onto the rooftops so the top of the city will be lush and green and inhabited by all kinds of species.

McDonough explains, "We lay the city out so everyone can move in parks without crossing lanes of traffic, the buildings have daylight lighting, the university is at the center, and everything has high-tech connectivity." He goes on to describe his vision of converting waste products into energy: "Waste is energy; methane will be used to cook food. A quarter of the city's cooking will be done with gas from sewage. The main energy systems will be solar energy. China will be the largest solar manufacturer in the world."

Is this "sci-eco-fi"? McDonough says, "The Stone Age did not end because humans ran out of stones. It ended because it was time for a re-think about how we live."

Thus, the visualizer imagines the future and then works backward incrementally to the present, to envision the steps taken to produce that image. Envisioning the future breaks down into four steps: (1) Identify the problem or goal, (2) set a solution or achievement date, (3) visualize the problem solved or the goal reached, and (4) come back from the future.

Step 1 Identify the Problem or Goal

I already discussed ways to identify problems or goals in chapters 6 and 7. You can use the steps in the Problem Articulation process, the Idea Mapping approach, the Smart Question approach, or the Six Universal Questions approach.

Step 2 Set a Solution or Achievement Date

You need to decide when the problem must be solved or when the goal should be achieved. The problem or goal might be a long-term one, such as sales levels you'd like to reach in five years. Or your goal may be a short-term one, like solving ongoing problems of organizational miscommunication.

Step 3 Visualize the Problem Solved or the Goal Reached

Here's the essence of this approach. Just as you might picture a putt made or a basketball shot swished, close your eyes and picture what things will be like if—*when*—the problem is solved or the goal is reached. Don't picture "near misses" or "maybes"; picture only success.

Insisting on a rigid or narrow picture of the future, such as the precise mix of sales in five years or all the steps you anticipate your competitors making, is probably self-defeating. Free your thinking by concentrating on the overall picture of the future, seeing your place in it, and then sketching the specific details that make sense in that setting. Describe a complete scenario, depicting your organization *now* in the future.

One useful technique is to write a short newspaper article describing the future as the *present*. What's the headline? What are the news media saying *right now* about your organization's performance? Did it make the nightly news? If so, what did the news anchor say?

Step 4 Come Back from the Future

Once you have envisioned the future, you have to return from the future incrementally—one step at a time. Try to picture all the moves you or the organization has to make to achieve your future goals, and then put in place the mechanisms and practices needed to make that future a reality.

As long as you're time-traveling, revisit the past to see where the problem came from in the first place. Maybe what's causing the problem today was a great idea back then, but the conditions—technology, your competition, the economic climate—have changed. Just think back to pre-1990: no e-mail, no MP3 players, no Web stores, no DVD player in any home.

Executives at Apple Computer use this device to decide on products to launch. After attending some of my seminars in creativity, new product development managers at Apple have shared with me their "Back from the Future" planning. The Apple executives envision what the industry will be like, what consumers will be demanding, what the competition will be doing. They identify a desirable and reachable goal for Apple in this future computer industry and then work backward, step by step, to the present day, keeping track of the precise steps needed to achieve their goal.

In the late 1990s, Apple's vision of the future focused heavily on downloading media—whether it was music, movies, or television shows—and displaying it on handheld devices and computer screens, as well as projecting it in your family room. As the company thought back to the present, they knew they first had to create the media marketplace that is now called iTunes, that is, create a market for the products they wanted to introduce. What then followed was the iPod player and later the video player.

The Back from the Future process is a rich breeding ground for ideas. By reframing their problem or goal, the Apple execs gained a perspective unlike any they would normally have had.

Another superb example of Back from the Future planning is the process initiated by Smith & Hawken, the highly successful mail-order marketers of fine gardening tools, as described by Peter Schwarz in his book *The Art of the Long View.* Smith & Hawken's managers projected their firm into the future from the late 1970s, when the company was just starting out. They made plans based on three different broad scenarios for the future of the Western world's economy. In one scenario, economic growth, consumption, and materialism continued unabated. In another scenario, the world faced economic depression, famine in the developing world, crisis in the environment, and shortages of natural resources. The third scenario projected a basic shift in Western culture toward harmony with the environment, consumption of natural foods, and an emphasis on inner, personal growth.

The next task facing Smith & Hawken was to project the impact of these scenarios on the garden tool market. In the first scenario, gardening would be popular as a status symbol for the affluent—"beautiful gardens" for "beautiful homes." The growing affluent class would have no problem buying the beautifully made, high-quality, relatively expensive tools offered by Smith & Hawken. Under the second projection, gardening would be necessary for survival. The company's products would be in demand because people would need tools that could stand up to heavy use. In the third scenario, "many affluent people would take up pleasant, ecology-conscious hobbies." Gardening would be popular as a meditative activity that promoted spiritual growth as well as the growth of food and flowers.

Each scenario projected a strong market for sturdy, well-made, high-end garden tools. The next step was to determine how the different prospective markets might affect marketing strategy. Under all three projections, the planners decided that mail order was preferable to distribution through retail outlets for Smith & Hawken's specialized products. In the first case, affluent consumers would be too busy to shop in stores; in the second, stores would tend to have problems surviving; and in the third, mail-order selling would appeal to the *Whole Earth Catalog*–oriented type of consumer.

As it turned out, all three scenarios emerged in the 1980s. Yuppies; a large segment of struggling, working poor; and "New Agers" all lived side by side, so that each of the projections was correct in some respect. Smith & Hawken went from $200,000 in sales in its first year to $1 million within three years to being acquired in 2004 by the Scotts Miracle-Gro Company, the leading supplier of consumer products for lawn and garden care.

To help you do your own Back from the Future planning, I've prepared an Envision the Future Action Sheet at the end of this chapter. You'll find that it's extremely useful to pass out at meetings when you need other people to come up with some great ideas.

Is What You See What You Get?

I gained an interesting perspective on the Envision-the-Future approach from Joe McMoneagle, author of *Mind Trek: Exploring Consciousness, Time, and Space through Remote Viewing* and widely considered one of America's most reliable "remote viewers." *"Remote viewer,"* McMoneagle observes, "is a nice way of saying 'a psychic'"—in this case a psychic who works under strict scientific protocols and who has been the subject in many published experiments. McMoneagle also looks into the future for private and corporate clients.

A remote viewer has demonstrated the ability to see things, places, and events far removed in time or space. Regardless of one's beliefs about such abilities, McMoneagle's ideas mesh with our emerging consensus about visionary techniques and illuminate the process by which we all go about trying to create a better future. Almost any of his statements can be taken either literally or metaphorically, with similar results.

For example, McMoneagle thinks it's important to demystify the process of looking into the future:

Envisioning the future is a natural ability—all men and women have at least some capacity to do it. Some become players of the Stradivarius, so to speak, and others never get more than squeaks out of the fiddle. The degree of success is determined by the openness that you want to apply to the process.

You make mistakes when you start—it's a learning process, because you're learning a new way of thinking about things.

McMoneagle sees a direct relationship between how we envision the future and how things will work out. He believes that "We do, in fact, create our realities"—literally, through our intentions—and that "the only limitation on what the future might be occurs in our own minds—the birthplace of limitations."

If so—and even if not literally so—it behooves the person envisioning the future to project a positive view of the future and not to block the view with unnecessary assumptions. As McMoneagle said:

Expectations can actually get in the way. There seems to be a point where you can know too much about your problem. It's as if you leave yourself with only so many options. If you're envisioning the solution to a problem, there seems to be a point at which you want to let creativity take care of it. In other words, you don't want to get your feet stuck in some kind of rut, going in one direction.

That step when you say, "What's it going to be like ten years from now?" should probably be done first, before you consider anything else, any details. Then nothing gets in the way; you haven't "prebuilt" the roads or directions that you will allow. Were you to try to cover all the bases first—assuming all the things you know in the present, and then overlaying them onto your vision of the future—you'd be stuck with roads going north, south, east, and west—when it may be that there's no road at all and what gets you there is a path of a different nature.

Use the Envision-the-Future approach, either on your own or in a meeting. I guarantee that you'll come up with ideas, many of which will be unexpected, and a few of which could change your life.

GREAT IDEA ACTIONS
ENVISION THE FUTURE

Visualize your problem as solved and then work backward from the solution to the steps needed to achieve it.

Step 1 State your problem.

Step 2 What is your solution deadline?

Step 3 Visualize your ideal solution.
Project yourself mentally to a point in the future where the problem has been solved. Explore how it looks "out there" with the problem solved, and finally describe how the problem was overcome.

Step 4 Stay in the future.
What are the news media saying about your performance? Write a headline and a brief newspaper story or thirty-second news brief.

Step 5 Record the phases leading up to your solution.
Staying "out there" in the future, turn around and look back toward today. What were the main stages or events that led to the problem's being solved?

Step 6 Overcome the barriers.
What were the major barriers overcome at each key stage in the solution process?

Step 7 Sketch the Solution.
Now come back to the present and create a "first draft" of how you would solve the problem, based on your vision of the future.

C H A P T E R   9

Yin/Yang

Thinking in Opposites

The sun rises, the sun sets. Everything goes to its opposite.
Look at your problem backwards, forwards and upside down.
—*Tao Te Ching*

Big: Little. Up: Down. The world is a world of opposites. Life is full of paradoxes, and any attribute, concept, or idea is meaningless without its opposite.

Thinkers and achievers have always been aware of the interplay of opposites. They have realized that ideas don't travel in straight lines. According to physicist Niels Bohr, geniuses mentally reverse their thinking by asking the simple but powerful question, "What would we *never* do?" Similarly, Jim Collins points out in his best-seller, *Good to Great,* that "Great companies did not just focus on what to do to become great, they focused equally on what *not* to do and what to stop doing." When you hold opposite opinions at the same time, you suspend your thought and your mind moves to a new level. This swirling of opposites creates the conditions for a new point of view to bubble freely from your mind.

Creative Leadership

Creative leaders are part alchemist, part diplomat. They are always looking for imaginative ways to help people achieve their vision and harness their organization's creative energy and creative tension.

At the heart of creative leadership is the ability to see and bring together opposites—whether it is a vision back to a viable path for a wayward organization, simplicity for a complex task, consensus to end a conflict, or revenue from a budget cut. Creative leaders employ the following key principles of opposite thinking:

> "The further backward you look, the further forward you can see."
>
> —Winston Churchill, British prime minister

1. Creating dynamic new ideas by reaching out to people of all viewpoints and not allowing opposing views to cancel each other out.

2. Creating time for innovation by abandoning old and outdated programs and policies that get in the way.

3. Breaking those old rules from elementary school and replacing them with guidelines for collaboration, improvisation, and reflection.

Creative Destruction

Creative destruction has become the most fashionable catchphrase today for describing our ability to challenge our assumptions. Coined by Joseph A. Schumpeter, an early twentieth-century economist, it suggests that capitalist economies grow by creating new businesses that then destroy the old ones. Pablo Picasso understood this necessary turbulence when he said, "Every act of creation is first of all an act of destruction."

In 1853, at a Saratoga Springs resort, a customer kept returning his fried potatoes to the kitchen, complaining that they were too thick. So the enraged chef sliced the potatoes razor thin, and Saratoga chips—now called potato chips—were invented.

In 1874 there was a ban on "sucking soda" on Sundays. Robert Green, a Philadelphia soda fountain maker, invented the ice cream soda and ran his own shop. He got around the ban by serving ice cream on Sundays with sweet syrups on top but no soda water—hence, the sundae.

Creative destruction is the middle name of the entrepreneur who can cut prices, boost sales, and still earn a healthy profit—until rivals figure out how to mimic the innovation. Earnings then decline until another wave of creative destruction sweeps aside the old. It is a cannibalistic vision that is the essence of market capitalism and an awesome revolutionary force.

Entrepreneurs tear down the old order every day, in business and science, literature, art and cinema, politics and the law. Our parents had grocers and milkmen deliver to their home. Then we invented supermarkets and Sam's Club and bought minivans to carry it all home. Now we can order groceries online and we are having them delivered to our homes once again.

So if you need to see the world differently, challenge an assumption by forcing yourself to see the opposite. Let's take a look now at some interesting opposites in the world around us.

Opposites in the Arts

In the arts, opposites drive the creative process. The poet Samuel Taylor Coleridge observed that the power of the poet "reveals itself in the balance or reconciliation of opposite or discordant qualities." Thinking in opposites must have influenced Leonardo da Vinci when he painted his masterpiece— not simply because the enigmatic smile of *Mona Lisa* closely resembles an upside down image of da Vinci's scowl in his own self-portrait, but in a larger sense because of the tension between the expected convention of a smile and the subject's unforgettable expression.

> "The heart of every creative act is to bring together opposites—wet paint to dry paper, color to empty barren spaces, feeling and thought into a void. So the artist is also a diplomat who reaches out to whatever is the "other" and creates unity."
>
> —Shoshana Alexander, *Women's Ventures, Women's Visions*

Opposites in the Marketplace

Every day a product or service is eclipsed at its prime because another changes the rules. Motels were not created by the urban hotel industry; rather, they began as mom-and-pop motor courts on the outskirts of town, sparked by the surging growth in automobile ownership. Desktop publishing did not grow out of the over thirty thousand printing companies in the United States. Quicken® accounting software was not created by one of the Big Six accounting firms. MinuteClinic®, the nationwide fifteen-minute medical clinic, was not the brainchild of a hospital or medical center. While these innovations would never wipe out their precursors, they did take a chunk out of their profits, causing them to seriously re-think their operations and future sources of profitability.

> " I watched where the cosmetics industry was going and then walked in the opposite direction.
>
> —Anita Roddick, founder, The Body Shop

Executives at a company manufacturing baby-bottle nipples faced a dilemma of corporate life–threatening proportions. Births were down. Breastfeeding was up. Sales were off. Either they had to find new consumers for baby-bottle nipples or they had to find new consumers for something else. Looking at the problem from the opposite perspective, they began to describe not only what a baby-bottle nipple *was,* but what it *was not.* It was small; it was not large. It was used by babies and their parents who wanted those babies; it was not used by couples who did not want babies. It had a hole in the end so the milk could come out; it was not totally solid to prevent the escape of liquids. *Not* large, *not* solid, *not* used by couples who did not want children. Thus did they solve their problem.

They started manufacturing condoms.

Considering the opposite allowed a greeting card manufacturer to turn on a dime when anthrax-laden envelopes struck fear in the public. The answer was simple: Drop the envelopes and return to the days of the holiday postcard.

A company with 28,000 miles of unused oil pipeline wanted to move into new businesses. To come up with new sources of revenue, they thought backward—in opposites. Instead of pumping something through the pipeline, they could install something that would just sit there and not move at all:

the networks of fiber-optic cable needed for the new long-distance phone companies. Companies like MCI Communications were only too happy to "pump" phone calls through the otherwise empty pipes.

Jack Welch, the former CEO of GE and the author of *Winning*, was once the undisputed authority in management. But the cover of the July 2006 *Fortune* magazine declared, *"Sorry, Jack . . . your rules don't work anymore."* *Fortune's* lead story was that today's smart CEOs are following an opposite set of rules:

NEW RULES	JACK'S OLD RULES
1. Agile is best; being big can bite you.	1. Big dogs own the street.
2. Find a niche; create something new.	2. Be No. 1 or No. 2 in your market.
3. The customer is king.	3. Shareholders rule.
4. Look out, not in.	4. Be lean and mean.
5. Hire passionate people.	5. Rank your players; go with the A's.
6. Hire a courageous CEO.	6. Hire a charismatic CEO.
7. Admire my soul.	7. Admire my might.

Jack Welch was a big believer in the process of creative destruction; just one year after his book of rules, *Winning*, was published, he became its newest victim.

Creative Construction

Rather than view everything in terms of creative *de*struction, with its winner-takes-all overtones, I like to think in terms of creative *con*struction. That's seeing the future trends and then identifying what is correct with both approaches. Viewing Rule #1 above in this light, the best solution is to have the deep pockets of a big dog and the agility and passion of a scrappy entrepreneurial terrier.

My first employer, W. L. Gore & Associates, comes to mind in this connection. Gore is considered one of the most innovative companies in the world, and now has around seven thousand employees; yet most of its manufacturing plants have only 150 employees. Bill Gore used to say, "We build a facility with 150 parking spaces and when our employees are forced to park on the grass, we build a new facility a couple miles away." Bill wanted to keep the spirit of the entrepreneurial company with the clout of the global "Gore-Tex: Guaranteed to Keep You Dry" brand.

How to Spot Opposites

To see the opposite, indeed, constitutes one of the primary techniques of idea making. Successful Idea Generators routinely look at problems in completely "opposing" ways. They look to see not only what a problem or idea *is,* but what it *isn't.*

There are two fundamentally different types of problems: convergent problems and divergent problems. Convergent problems have a clear solution, and the more you study them, the more the answers converge into that one solution. Divergent problems have no single solution. The more they are studied, the more answers you come up with, some of which may contradict one another.

When facing a divergent challenge, such as writing a three-year action plan during a turbulent time, I like to tap into the wisdom of the ancient Roman God Janus. Janus had two heads and looked backward and forward at the same time. The month of January was named after him, along with the term *Janusian thinking,* which is the ability to conceive of two or more opposites existing simultaneously.

> ❝ Life can only be understood backwards; but it must be lived forwards. ❞
>
> —Søren Kierkegaard,
> Danish philosopher

Roman God Janus

When approaching a new challenge or a New Year, try employing Janusian thinking and asking the following questions:

1. What should we start doing?

2. What should we stop doing?

3. What should we do differently?

4. What should we keep on doing?

These four questions work extremely well in brainstorming strategic plans for a coming year or another time frame. The great idea comes from the intersection of the opposite thoughts during the brainstorming process. To facilitate maximum intersection, during seminars, I place these four questions on large sheets of poster paper taped on the four walls of the room and then turn the attendees loose to fill in the answers.

Brainstorming the Spiral

If you were in the food business, it would be useful to chart how groceries have been sold over the last fifty years. As I mentioned earlier in this chapter, fifty years ago grocers used to deliver your goods to your home. Then you went to the supermarket. Then convenience stores were created, offering provisions close to the customer's home. Then along came Sam's Club and Wal-Mart, which once again employed the model of customers traveling to purchase their groceries. Finally, Internet-based grocers like Pea Pod and WebVan, which deliver goods directly to customers' homes, were born.

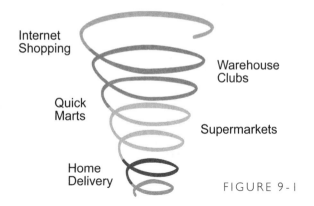

FIGURE 9-1

The graphic that best depicts the development of these opposite models over time is the spiral (see Figure 9-1). The spiral is an ideal way to view opposites: Moving upward on the spiral allows you to continually envision the next opposite direction. Moving downward on the spiral can represent returning from a future strategy, or a freefall when two opposite thoughts, ideas, or people conflict and cancel each other out. The most challenging job of a creative leader is to tune the spiral so that the opposite paths resonate with each other rather than canceling each other out.

Here's another way to think about the spiral. If you label the spiral with your *current reality* at the base and your *vision* at the top, it graphically represents the gap between your vision and your current reality. This gap can be your source of creative energy—I like to call it my *creative tension*—in solving a problem. If there were no gap, there would be no need for any action.

You'll find that ideas flow easily and this visual play of opposites energizes your brain. By looking at opposites together, you suspend your regular habits of thought and your mind moves to a new level.

How to Create Opposites

The Idea Generators of this world routinely look at things from several perspectives. Though they may not know it, they use the creative tension of opposites in a systematic way:

1. They tend to change positive statements into negative ones.

2. They try to define what something is *not*.

3. They try to figure out what everybody else doesn't do.

4. They change the direction or location of their perspective.

5. They flip-flop results.

6. They turn defeat into victory or victory into defeat.

7. They create oxymorons.

8. They challenge ingrained assumptions.

9. They ask, "What would we never do?"

Let's consider each device in turn.

Make the Statement Negative

The first technique is the most obvious one, but it contains some nuances that you might not have thought about. All languages contain negative expressions, enabling the speaker or writer to turn a positive expression into a negative one. Placing *no* or *not* before nouns, verbs, adjectives, and adverbs turns the positive into the negative.

Consider a manufacturer with a quality-control problem, a problem that irked and hassled its customers. Here's a positive statement—with a noun, a verb, an adjective, and an adverb—describing the problem:

All hassled customers complain loudly.

Now watch what happens when each element of the sentence is turned into a negative. Following each revised statement are the mental musings of an Idea Generator.

*All hassled customers do **not** complain loudly.*

Hmmm . . . if they do not complain, maybe they compliment us, maybe they thank us? How do we get a hassled customer to thank us? Ahhh, call her and solve the quality problem immediately, maybe even before she knows there's a problem.

Not *all hassled customers complain loudly.*

Whoops, there must be many hassled customers who just take their lumps, never complain, *and* never return. We've got to survey our customers and see if there are any we need to follow up with.

*All hassled customers complain **not** loudly.*

Uh-oh . . . if they don't complain loudly, they complain softly. Not only here but elsewhere. There goes the word-of-mouth advertising so crucial to our success. We've got to identify our hassled customers and actively intervene so they are assured of our future quality and feel that we're a reliable supplier.

You can readily see how the device of making the statement negative alerted the Idea Generator to some very real problems in dire need of creative solutions.

Using *no* and *not* isn't the only way to make statements negative. Don't forget the handy device of antonyms. If something is fat, think about it as thin. If it's old, imagine it new. If something is up there, look at it down here. Become accustomed to using your word-processing program's thesaurus feature, which can give you immediate access to antonyms.

The "What If . . ." Compass is a device I use to facilitate thinking in antonyms. When I've got a problem, I just ask "What if I _____," and then I plug in each one of an opposite pairs of actions. By answering "What if," I invariably come up with some great ideas.

Here's a list of opposing actions:

What if I . . .

Stretch it	Shrink it
Make it romantic	Make it heart-breaking
Combine it	Separate it
Appeal to kids	Appeal to seniors
Winterize it	Summerize it
Illuminate it	Darken it
Speed it up	Slow it down
Go clockwise	Go counterclockwise
Sharpen it	Dull it
Freeze it	Melt it
Misspell it	Spell it correctly
Sweeten it	Sour it
Balance it	Unbalance it
Tighten it	Loosen it
Force it	Relax it
Build it up	Tear it down
Tie it	Untie it
Jump over it	Go under it
Raise the price	Give it away
Put it to music	Put it in pictures
Add nostalgic appeal	Add future appeal
Make it stronger	Make it weaker
Make it portable	Make it stationary
Personalize it	Depersonalize it
Exaggerate it	Understate it
Add sex appeal	Remove sex appeal
Make it simple	Make it complex
Fill it up	Empty it
Make it breakable	Make it unbreakable
Make it funny	Make it serious
Moisten it	Dry it
Cushion it	Prick it
Make it disposable	Make it reusable
Make it fly	Make it float
Do it backward	Do it sideways
Magnetize it	Demagnetize it
Make it invisible	Make it visible
Go forward	Go backward

A "What If . . ." Compass Action Sheet appears in the Great Idea Actions section at the end of this chapter, so you can try this technique for yourself. Hopefully, it will lead you to some great ideas!

Another linguistic tool for Opposite Thinking is to use the prefixes that form opposites: *Un-, non-,* and *dis-,* when added to the beginning of a word, will yield an opposite meaning. We saw this in the marketplace with commercials portraying 7 Up as the "Uncola." We see it in business with the differentiation of profit versus nonprofit.

The Negative Definition

Great ideas often come from thinking about what something *isn't*. We look not at what a problem is but at what the problem is not. The English language itself encourages this approach to thinking with what is called the *correlative conjunction*. Without getting too steeped in grammar, one example of this is the "not . . . but" construction, in which *but* acts as a correlative conjunction. As I stated above, we look not at what a problem is *but* at what a problem is not.

The Negative Definition device is, of course, quite simple. Just plug in the word or phrase you're trying to define and define what it is *not:*

> **[Word] or [Phrase] is not a . . .**

Jot down as many things as you can think of that the problem is not, and you'll be surprised at the insights you gain.

Here's a recent example. My problem is that my flight to Minneapolis is canceled at the last minute due to the weather and I can't get to the city to give my early-morning talk. Instead of looking at what the canceled flight *is,* I look at what the canceled flight *is not*.

> **The canceled flight is not . . .**
> **life threatening.**
> **the only way to get there.**
> **me losing my voice.**
> **intentional.**

Looking at what the canceled flight is *not* calms me down so I can plan an alternative course of action. I can look into other carriers or a charter service. I can line up a telecourse or WebEx presentation. After all, I still have my voice, my PowerPoint, and, hopefully, a broadband connection. I can look for a replacement speaker or offer a discount to present my talk at a later time. Most important, I learn that the situation is not my fault, so my conscience is clear and my mind can start brainstorming other issues.

Doing What Everybody Else Doesn't

Anyone who is a parent has heard this lament: "But everybody else does it!" Ah, peer pressure. In the marketplace, of course, it's called *competition*, and certainly everyone playing in the marketplace keeps a close eye on what the competition does, what the consumer does, what the government does, and so on.

But you can flip-flop this perspective and think about "What everybody else doesn't do" instead. This opposite perspective will help you identify those niches that no one else has discovered. You look not at what manufacturers are making, buyers are buying, teachers are teaching, and regulators are regulating. Look instead to see what they are *not* making, buying, teaching, or regulating. By seeing what is *not* happening, you might just uncover what *ought to happen,* or the next big thing no one can do without.

We need not look far to find examples of the Everybody-Else-Doesn't approach to idea making. Apple Computer saw what IBM was *not* doing. IBM was not making small computers for the little guy. Naturally, the little guys were not buying small computers because no one was making them. Apple proceeded to do just that. The Japanese saw quite clearly what Detroit was not doing. The Big Three were not producing small, fuel-efficient cars. The Japanese started doing just that and changed the way the world does business. The MinuteClinic® saw that hospital emergency rooms and physicians' offices were overcrowded and that long waiting times were a major complaint of patients. The MinuteClinic® (with the slogan, "You're sick . . . we're quick") offers fifteen-minute visits for common illnesses, such as strep throat, bronchitis, ear infections, and sinus infections, and no appointment is needed. It's open seven days a week and located inside or near a pharmacy.

Peter Lynch, author of *One Up on Wall Street: How to Use What You Already Know to Make Money in the Market,* uses this approach in predicting when the stock market will turn up. In his words: "When ten people at a cocktail party would rather talk to a dentist about plaque than to the manager of an equity mutual fund about stocks, it's likely that the market is about to turn up."

I've used the Everybody-Else-Doesn't approach many times in my business life. Once I was owed a considerable amount of money and discovered to my horror that my debtor was about to move out of town. I sat down and thought about what everybody else *does* do to recoup their money in order to get a handle on what everybody else *doesn't* do. Everybody else sends a formal invoice (so I'll send a cartoon of myself lying on the floor with a giant knife stuck in my back and caption saying, "I trusted you."). Everybody else sends the invoice to the office where the secretary opens it (so I'll send the cartoon to his home where he or his family will open it). Everybody else sends an invoice in a neatly typed, business-size envelope (so I'll send my cartoon in a three-foot-wide package with a hand-addressed mailing label). Everybody else sends an invoice through the mail (so I'll send mine by next-day UPS so it'll be sitting on his doorstep when he gets home from the office).

My Everybody-Else-Doesn't approach to Opposite Thinking really paid off. Not only did I collect my bill, but I turned those collection cartoons into a novelty item, marketing them to stationery stores across the country. Stories about the cartoons appeared in many U.S. newspapers and then spread to Japan, Germany, and even Pakistan.

Changing Directions or Locations

The Change Direction or Location approach to idea making requires you to do one of two things: Either you physically change your perspective by getting off your, uh, chair, and going somewhere else, or you mentally change the way something works or the direction something takes or the vantage point from which you watch something work.

After a lifetime spent cleaning out clogged arteries, Dr. Toby Cosgrove took over as the new CEO of the Cleveland Clinic in 2004. As he walked around the hospital, he noticed that some of his employees were in poorer physical condition than the patients. He walked some more and discovered where many of them were eating—the McDonald's located right there in the hospital food court. He challenged McDonald's to create a heart-healthy menu. What the media called a "food fight" led to McDonald's now offering veggie burgers and carrot sticks exclusively at the Cleveland Clinic.

The "Managing by Wandering Around" technique, made famous by Hewlett-Packard, relies on physically changing one's perspective. The manager mingles with the people he directs, watches what goes on, talks to people about their problems, and then comes up with some great ideas.

Mentally changing perspectives requires a highly developed imagination. If you usually look at things from the top down, look at them from the bottom up. If you're on the outside, mentally go inside and check things out. If something goes left to right, try making it go right to left.

IBM literally used this Change Direction approach when it revolutionized typewriters back in the 1970s. Are you old enough to remember the manual Underwoods and Remingtons with the black-and-red cloth ribbons? The entire carriage holding the paper moved from right to left as the stationary keys typed the line from left to right. IBM changed all that by reversing the directions. The company figured out how to keep the paper still and move the typing element. The paper stayed put, and the typing ball moved from left to right. Typewriting was never the same again.

Flip-Flop Results

If your desired result is *better morale,* flip-flop this result and think about producing the opposite—really rotten morale. What would it take to make everyone go screaming from the room, refusing to work at such an awful place? By envisioning the flip side of your desired result, you begin to look at the problem from the completely opposite perspective.

This approach, of course, is nothing new. Ever heard of the Devil's advocate? If you want to increase sales, think about decreasing them. What would you have to do to produce truly awful sales? Changing your perspective in this way often produces some great ideas.

Leaders in the New England office of the U.S. Environmental Protection Agency once executed a brilliant example of flip-flopping results, as well as doing what everyone else doesn't. They developed a public awareness campaign called "How to Destroy the Earth." Its tips included:

1. Leave lights on

2. Photocopy everything

3. Buy overpackaged products

4. Ask for plastic supermarket bags

5. Drive everywhere (don't walk, bicycle, or take public transportation)

6. Reach for paper towels (why use one made of cloth that's reusable?)

7. Pour used motor oil into the ground

8. Mow your lawn daily

9. Throw leaves out with the trash

10. Put off that tune-up ("if only 100,000 car owners followed this simple tip, we'd add ninety million pounds of greenhouse gases to the air")

The campaign drove its message home with this opposite punchline: "You can save the earth by knowing what you are doing to destroy it."

Snatching Victory from the Jaws of Defeat

The Idea Generator will often snatch victory from the jaws of defeat. When you're staring defeat in the face, just ask, "What did I learn from this defeat?" We learn from trial and error, not trial and rightness.

In 1970, just out of college and working for W. L. Gore & Associates, I was asked to create some medical applications from our new material called Gore-Tex®. Since Gore-Tex® was smooth, slippery, breathable, and could be made "hospital clean" by wiping it down with alcohol, I recommended creating a hospital bedsheet out of the material to eliminate bedsores. Everyone loved my prototypes and, being twenty-one, I was thrilled to be able to sleep on my bed for months without having to change the sheets. Also, food wiped off without a trace after late-night pizza breaks.

Unfortunately, the in-hospital test market results weren't nearly as favorable. When the patients started slipping out of bed, the test was stopped. Bill Gore asked me one of the most memorable questions of my life: "We know what went wrong, but what went *right* with the sheet?" I explained that the medical staff loved the concept of Gore-Tex® and had ideas for face masks, surgical gowns, and the like. Thus my career as a new product developer was born. I just heard that there are up to one thousand medical products with a Gore-Tex® component.

Last year, I was presenting a talk at a plastic surgeons conference and told the bedsheet story. The head of a burn unit came up after my talk and proudly mentioned that his unit had just started using Gore-Tex® bedsheets on the burn center beds. He said that the beds had rails on them, so slippage was not an issue, and that the sheets worked just fine to reduce bedsores. It took thirty years, but my first idea actually worked!

Create an Oxymoron

An *oxymoron* is defined as a combination of apparently contradictory words or phrases that describe a paradoxical truth.

> "The curious paradox is that when I accept myself just as I am, then I can change."
>
> —Carl Rogers, psychologist

The advertising industry uses the oxymoron to capture our attention. When a form of packaging was invented to prevent dehydration and decomposition of foods stored in electric freezers, advertisers came up with the oxymoron *freezer burn* to describe the problem the packaging would solve.

Using an oxymoron to describe your own paradoxical qualities is very helpful because it names in a truthful and easy-to-relate-to manner the tensions you are trying to deal with as a result of your own personality and individual characteristics.

Here's an insightful exercise from Dr. Charles Handy, author of *The Age of Paradox*. Dr. Handy encourages you to discover your *high-performance paradox*. List your six most positive characteristics. Then list your six greatest shortcomings. (It's always great to ask an ex-spouse for these!) Finally, match a positive with a negative and see if you can create your own high-performance paradox. To give you an actual example, I am sharing my personal characteristics, as seen in Figure 9-2.

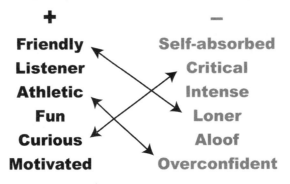

Pairing *friendly* and *loner* helped me see that when I come off the road from speaking, I need time to recharge before I can be friendly at a neighborhood party.

Matching *athletic* and *overconfident* explains my love of skydiving—and all of the weekend injuries I've sustained from my pursuit of sports.

But the breakthrough was the pairing of *curious* and *critical*. My high-performance oxymoron is "Be curious first, critical second." If I'm critical first, my creativity gets buried (and only resurfaces when I take my next shower).

CREATING YOUR OWN OXYMORON

Now it's your turn to find your "high-performance paradox."

List your six most positive characteristics. Then list your six greatest shortcomings. Then match a positive with a negative and see if you can create your high-performance paradox.

Positive	Negative
1.	1.
2.	2.
3.	3.
4.	4.
5.	5.
6.	6.

You can also use this exercise to describe the strengths and weaknesses of your department or your organization.

Challenging Assumptions

As I mentioned in chapter 3, top executives at Steelcase, Inc., wanted a design for their corporate development center that would foster creativity. When commissioning their design from the architects, they challenged the assumption that a center is divided into departments. The resulting plans produced an environment that requires finance to mingle with sales, product design, and advertising. The "clustered teams" design brings together four members, one from each department. According to Steelcase, the center is now a laboratory of innovation.

In the 1990s, I was asked to adapt the GE Work-Out! continuous improvement process to the hourly factory workforce. Several underlying assumptions surfaced rapidly:

1. The factory workforce could never sit through a two-day course, so reduce it to one day.

2. The factory workforce could never make presentations to management; they just don't have the presentation skills. So eliminate that part of the training.

3. The factory workforce will never speak out if their supervisors and team leaders are in the room, so only include employees from the first three pay levels.

Naturally, we challenged many of these assumptions. And we produced one of the most empowering training programs of my career. It featured a cross-functional and multilayered mix of factory employees interacting and presenting for two consecutive days. We invited supervisors and team leaders to help with presentations, and you couldn't tell the "ties" from the "hourlies" because everyone in attendance was required to wear a GE T-shirt—even the executive vice president of manufacturing.

We instructed the factory workers in the use of various visual aids for their presentations. Many of their presentations turned out to be more to the point and more emotionally compelling than those produced by the management-level personnel.

The closing comments of the director of operations to the factory employees summed up the powerful effects of challenging these ingrained assumptions: "You blew management away with your great presentations. We've known that you have the answers to help us. We just didn't know how to listen for them. I'm so proud of you." As he turned to walk back to his seat, I noticed tears in his eyes. And in everyone else's. A wall had come crashing down.

What Would We Never Do?

This is my favorite question to challenge an ingrained assumption. It takes you out of the box faster than any other technique I know. When leaders at SC Johnson added their Glade scent to their Windex product, they had a big success. Then their new product director asked, to which of our products would we never add potpourri scent? The answer—Raid Bug Killer—came screaming back.

Go to the supermarket and look at the Raid product line. A number one seller is outdoor fresh–scented Raid—and it kills bugs dead.

Challenging assumptions, as you can plainly see, is quite simple. To come up with ideas, you must reframe your problem or situation. Challenge the normal assumptions you make when dealing with such problems or defining such goals. Try the following steps:

1. Define your problem.

2. Write down all assumptions that you would ordinarily make in relation to that problem.

3. Challenge each assumption by making it a negative or an opposite. If you assume that centers are broken into departments, assume the opposite—that they're not—and analyze what might happen if the assumption were false. If you assume that hassled customers only complain, assume the opposite—that they express gratitude. You may then be able to imagine how this would be possible.

Un-creation, *Re*-creation

Looking at the world creatively is really a matter of *re*-creation, which implies a certain amount of *un*-creation—undoing, if only in your imagination, things that "Everybody knows are so." If our assumptions were all true, we would never be surprised, and nothing new would ever be created.

Every assumption we have is an opportunity for change, fun, improvement—an opening for your great idea.

GREAT IDEA ACTION

THE POWER OF OPPOSITE THINKING

After stating a problem, come up with some great ideas by (1) making the statement negative, (2) coming up with a negative definition, and (3) figuring out what everybody else doesn't do.

PROBLEM STATEMENT:

Step 1 Make the statement negative. Make various parts of the statement negative by adding *no, not, non-, un-, dis-,* or an antonym to the statement.

Step 2 Define the problem's opposite. First define what the problem is and then define what it is *not*.

Step 3 Do what everybody else *doesn't*. Write down what everybody else is doing (competitors, customers, government, private sector, and other relevant players). Then write down what they are *not* doing.

Doing	Not Doing
1.	1.
2.	2.
3.	3.

Step 4 Pick a possible solution.

GREAT IDEA ACTION
THE "WHAT IF . . ." COMPASS

Briefly describe your problem. Then pick two opposing actions, such as "increase it/decrease it" from the list of opposing actions given earlier in this chapter on page 134. Complete the "What If . . ." question as many times as you can and show the various results.

PROBLEM STATEMENT:

Step 1 Ask yourself, What if I . . . _____
      Results

          1.

          2.

          3.

          4.

Step 2 Ask yourself, What if I . . . _____
      Results

          1.

          2.

          3.

          4.

Step 3 Write down ideas that will help solve the problem.

GREAT IDEA ACTION
CHANGING PERSPECTIVES

Briefly describe your problem. In the space provided, come up with some great ideas by (1) changing the direction of the process or your perspective in viewing the problem, (2) changing the results to exactly the opposite, and (3) transforming the problem into an opportunity.

PROBLEM STATEMENT:

Step 1 Change directions or locations. Write down changes in the direction of the process or in your vantage point in viewing the problem.

Step 2 Flip-flop results. State the exact opposite of the results you are experiencing. Note how you could produce these opposite results.

Step 3 Snatch victory from the jaws of defeat. Take the problem and turn it into an opportunity. How can you profit from the problem?

Step 4 Record your new ideas. After studying your notes, write down three ideas that will help solve the problem.

　　1.

　　2.

　　3.

GREAT IDEA ACTION

CHALLENGING ASSUMPTIONS

Write down your assumptions relating to the problem stated below. Then challenge each of these assumptions and jot down ideas that spring from each challenge.

PROBLEM STATEMENT:

Step 1 Write down three assumptions that we ordinarily make when confronted with this problem.

1.

2.

3.

Step 2 Now challenge each assumption by stating its opposite or by assuming the negative.

1.

2.

3.

Step 3 Write down potential advantages that could spring from your challenges to these assumptions.

1.

2.

3.

Step 4 After studying the challenged assumptions, write down any suggestions you could use to solve the problem.

A Curveball

Metaphorical Thinking

*So much of leadership is music from the heart ... The leader
of a jazz band has the beautiful opportunity to draw the
best out of other musicians ... Jazz, like leadership, combines
the unpredictability of the future with the gifts of individuals.*
—Max DePree, Leadership Jazz

Highly creative people often use comparisons—similes and metaphors—
to help define problems and to think about possible solutions. They
look at their problem, define it, and perhaps even give it a name. They then
think metaphorically, ruminating about what their problem is like. To create
a simile, for example, you need only say:

My problem is like a _____.

I use *metaphor* here in a broad sense, referring to similes, metaphors,
and other figures of speech that create comparisons between things.
Thinking metaphorically serves several important functions:

1. Metaphors enable you to go beyond the limits of standard solutions through divergent thinking and to move away from the problem so you can see the bigger picture.

2. Metaphors focus your mind on the relationships among ideas, images, and symbols.

3. Metaphors make complex issues easier to understand.

4. Metaphors create tension, rooted in collisions of ideas, and fusion, an integration of ideas.

5. Metaphors turn one idea into two or more.

Blasts from the Past

We've always used metaphors to describe our problems and guide decisions in the workplace. The resulting metaphors have infused our language with colorful and incisive images.

When industrialization became entrenched in the early twentieth century, we used the machine metaphor and spoke in terms of keeping the machine "well oiled." When faced with problems, we "hammered out the details."

As war consumed much of the first half of the twentieth century, military metaphors assailed the workplace: "Let's win the battle in the trenches!" "Let's hit them with both barrels!" The notion of overcoming hostile competition had been added to our formula for success.

By the 1950s, competition in warfare was replaced by a more civil form of competition—the athletic arena. Our organizations mirrored the structure of athletic teams and our motivational cry was for "team spirit." Strategic language sounded as if it came from a locker room. A commonly heard warning was this: "Watch out! They might throw us a curve!" While on the playing field, we still found the competition hostile, because someone had to lose.

Playing with the Sports Metaphor

From "dropping the ball" to being an "armchair quarterback," we use sports metaphors in the classroom, at home and at work. When your goal is team building, the sports metaphor offers valuable insight. To create a winning team, you need to ask these questions:

1. Is our team playing the right game?

2. Does our team have the right players?

3. Is the coach's leadership style right for our team?

By definition, a team is two or more persons with a shared goal that cannot be accomplished effectively by one person acting alone. To help expand your use of the sports metaphor, I've organized a comparison of three popular team sports.

SPORTS METAPHOR MATRIX FOR BUSINESS

STYLES OF:	FOOTBALL	BASEBALL	BASKETBALL
Coaching	Call right plays	Choose right players	Develop self-correcting team
Communication	Top down	Up and down	Up, down, and among players
Leadership	Authoritarian	Laissez-faire	Participative
Team	Loyalty-based	Autonomy-based	Interdependence
Success	Consistent execution	Big individual plays	Continuous adaptation
Player	Waits for decision	Self-directed	Proactive, interdependent

TYPE OF:			
Organization	Manufacturing Fast-food industry	Sales organizations Technical units	High-tech firms Project teams
Environment	Consistent, structured Centrally controlled	Changing, unstructured Individual concentration	Rapidly changing Calls for group creativity

Malcolm Gladwell, author of *The Tipping Point: How Little Things Can Make a Big Difference,* points out in an interview in *The New Yorker* (July 22, 2002) that the meaning you derive from a sports metaphor is dependent on the sport that you pick. Gladwell says, "I think, for instance, that you can build a winning baseball team just by snapping up individually brilliant players. . . . But basketball, or football, is a different story. I tend to think of corporations as more like basketball teams than baseball teams."

My good friend and Nike Katalyst Kevin Carroll best exemplifies using the sports metaphor in your life. He has just written a wonderful little book called *Rules of the Red Rubber Ball: Find and Sustain Your Life's Work.* It tells his own motivational, up-by-the-bootstraps story of going from the inner city streets to the trailer park to the military to the Philadelphia 76ers and finally to Nike. The whole time the constant remained his vision, passion, and commitment to playing with the red rubber ball. In his book, Kevin describes his unique way of exercising his creative muscles and solving problems with fresh ideas through sports:

> *To stretch my creative muscle, I dedicate time to an activity that eliminates outside noise and forces me to focus on the moment. For me that activity is exercise. I don't work out in a gym—that's too East—instead, I work out in my surroundings, mainly, the city streets. I've created what I call the urban obstacle course, and anything outside—a car, a stoop, a street sign—becomes potential exercise equipment. I hang from light posts to do leg raises; I balance on sidewalk curbs; I jump over fences and cement barricades; do pull-ups at bus shelters; and use the jungle gym at a local playground for sit-ups. Not surprisingly, I also solve problems and get fresh ideas when I'm working out. When my body is busy, my mind is free.*

At the end of this chapter I have included a Great Ideas Action Sheet to help you use the sports metaphor in your life and work.

In the Groove

As we move through the information age, successful organizations are making the transition to the next step in metaphors. Organizations are beginning to "march to a different beat." Now we're *improvising. Improvisation* is at the heart of today's favorite type of metaphor—the music metaphor.

Management guru Peter Drucker, using the music metaphor, compares the successful information-based corporation to a symphony orchestra. This metaphor requires highly talented specialists to perform at their peak to play great music together.

Peter Senge, author of *The Fifth Discipline: The Art and Practice of the Learning Organization,* uses a jazz analogy to describe this new approach to management:

> *Jazz musicians know about alignment. There is a phrase in jazz, "being in the groove," that suggests the state when an ensemble*

"plays as one." . . . Outstanding teams in organizations develop the same sort of relationship—an "operational trust," where each team member remains conscious of the other team members and can be counted on to act in ways that complement each other's actions.

Gary Muszynski, founder of the leadership-training group One World Music, says that getting a group emotionally "into a groove" calls for a leader who knows how to create resonance and empathy—a felt connection with others. Muszynski's mission is "transforming organizations one beat at a time" through interactive workshops with titles like "Synergy through Samba" and "Leadership Jazz."

Mastering the Music Metaphor

Managers and musicians, CEOs and conductors—they're surprisingly similar. An orchestral score is much like the five-year plan—a blueprint for both large and small organizations. The musical notes guide the conductor and the musicians, just as organizational guidelines direct executives, managers, and staff.

> I don't lead musicians, man. They lead me. I listen to them and learn what they do best.
>
> —Miles Davis

All musical ensembles, from small jazz combos to rock bands to large symphony orchestras, require organization and cooperation. Each group typically has a leader: The conductor of a large orchestra leads the group in its musical interpretation and coordinates the members' individual efforts during performance; the small jazz combo often relies on a soloist to synthesize the overall effect and sound.

The music metaphor applies especially well to organizations, for much of today's music incorporates flexibility and innovation. Jazz thrives on creative tension. According to Miles Davis, musical innovation arose from a friction between his technique and the band members' evolving sense of community and purpose.

Jazz musicians constantly seek a new sound, a new combination, a new feel, a new expression. If we accept change as a premise for the future of our world, then that same desire to explore new sounds, feels, or combinations is the key asset organizations need to keep pace with the changing marketplace of goods, services, and political ideas.

Talking in Music

The music metaphor permeates our language today with an array of sayings that evoke many moods and meanings. Have you ever caught yourself asking how a given plan will be *orchestrated* or what *mode* it's in? The following phrases have already worked their way into our standard office vocabulary:

> *You're marching to a different drummer.*
> *We've got a lot of dissonance here.*
> *We're playing in harmony.*
> *Our division is out of tune.*
> *Let's improvise.*
> *Let's try it in a different key.*

Applying Music Metaphors

You can use music metaphors in any situation simply by thinking of your problem with the mind-set of a musician. This metaphor is best suited for situations that require harmonizing of conflicts or different points of view.

In 1998 IBM held its first online, twenty-four-hour brainstorming "Jam," which involved research labs from around the world. In 2001 every IBM employee was invited to join an online seventy-two-hour WorldJam to explore ideas on establishing a set of core values that define what being an "IBMer" means. In July 2006, I actively participated in the company's Global InnovationJam, which focused on generating ideas in four areas:

1. Travel and transportation in an increasingly mobile society

2. The science and business of staying healthy

3. Balancing economic and environmental priorities for a better planet

4. The changing nature of global business and trade

The IBM InnovationJam Web site states:

> *Jams are born from a simple premise—the expertise of 330,000 smart people with a broad range of experience is a powerful way to run a business. These IBMers possess insights, perspectives, and knowledge of best practices that could never otherwise be*

captured. Jams are like the spontaneous improvisation of a jazz ensemble, jams are active. They're egalitarian. They're both organic and structured. They have a focus and a goal, yet offer participants the freedom to pursue trains of thought and hop from idea to idea. And they're a lot of fun.

As you can see, IBM's use of the jazz analogy to generate ideas was a perfect fit. If instead they had said, *let's all think like a baseball team and play nine innings,* the brainstorm probably would not have been as successful.

Try completing the Great Idea Action Sheet on page 161 to see how music metaphors might harmonize your office environment.

A Walk in the Woods

Great thinkers often turn to nature for inspiration. Louis Pasteur, for example, noticed that the skin of grapes had to be broken before the fermentation process of winemaking could begin. Pasteur then realized that human skin had to be broken before infection occurred—a great leap from the nineteenth-century theory that infection was caused by internal poisonous gases.

Thomas Edison used the nature metaphor to invent whole systems, such as a lamp, a conduit, an electric grid, and a dynamo. In his words: "Nature doesn't just make leaves; it makes branches and trees and roots to go with them." Charles Darwin used branches to illustrate his "tree of life," which led to his theory of evolution. And, of course, Sir Isaac Newton, while in a contemplative mood, was inspired by the fall of an apple to formulate the laws of gravity.

In fact, the next metaphorical frontier most likely lies in nature. As ecological political movements begin to capture the attention of the middle class, as the media explore the hazards facing Mother Earth, and as extreme weather events increasingly prompt national and international concern, I believe that the next operative metaphor will emphasize "nature's way of doing things." For, unlike our former metaphors of war and athletic prowess and their emphasis on one side winning and the other side losing, nature offers a long-term win/win metaphor in which all parties benefit.

Looking at your problem or goal through the eyes of nature instills a sense of global interdependence and cooperation, and it's a useful technique when you need to expand your horizons. Try it out in the Great Idea Action Sheet at the end of the chapter.

Win/Lose versus Win/Win Metaphors

While military and sports metaphors promote competition, nature and music metaphors inspire cooperation. Therefore, these two different types of metaphors produce strikingly different reactions within an organization:

WIN/LOSE (MILITARY & SPORTS)	WIN/WIN (NATURE & MUSIC)
Immediate motivation	Incremental motivation
Revolution	Evolution
Competition	Cooperation
Inspiration	Contemplation
Mission statements	Vision statements

Both types of metaphors have their place in history and in fulfilling our present managerial needs. Skilled communicators and Idea Generators mix and pace their use of these two types of metaphors, prompting short-term gains with the win/lose metaphor and fostering long-term cooperation with the win/win metaphor.

Half-Full Cans of Paint

Jack Welch, former CEO of General Electric, declared war on junk work and, in eliminating it, decided to make speed, simplicity, and self-confidence GE's mantra, and the standard way of running its worldwide businesses.

Welch used a most effective metaphor to describe the need for speed, simplicity, and self-confidence. He asked a group of top managers how many had relocated within the past ten years. Most raised their hands. He then asked how many had moved half-full cans of paint and pairs of stained sneakers used to stain wooden decks. Most raised their hands. He then asked how many had *used* those cans of paint and sneakers *ever* in their new homes. Only a smattering of hands went up.

Welch then pointed out that the same thing happens when people change positions in a company like GE. They take once-crucial reports, approvals, meetings, measurements, and policies with them to their new jobs, where they're no longer necessary or a good fit. It was these, Welch believed, that slowed people down. What was needed instead was a healthy "spring cleaning."

This spring cleaning, called Work-Out!, was put in place as a ten-year plan at General Electric. To speed up people's performance, GE insisted on a new mind-set of continuous improvement by finding a better way every day.

By focusing people's minds on the metaphor of half-full paint cans, stained sneakers, and spring cleaning, the General Electric CEO managed to create an environment of speed and self-renewing innovation.

Juggling: A Metaphor for Workaday Life

Juggling requires maintaining a balance between focusing on essentials and letting go of the unnecessary. Successful jugglers (like people in business, government, the professions) must focus on the pinnacle of their toss (their goals, their vision) and trust that their hands (their people, customers, clients) can throw and catch at the same time. Jugglers (as well as people in business, government, the professions) who are preoccupied with the motion of their hands are actually setting themselves up for failure. They drop the ball. The same preoccupation can prevent you from communicating and realizing your vision. You, too, drop the ball.

In order to get GE employees to feel what it's like to focus on a shared vision while going about their daily tasks, I teach them the art of juggling. I emphasize that the juggler must concentrate on the apex of the toss, which I liken to a shared vision. If jugglers stop looking at the shared vision and lower their eyes to their hands, they start dropping things, and everything begins to go awry.

Juggling is also a good way to loosen up a situation—and yourself. John Ahlbach of the National Stuttering Project recommends juggling as a way for speech pathologists to work with kids in school—to create rapport, improve the juggler's self-image, teach a new behavior, distract children from the stuttering problem, make therapy more fun, and break "a few handheld objects in your office you didn't want anyway."

And, he says, "Juggling makes that ordinary trip to the produce market a real adventure."

— E X E R C I S E —

HOW TO BECOME A JUGGLER

Get out three tennis balls or beanbags and get ready to become a juggler.

Step 1
Start with one ball or beanbag in your throwing hand.

Step 2
Throw it from hand to hand with scooping, underhand throws. Say, "Throw" when you toss it, to distract yourself from worrying about catching it; trust yourself to catch and focus instead on throwing. The pinnacle should be slightly above your head. Keep your eyes focused at the top of your toss and your hands down at waist level.

Step 3
Now face a wall and put a ball in each hand. The wall forms a visual plane for your tossing pattern so that the balls don't get way out in front of you. Start tossing from your dominant throwing hand and say, "One." When that ball reaches its peak, say, "Two" and throw the second ball with your other hand. The two balls will cross in the air and change hands.

Step 4
Pay attention to the arc of your toss. You are probably throwing the second ball to the side or out in front of you. Keep going. It just takes some more practice to get your toss under control.

Step 5
Now start with two balls in your dominant throwing hand and a third in your other hand. Start tossing with your dominant hand and say, "One." Say, "Two" when the ball reaches its peak and toss the second ball, held in your nondominant hand. When that ball reaches its peak, say, "Three," and toss the third ball, held in your dominant hand. When that ball reaches its peak, say, "Four," and keep going.

Step 6
If you are having difficulty releasing the third ball, make a pact with yourself that, no matter what, you will throw that ball. Don't try to make perfect tosses or to catch every ball. Dropping the ball is a metaphor for progress.

For more on applying juggling to your life and business, read *More Balls than Hands* by Michael Gelb. For more thorough juggling instructions, see *Juggling: From Start to Star* by Dave Finnigan.

What's the "Right" Metaphor?
A Sandwich or an Appliance?

According to Kurt Ling, the former VP of innovations at Simmons Mattress:

From a company perspective, we always say building beds is like a sandwich. You stack up layers of coils, foam, and fiber between the bun. However, consumers can readily tell you that buying a mattress is either like the utility purchase of buying appliances or the comfort purchase of buying running shoes.

So whose metaphor is correct? Both! One metaphor represents the views of those who design and manufacture the mattress. The other represents the perspective of the customer, who sees this purchase in terms of its utility or its comfort. The key is for the manufacturing and sales folks to understand and appreciate the metaphor that reflects the buying experience of the customer.

So Kurt and I brainstormed. If the consumer thinks the mattress purchase is akin to the purchase of an appliance, why don't we ship the mattress in a box like the one an appliance comes in? Usually a mattress is shipped in plastic, which is ripped off at the customer's home and can become a choking hazard for children.

Since kids love to play with empty cardboard appliance boxes, why don't we create a mattress shipping box that can be turned into a kid's fort? We could then put Simmons logos on the box so that when the kids are playing in the fort outside, the whole neighborhood knows this family just purchased a new Beautyrest mattress.

As you can see, creating metaphors can be quite effective as an approach to idea making. The process is simple:

1. Describe your problem.

2. Distill the problem down to a single word or phrase.

3. Dream up some metaphorical ideas by completing this simile:
    [Word] is like a . . .

4. Use the metaphorical image and try to solve the metaphorical problem.

5. Be ready. All sorts of ideas will emerge from this process.

GREAT IDEA ACTION

WHAT GAME ARE YOU PLAYING?

Compare the style of your organization with the three team sports cited in this chapter (football, baseball, basketball)—or with any sport familiar to you—or expand the metaphor to create a hybrid sport that best describes your organization.

Step 1 Fill out the sports metaphor chart below.

Your Style of:	**Similar Sport:**
Coaching_____ _____	_____
Communication_____ _____	_____
Leadership_____ _____	_____
Team_____ _____	_____
Success_____ _____	_____
Player_____ _____	_____

Your Type of:

Organization_____ _____	_____
Environment_____ _____	_____

Step 2 Now answer these questions:

1. What are your strengths as a team?

2. What are your weaknesses as a team?

3. What would a half-time locker room talk sound like?

4. Do you have superstars? Benchwarmers?

5. Is your coaching style right for the game?

6. How do you celebrate when you win?

7. How do you console and motivate the team when you lose?

Step 3 Review your answers and on another sheet of paper write up your game plan for winning.

GREAT IDEA ACTION
USING THE MUSIC METAPHOR

Create a music metaphor Idea Map to come up with suggestions for managing stress in the office.

Step 1 Complete the following analogy:
Stress in our workplace is like what in music: _____

Step 2 Idea Map your music metaphor on another sheet of paper.
Put your music metaphor in a circle in the center of your paper and start Idea Mapping. Write down as quickly as you can words associated with your music metaphor; put these words all around the center circle. Look for new associations. Draw arrows from one word to another, connecting your key thoughts. Add more words as necessary.

Step 3 Look for the main concepts and patterns in your Idea Map.
Assign geometric symbols to your main concepts and "cluster" your words by putting the respective symbol around each related word.

Step 4 Create an Idea Outline.
Now transcribe your Idea Map into either a "cluster" or a Roman-numeral outline.

Step 5 Record your ideas. Write down four ideas that can help you manage stress in your office.

       1.

       2.

       3.

       4.

GREAT IDEA ACTION
USING THE NATURE METAPHOR

Create a nature metaphor Idea Map to come up with suggestions for improving communications in the office.

Step 1 Complete the following analogy:
Effective communication is like what in nature: _____

Step 2 Idea Map your nature metaphor on another sheet of paper.
Put your nature metaphor in a circle in the center of your paper and start Idea Mapping. Write down as quickly as you can words associated with your nature metaphor; put these words all around the center circle. Look for new associations. Draw arrows from one word to another, connecting your key thoughts. Add more words as necessary.

Step 3 Look for the main concepts and patterns in your Idea Map.
Assign geometric symbols to your main concepts and "cluster" your words by putting the respective symbol around each related word.

Step 4 Create an Idea Outline.
Now transcribe your Idea Map into either a "cluster" or a Roman-numeral outline.

Step 5 Record your ideas.
Write down four ideas that can help you improve communications in your office.

1.

2.

3.

4.

GREAT IDEA ACTION
CREATE A METAPHOR

Write down metaphors that describe or characterize a problem you are experiencing. Based on the metaphors, suggest positive ways to help solve the problem.

Step 1 Describe your problem:

Step 2 Reduce the problem to a word or short phrase:
Word:

Phrase:

Step 3 Insert your word or phrase to produce appropriate analogies:
[WORD] is like a:

[PHRASE] is like a:

Step 4 Pick the analogy that gives you the freshest perspective.
Use it to generate several metaphorical solutions.

      1.

      2.

      3.

Step 5 From the above solutions, write down two ideas that can help you solve your problem.

      1.

      2.

Pass Notes

Borrowing Ideas from Others

I've got to be careful here, because there is Okay Borrowing and Not Okay Borrowing.

Okay Borrowing is simply borrowing an idea from someone else and improving on it. Okay Borrowing has been going on in the world of commerce for thousands of years and, if we're to progress as an economic superpower and as a civilization, must go on indefinitely into the future.

Among the innumerable fields that reflect the benefits of Okay Borrowing is small appliances. In the 1920s, designers at Hamilton Beach borrowed the idea behind the vacuum cleaner, combined it with their small food blender motor and—voilà! The portable hair dryer was born. Waring then borrowed the idea behind the malted-milk blender from Hamilton Beach and introduced it into bars to make mixed drinks. In the late 1950s, Oster borrowed the blender idea and introduced a new style of cooking where all ingredients are blended together, called "Spin Cookery."

Not Okay Borrowing has also been going on since the dawn of time. It's called plagiarism, trademark infringement, patent infringement, or copyright infringement. In a word, stealing.

The difference between Okay Borrowing and Not Okay Borrowing is crucial. It might very well mean the difference between unbounded market success and a term in jail. Basically, it's Okay to take somebody else's idea and use it. For example, if McDonald's shows that there's a market in fast-food hamburgers, then it's perfectly Okay, indeed, beneficial to the marketplace, for Hardee's and Wendy's to start up fast-food hamburger franchises. The fast-food hamburger idea itself is too broad for anyone to own, as is the idea of franchises.

But the expressions, formulations, and emblems particular to McDonald's implementation of the idea—for example, the golden arches—*can* be protected by a trademark at the U.S. Office of Patents & Trademarks. Advertising copy, packaging, and the like can also be protected by copyright. So someone other than McDonald's using golden arches to sell hamburgers is a Not Okay form of Idea Borrowing.

The wise Idea Generator will make it a habit to become exposed to the ideas of others, to identify good ideas, and to adapt them for her own purposes. A 2002 *New York Times* news story confirms that creative people are great observers and make time for their Okay Borrowing, pointing to the research habits of a popular comedian: "For three hours every day, Jerry Seinfeld wanders around his neighborhood—people-watching, sliding in and out of shops, pausing on a park bench—looking for the seed for a good stand-up routine."

Creatively Borrowing Creativity

At one time, all employees at Nissan Motors were required to drive Nissan cars. That made perfect sense, according to top management. It would certainly hurt the image of the company to have its employees tooling around in competitors' cars.

No longer. Now Nissan's top management allows employees to own anyone's cars, and encourages employees to test-drive the cars of competitors, to visit competitors' showrooms, to look carefully at the ideas developed by others. They've dropped the mind-set that if it's not invented here, it can't possibly be any good.

Several years ago, I was taking a tour of the manufacturing facilities of clothing manufacturer Lands' End. I commented that everyone was wearing Lands' End clothes. The executive giving me the tour smiled with pride. Later that day in my creativity session, I asked the audience to imagine a possibility: What if one day a month, everyone were expected to wear competitor's clothes? What could we learn from wearing the clothes of L. L. Bean or the Gap or Banana Republic? The attendees immediately realized that they had been missing a learning opportunity for Lands' End and, hopefully, implementing this idea will provide ongoing insights.

Recently, I was having dinner with the management team of a major mattress manufacturer, and I asked what mattresses team members slept on. Everyone slept on one of the company's top-of-the-line models. I then asked if any of them had slept on the new Swedish foam mattress or the new air mattress advertised heavily in TV infomercials? One of the executives responded that he had sat on one of the Swedish foam mattresses once.

I then asked if any of them slept on their company's low-end models. They all said no. Not surprised, I asked, "You're a mattress manufacturer with a lot of competitors. Wouldn't you all learn something from sleeping on a competitor's mattress, or a mattress in your product line that your average customer sleeps on?" There was complete agreement and we then brainstormed a "musical mattress" program for them, whereby a new mattress by one of their competitors—or one of their own lower-end models—is delivered and installed in each of their homes a couple times per year. They get to sleep on it and evaluate it and share their insights with the company and their families. The bottom line is that competitive analysis isn't just for the marketing or product-development folks; it's a strategy for everyone in your company and everyone in their families to utilize.

Successful innovators recognize the value of borrowing ideas and resist what others have called the "Not-Invented-Here" (NIH) syndrome. People get so hung up on the NIH syndrome that they close their eyes to ideas developed elsewhere. Why? Arrogance explains the syndrome to a large extent ("No one's widget is as good as ours."). Other likely causes include the Protestant work ethic, which decrees that if it's free, or if it didn't require Herculean effort, it can't be worthwhile; and a sense of false pride, which leads organizations to fall into the trap of thinking, "What *we* do is important; what *they* do can't possibly measure up."

Whatever the source, the time to root it out once and for all is *now*. To help you along, I've listed ways you can creatively and ethically borrow ideas.

Roll the Dice

This is my favorite technique for borrowing ideas. I first make a list of the six places or people from whom I think that I can borrow an idea. Then I roll a die to see what number comes up. Using the list found in the exercise on the next page, if I roll a three, then I would need to think like the folks at Apple Computer. What can I learn from their marketing and design practices? What advice would Steve Jobs give me?

Once I've got some new thoughts, I roll the die again.

"THINK LIKE _____" EXERCISE

Roll a die and "think like . . ." the associated company. Brainstorm for 10 minutes and roll the die again.

#1 WAL★MART

#2 Google

#3

#4 TOYOTA

#5 The Ritz-Carlton®

#6 STARBUCKS COFFEE

Become Your Competition's Customer

Do your competitors maintain mailing lists? Do they send out promotional pieces or newsletters? Are *you* on their lists? I'm serious. You should receive your competition's promotional mail. That way, you'll keep up with their new ideas and sales strategies.

Examining how your best competitors operate and manage their businesses is sometimes easier than analyzing your own operation. The purpose of benchmarking is not to set your own performance targets, but to get outside your organization's own assumptions and habits to see other patterns of success.

Visit Great "Showrooms"

I love to walk into a Build-a-Bear Workshop or a Whole Foods grocery market. These are showrooms that create a consumer experience and are reconceiving entire brand categories, not just displaying products. I recently got ideas for my Children's Hospital client from a walk through a Build-a-Bear store and ideas for my technology services client from a visit to an Apple store.

Start a Borrow File

Whenever you see an ad, a direct-mail piece, a quote, a passage in a book, or a comic strip that makes you see things in a different way, clip it out and put it in your Borrow File. Periodically review your Borrow File in search of new angles or new ways of approaching old problems.

Announce a "Not-Invented-Here" Contest

To encourage those around you to get out of the rut caused by the NIH syndrome, start a "Not-Invented-Here" contest. Have people submit ideas borrowed from various sources.

You might include the following prize categories:

Most Easily Implementable Idea

Best Idea from a Family Member

Best Idea from a Foreign Company

Best Idea from a Friend

Best Idea from a Competitor

Become a Part of the Marketplace

Sony demands that its research-and-development people and marketers spend 25 percent of their time out of the office in the consumer marketplace. This policy has paid handsome dividends. Years ago, a Sony engineer was watching the growing trend of California's youth going up and down the California coast on roller skates—alone. The engineer put two and two together. Youth . . . alone . . . on wheels . . . with no music. Fast-forward to the revolutionary Sony Walkman, and now, of course, to the Apple iPod.

Read a Biography of a Person You're Trying to Emulate

As you're sitting at your desk, stuck for a fresh approach to a talk you have to give tomorrow, think how creative it would be to have Thomas Jefferson take over your assignment for a while. Although you can't give Jefferson a call and make arrangements for a working lunch with him, you can do the next best thing by reading biographies of great and inspirational people. Try such topics as history, philosophy, politics, science, and sports.

Take a Problem to the Movies

When you sit down to solve a problem all by yourself, when you stare at the wall determined to come up with some innovative solutions, oftentimes you fail. Instead of trying and trying and trying again, take a break! Recognize that creativity does not come just from within, but from the outside as well. A scene, a sound, an odd object can spark that idea you've been looking for. Be open to this kind of outside influence and you'll be shocked at how often an idea will occur to you, seemingly out of the blue.

When I need ideas, I'll often sit down and watch a movie. My goal is to come up with ideas I can use. This "focused observation" has worked wonders for me on many occasions. Sometimes I even take a problem with me to the golf course. I then look for ideas in the context of greens, sand traps, fairways, divots, tees, birdies, bogeys, and pars.

Start a Campfire

With the advent of e-mail, text messaging, and instant messaging, technology has become the campfire around which we now tell our stories. In cyberspace, we share our lives, our dreams, our photos, our music, and our stock picks.

At the touch of a button, from almost anywhere in the civilized world, we can exchange ideas with others. The opportunities for collaboration have never been so great, and the chance to create a breakthrough in thinking never more readily available.

If you want to increase the world's receptivity to your ideas, become a great listener to the ideas of others. Figure out which ideas work and which don't. Listen for ideas that build on your idea. Listen for the pitfalls. Listen for the energy surging through other people's thoughts. Be attuned to the possibilities.

As the world-famous golfer Arnold Palmer said, "The secret to great putting is having lunch with great putters." This makes perfect sense, because great putters talk about their techniques and recount their hours spent practicing putting, both on the green and in their minds.

If you could build a campfire to share your ideas, whom would you invite?

GREAT IDEA ACTION

WALK IN OTHERS' SHOES

Consider the issue at hand from the viewpoints of others involved in or at the source of your challenge to help "borrow" solutions to your problem.

PROBLEM STATEMENT:

Step 1 Write down the identities of three people who ordinarily are associated with the problem.

    1.

    2.

    3.

Step 2 Now describe the problem from their points of view.

    1.

    2.

    3.

Step 3 After studying the identities of these three people and their differing perspectives, write down suggestions you could use to solve the problem.

GREAT IDEA ACTION

WALK IN COMPETITOR'S SHOES

Put yourself in your competitors' place to help "borrow" solutions to your problem.

PROBLEM STATEMENT:

Step 1 Write down the names of three competitors who could help you solve the problem.

   1.

   2.

   3.

Step 2 Now describe the problem from their points of view.

   1.

   2.

   3.

Step 3 After studying the identities of these competitors and their differing perspectives, write down suggestions you could use to solve the problem.

The Brain Gym

Overcoming Mental Blocks

Has this ever happened to you?

You're at a party, talking to a small group of people. A friend walks up. You want to introduce her, but your mind goes blank. You can't remember her name!

You're in a heated debate with your boss. Just when you're about to make the winning point, your mind goes blank. You can't think of a thing, even though you can "feel" the argument you were about to make.

You're writing an important report. As you turn to the next blank page, your mind goes blank as well. Words won't come, even though you knew (just a moment ago) what you wanted to say.

It never fails, of course—after your embarrassed friend leaves or your boss wins the argument or your report misses its deadline—you remember your friend's name, you know those winning arguments like the back of your hand, and your report writes itself in your mind. Good old 20/20 hindsight. We're all blessed with that ability to know what we should have done. But we're not as well endowed with the knowledge of what to do when the mental block occurs.

A mental block usually crops up when you're looking for an immediate answer in a direct, linear way, yet your brain needs time to free-associate for the solution. If you were to equate your brain with a telecommunications system, its capacity could be likened to the total number of phone circuits in the world, multiplied fourteen hundred times. With this vast array of interconnected lines, your plea for a direct answer is often met with call waiting or voice mail. To get your answer, you need to make the call on an open line, one of many in your mind. For some reason, however, we seem to pick the line already jammed with other calls. We need ways to find that open line.

Metaphors Left and Right

To Plato, the brain was a block of wax. In his words: "Imagine a block of wax with thoughts imprinted into it." To Aristotle, the brain cooled the blood, while thinking took place in the heart. In more modern times, we tend to think of the brain as a giant computer, complete with input, output, software, and the equivalent of a gazillion computer chips.

Most images we use today to describe creativity and the work of the brain rely heavily on the increasingly familiar divisions of function between the "left brain" and the "right brain." Researchers have discovered that the left and right hemispheres of the brain process information in contrasting ways; they have individual styles of thinking while still managing to work in a complementary way. As many readers already know, the left hemisphere specializes in verbal, logical, and analytical thinking. Its favored way of thinking is linear: first things first. It excels in the three Rs: reading, writing, and arithmetic. An apt example of left-brain thinking is balancing your checkbook. A sense of satisfaction comes from reconciling the numbers.

The right hemisphere specializes in nonverbal, visual, spatial, and perceptual thinking. It prefers nonlinear thinking, and relies on simultaneous information processing. The right brain excels at seeing patterns and relationships, and is undaunted by ambiguity and paradoxes; some might say it even thrives on the tension of unresolved issues. An apt example of right-brain thinking is highway driving. Successful driving requires the skill of simultaneously processing divergent visual and other perceptual information. The sense of satisfaction comes from all the free association that goes on in your mind while driving without conscious monitoring. How often have you driven a familiar route and suddenly realized that you don't remember passing a particular scene or noteworthy landmark?

The left and right sides of the brain share and communicate their views by means of a nerve bundle called the *corpus callosum*. Throughout the day, the two sides work cooperatively. When you're playing music, the left side reads the music and keeps the beat while the right side handles tone, melody, and expression.

In the creative process, the left side tends to be "fact friendly," while the right side is more "idea friendly." We need both sides interacting in a complementary way to come up with creative solutions to problems:

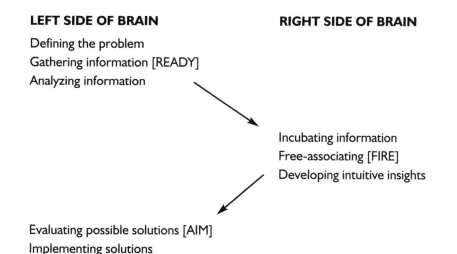

LEFT SIDE OF BRAIN

Defining the problem
Gathering information [READY]
Analyzing information

RIGHT SIDE OF BRAIN

Incubating information
Free-associating [FIRE]
Developing intuitive insights

Evaluating possible solutions [AIM]
Implementing solutions

You can readily see how these left-right brain functions reflect our "Ready, Fire . . . Aim!" model of creative thinking. Getting ready and defining the problem is basically a left-brain exercise. Using one of the many idea-generating techniques described in earlier chapters—firing off in divergent directions in the brainstorming process—is a right-brain exercise. And aiming and choosing a solution is another left-brain exercise, informed now, however, by the right brain.

The following chart should help put many of these left/right functions into better perspective:

INFORMATION PROCESSING IN THE BRAIN

	LEFT SIDE OF BRAIN	RIGHT SIDE OF BRAIN
Historical Perspective	Yang	Yin
	Ego	Id
	Conscious	Subconscious
	Mind	Spirit
Information Gathering	Thinking	Feeling
	Sensing	Intuition
Remembering	Words	Images
	Numbers	Patterns
	Parts	Wholes
	Names	Faces
Expressing	Verbal	Nonverbal
	Talking	Dreams, gestures, gut feelings
	Counting	Drawing, singing
	Writing	Doodling
Thinking	Analytical	Visionary
	Linear	Spatial
	Logical	Analogical (thinking in analogies)
	Rational	Free associating
	Sequential	Simultaneous
	Vertical	Lateral
	Convergent	Divergent
	Deductive	Inductive
Perception	Black/White	Gray
Performance	Intentional	Reflex
	Execution	Visualization
Management	Rules, procedures	Shared vision
Organization	Financial Assets	Values
	People	Commitment
	Raw Materials	Ideas
	Technology	Innovation

Hemispheres and the Body

Neurophysiological research shows that, at birth, the hemispheres are separate but equal: If one hemisphere is damaged in infancy, the other one can take over all its functions and the child will grow up with normal abilities. This capability is called *plasticity* of the brain. However, by age seven, the two hemispheres have specialized, and injury to the left hemisphere will adversely affect the verbal abilities and the control of the right side of the body. Injury to the right hemisphere will diminish spatial abilities and the control of the left side of the body. Thus, with specialization, each hemisphere governs control of the *opposite* side of the body.

Hemispheres and Overcoming *Senior Moments*

Have you ever walked into a room and immediately forgotten why you walked in there? This is sometimes referred to, humorously, as a *senior moment*. Dr. Lawrence Katz, a professor of neurobiology at Duke University Medical Center, recommends the following pattern-breakers to stimulate your brain so that you have fewer of these moments. He calls this *neurobics*—think aerobics for the mind—the neuroscience of brain exercise.

> "We spend more time trying to keep our stomach flat and thighs thin than our mind sharp. We snack on "veggies" while our brain snacks on junk TV."
>
> —Dr. Lawrence Katz, Duke Medical Center

1. Brush your teeth with your nondominant hand.

2. Listen to a new radio station on the way to work.

3. Watch a different newscast on TV.

4. Move your watch to your opposite arm. (Sound familiar?)

5. Sit in a different seat at meetings or at the dining table.

6. Mix and match your clothing combinations.

7. Drive to and from work a different way.

8. Use your opposite hand to maneuver your computer mouse.

9. Adopt a new hobby.

What Dr. Katz is encouraging you to do is to try some exercises that make you feel distinctly uncomfortable—to make the nondominant side of your brain do things it normally doesn't do. By making that side of your brain control some motor functions, you prompt your entire brain to look at things in different, creative ways.

Here's a great idea for dinner tonight. Prepare your meal from scratch. Cut up the raw ingredients, grind the spices, stir, taste, stir some more. You'll be using both sides of your brain—rather than just mindlessly dumping ingredients into a container and putting the concoction in the microwave. Your brain will thank you; hopefully, so will your stomach.

The Power of Your Other Hand

If you're bogged down in a problem and need a jump-start, start scribbling with a pencil in your *other* hand or pick up a small object with your *other* hand. The unfamiliar muscular movements from the nondominant side of your body will trigger electrical and chemical impulses in the nondominant side of your brain. The net result? New connections—a new perspective—possibly a new idea.

If you're a bit skeptical after reading this section—well, I was too, until I began to use this technique in my creativity workshops. My workshop participants, so far, all report significant changes in the way they view routine problems, and significant increases in the quantity and quality of their proposed solutions to those problems.

"OTHER HAND" WRITING

The next time you encounter a mental block, try following the steps below to stimulate the opposite side of your brain and come up with a fresh approach to your problem:

Step 1
Take out a sheet of paper and, using your dominant hand, write down six words that describe you.

Step 2
Take your pencil out of your hand and for one minute focus your eyes on the center of this graphic mandala.

Step 3
Now, using your opposite hand, write down six different words that describe you. Be a kid again! Draw them all over a sheet of paper, not one on top of the other.

Step 4
What similarities and differences do you see between the two sets of words? Is one set more emotional than the other? Is one more honest or insightful? Did you generate words that you have never before used to describe yourself?

Opposite Responses

Answering a question with your nondominant hand is a proven counseling technique used to bring out childhood and emotional issues. Most people write opposite responses with their two hands. By *opposite,* I mean work versus home settings, analytical versus emotional traits, adult versus child experiences, or powerful versus vulnerable feelings.

Many executives now use this technique to ferret out their emotional response to a question. It definitely triggers the ability to see answers that normally would not have surfaced. To grasp these opposite thoughts, you don't have to be writing with your nondominant hand; you could just be squeezing a rubber ball with your nondominant hand and then capturing your new thoughts.

The mandala also helped you trigger opposite thoughts by taking you on a spatial journey in and out of the design. Focusing on the center of the mandala or on any stationary object is an excellent form of stress reduction.

Historically, the biggest proponents of using your other hand for additional answers were Michelangelo and Leonardo da Vinci. In *How to Think like Leonardo da Vinci: Seven Steps to Genius Every Day,* my good friend Michael Gelb suggests that we all cultivate ambidexterity:

> **When Michelangelo was working on the Sistine Chapel, he astounded observers by switching his paintbrush from one hand to the other as he worked. Leonardo, a natural left-hander, cultivated this same ambidexterity and regularly switched hands when working on** The Last Supper *and other masterpieces.*

While Michael Gelb was researching his book, he interviewed the renowned anthropologist Raymond Dart and asked him about ambidexterity. Professor Dart responded, "Balance the body, balance the brain. The future lies with the ambidextrous human!"

Let's Try Both Hands

To get some practice finding answers with your "other" hand, apply the steps given in the previous section to a specific question or problem. Write down answers or comments using your normal writing hand, then relax for a minute with the mandala, and write answers—all over the page—with your "other" hand. What similarities and differences do you see between your two sets of answers (other than messier handwriting)?

Determining Your Brain/Body Dominance

Our hands are only one body part that can help us overcome a mental block. Let's take a trip from our eyes to our feet to determine the dominance or nondominance of other pairs of body parts or of various sides of one body part. Once you know the dominant way that you move, all you need to do to break out of your mental block is to activate a nondominant body part.

Eyes

Most of us think that we focus on an object with both our eyes. Actually we use just one eye to focus on what we're doing or reading. To determine which eye is dominant, simply hold your thumb at arm's length out in front of you and use your thumb to block out a small object on a far wall, such as a light switch or corner of a picture frame. Do this with both eyes open. When the light switch is blocked out, then close your *right* eye. If your thumb is still blocking out the light switch, then it was your *left* eye that was dominant in focusing. If the light switch "moved," as it will for 60 percent of you now reading this book, then you focused on it with your *right* eye. Figure 12-1 on page 184 is a chart for you to keep score of the various more-dominant parts or sides of your body.

Determining which eye is dominant, for example, has become very beneficial for athletes, for it has been shown that right-handed batters with a dominant left eye have a significantly higher batting average—they don't have to turn their heads to see the ball! The same increased batting statistic is true for left-handed batters with dominant right eyes. One basketball coach told me about the dramatic improvement his team made in free-throw shooting when players determined their dominant eyes. It turns out that before shooting, his worst shooters were setting up the ball in front of their dominant eyes, thus misreading the location of the basket. Just moving the ball in front of their nondominant eye increased their shooting percentage substantially.

Wink

Wink one eye, then the other. Does one feel more natural to wink? If so, that's your dominant eye for winking. Don't worry if this eye is not the one you use for focusing. Mark down your dominance.

Smile

Smile at yourself while looking in a mirror. Which side of your mouth goes higher? If you can't tell, look for which side of your face has more wrinkles. The higher, more wrinkled side is your dominant one. Mark down your dominance.

Arms

Cross your arms with one arm on top of the other. Whichever one is on top is your dominant arm. Mark down your dominance.

Thumbs

Bring your hands together, interlocking your fingers, making sure you have one thumb on top of the other. Whichever thumb is on top is your dominant thumb. Now, separate your hands and bring them back together with the other thumb on top. Feels awkward, doesn't it? Mark down your dominance.

You're probably starting to see that not only do we do things in a dominant, patterned way, but we are also a mix of right- and left-side dominances.

Hands

Eleven percent of the U.S. population is left-handed, so mark down which hand you use for writing. If you were switched in grade school from left to right, you are still considered left-handed for the purposes of this exercise.

Legs

Cross your legs at the knee. Which leg feels more comfortable on top? That's your dominant leg—mark it down.

Feet

If I rolled a ball to you, which foot would you use to kick it? That's your dominant foot—mark it down.

Thoughts

This exercise will require help from another person. Ask a friend to ask you several questions in a row. Start off with a simple question, and then move on to a contemplative or analytical one. Have your friend observe whether your eyes move to the left or the right as you contemplate the answers to these questions. Do not have the friend stare at you because you'll stare back. Your eyes need to be relaxed to move.

If your eyes go up or down before they go to the side, that's natural. Your eyes normally go up when you are visualizing an answer to a question like "What was I wearing last Tuesday?" Your eyes normally go down when you are *feeling* an answer to a question like "Was the ocean real cold that day?" If your eyes don't move to one side or the other, allow yourself to be observed later at a more spontaneous time. Mark down whether your eyes moved to the right or to the left.

You can find out more about the relationship between eye movements and thoughts by researching articles or books on the science of Neuro Linguistic Programming (NLP).

Visualization

Close your eyes. Now visualize a circular wall clock on the wall in front of you. In your mind, reach out and take the clock off the wall and put it in front of your face. Now put one finger of one hand at twelve o'clock and one finger of the other hand at three o'clock. Open your eyes and note if three o'clock is on the right or left side of your face; mark down which side.

Mixed Dominance

If you saw the clock both ways on your face or if neither leg feels more or less comfortable when crossed on top of the other, then your dominance for that part of your body is mixed. On the chart, you can check both right and left sides.

Scoring Your Dominance

Count up the number of left- and right-side dominances. The usual score I've seen in my workshops is seven for the right side and three for the left. These body dominances then show the exact opposite brain dominance, because the left side of the body is controlled by the right side of the brain and vice versa. So if your body score is seven right-side and three left, then your brain dominance profile is seven left-side and three right.

Brain/Body Dominances

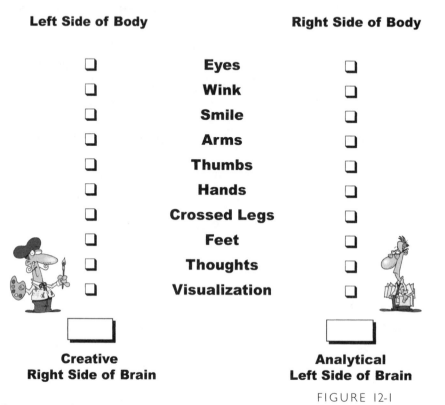

Left Side of Body		Right Side of Body
❑	Eyes	❑
❑	Wink	❑
❑	Smile	❑
❑	Arms	❑
❑	Thumbs	❑
❑	Hands	❑
❑	Crossed Legs	❑
❑	Feet	❑
❑	Thoughts	❑
❑	Visualization	❑

**Creative
Right Side of Brain**

**Analytical
Left Side of Brain**

FIGURE 12-1

Becoming Unstuck

The next time you feel stuck and want a fresh beginning, just cross your arms or legs in the nondominant way. When you're looking at a magazine, instead of browsing through the pages from left to right, go from right to left.

When going to the movie theater, you'll usually want to sit on the right side of the theater if your left eye is dominant, and on the left side if your right eye is dominant. This might explain the ongoing argument you and your spouse or date have when deciding where to sit—especially if it's true, as some people think, that couples tend to have complementary or offsetting patterns of brain/body dominance. To exercise the nondominant side of your brain, sit on the side you don't favor.

If you play tennis and want to play in what many athletes call the "zone," you need to be able to trigger the right side of the brain to assist you with the spatial concepts needed for success in tennis and most other sports. Between each point, just focus on your tennis racket strings. The spatial exercise of looking at the strings will trigger the right spatial side of your brain, will help eliminate distracting sounds from the audience, and will actually make the ball look bigger and slower.

This One's Really Healthful

You might also try the walk-a-mile-for-an-idea approach to overcoming mental blocks. Einstein walked a lot to help solve his problems. He sometimes grew so involved in thought that he would become lost in his own town of Princeton, New Jersey.

Fast walking seems to help jog forgetful adults' memories, according to a study conducted by Dr. Robert Dustman of the Salt Lake City Veterans Administration Medical Center. And Dr. Ted Bashore of the Medical College of Pennsylvania believes that aerobic exercise speeds up the brain's ability to process information.

This One's Fairly Weird

Pause for a minute and breathe only through your nose. If you pay really close attention to your breathing, you'll be able to figure out that you're favoring one of your nostrils over the other. To confirm which nostril is dominant (having more air going through it), close off one nostril and breathe. Then close off the other and breathe. When you figure out which one is now dominant, take your finger and close off that nostril. Feels strange, doesn't it?

I know you probably have better things to do, but several times today, pause for a minute and notice which nostril you're favoring in your breathing. Research shows that you will favor one nostril over the other for about ninety minutes and then switch to the other. This subtle rhythm, utilized in various yoga disciplines, was discovered more than five thousand years ago and is just one of our body's many ultradian rhythms—short cycles found in metabolic functions and perceptual abilities.

Recent research has shown that you can tell which side of your brain is dominant at any given time by observing which nostril you're favoring in your breathing. Right-nostril dominance shows left-brain activity; left-nostril dominance shows right-brain activity.

You know what's coming, don't you? Yes, research further shows that you can trigger the nondominant side of your brain by closing off your dominant nostril and breathing through your nondominant side for up to five minutes. The dominance switches every ninety minutes naturally, but you can spark the nondominant side with this exercise. You will not change the ninety-minute cycle, however.

I use this technique all the time. While sitting at my desk in need of a right-brain infusion, I close off my right nostril and breathe through my left nostril. Voilà! Naturally, I keep my finger discreetly on the *outside* of my nostril and try to look like I'm just leaning on my nose.

I'm not alone in my use of nondominant parts or sides to jog the nondominant side of my brain or to get a particular side of my brain working. I know some professional athletes who use the nose technique between golf shots or before skiing down the big slope. I even had a physician tell me he's using the device as a sleeping aid. When he has trouble falling asleep because of an overactive brain, he breathes only through his left nostril to trigger the right side of his brain. The right side, if you'll recall, is nonjudging and more dreamlike. I have borrowed the technique myself and can attest to its validity. It certainly beats counting sheep.

These Can Help in the Long Run

If you're left- or right-brain dominant, there are specific things you can do that will help you achieve balance, depending on which side you favor. Peak performance expert Maryellen Visconti recommends ongoing activities and routines that can bring out the potential of your lesser-used, nondominant side.

For example, if you're left-brain dominant, Visconti recommends:

Kite flying
Free-style dancing
Playing Frisbee
Learning to sail
Singing lessons
Joining a choir
Public speaking
Taking a course in storytelling

Finding a way to be with children (become a Big Sister
or a Big Brother)
Volunteering in a children's hospital
Drawing and painting
Using colored pencils/pens in note taking

If you're right-brain dominant:

Make miniature models
Start a stamp or coin collection
Keep daily checkbook balances (to the penny!)
Keep dated records of activities
Participate in competitive swimming, running, or
bicycling (where you have to be conscious of time)
Play golf
Read history books or novels
Join a history discussion group
Ballroom dancing
Learn chess
Paint (by numbers!)
Take a course in auto repair or financial investments
Chart the stock market
Learn a foreign language
Visit a science museum
Start an insect identification collection
Write, type, and file your ideas
Keep organized files of bills and correspondence

This One's Really High-Tech

Let's face it. We can learn all the creativity techniques in the world, but our mind will sometimes get stuck in a rut. We just can't get our brain in sync.

Don't give up. Borrow an idea from the latest brain research, which shows that nonverbal audio patterns have a dramatic effect on consciousness. According to Bob Monroe, founder of the internationally known Monroe Institute, certain sound patterns, when blended and sequenced together, can gently lead your brain into relaxation, sleep, concentration, or heightened creativity.

Using stereo headphones, Monroe sends separate sound impulses to each ear, prompting the two hemispheres of the brain to act in unison to "hear" a third signal—not an actual sound, but an electrical signal created by both brain hemispheres working together simultaneously. This coherent brain state is known as *hemispheric synchronization,* or *hemi-sync.* While this brain synchronization occurs naturally in everyday life, unfortunately, it typically lasts only for random, brief periods of time. The hemi-sync audio technologies developed by the Monroe Institute are designed to help you achieve and sustain this highly productive brain state.

The Monroe Institute makes hemi-sync technology available to the public in a number of ways, including intensive training programs for exploration and development of expanded states of consciousness. The institute offers numerous audio programs, dealing with accelerated learning, stress reduction, pain control, sleep enhancement, and (my favorite) heightened creativity. To learn more about this technology, visit the Monroe Institute at www.monroeinstitute.com.

Blockbusters

Mental blocks are natural in the creative process. Now you know some quick and efficient ways to overcome them. To help you further, I've prepared the following When-You're-Stuck Action Sheet.

GREAT IDEA ACTION

WHEN YOU'RE STUCK!

Here's all you have to do to get a lift from both sides of your brain:

USE YOUR NONDOMINANT BODY PARTS

Cross your legs the wrong way.
Interlock your fingers the wrong way.
Use your nondominant eye to read a short magazine article.
Write down some thoughts with your "other" hand.
Breathe through your left nostril for a right-brain jolt.
Breathe through your right nostril for a left-brain jolt.
Doodle or scribble with the "wrong" hand.

DO THINGS IN A STRANGE WAY OR DO SOME STRANGE THINGS

Drive to work a different way.
Close your eyes and daydream about your ideal vacation spot.
Make a short phone call to a friend and just catch up.
Browse through a magazine and just look at the pictures.
Walk around the mall and pretend that you have to get something.
Take a shower and sing the *Hallelujah Chorus*.
Do a crossword puzzle.
While pretending to analyze a spreadsheet, play a computer game.
Read a report that's been sitting on your desk for a month.

MANIPULATE YOUR TIME

Write down your thoughts as fast as you can. Then go back and edit.
Set a specific time limit for completing your task.
Divide your task into "doable" chunks and tackle them one by one.
Idea Map your problem and rapidly rank the ideas you generate.
Use an opposite Idea Map by answering this question:

    What would I *never* do to solve this problem?

THE THIRD STEP

Conclusion

All four steps that comprise this book focus on ways of removing obstacles to the generation of ideas. In cultivating creative *freedom,* the Idea Person removes the blinders that may have prevented the generation of multiple ideas (as opposed to the single "right" idea) and disarms the power of negative assumptions. In practicing *expression,* exercises like Idea Maps, by their very form, go beyond the obstacles presented by habitual, circumscribed, linear ways of thinking.

The obstacle to *creation* is, in a sense, reality itself—that is, *reality* as we assume it to be. The Idea Person does not accept this reality, even though she may be, and preferably is, highly realistic. The creative person "escapes" into *other* realities—worlds where the future happens right now, where everything turns into its opposite, where the things we believe are true just aren't, where the normal point of view is abandoned, everything is metaphorical, we trespass into other people's brains, and flip-flop our own. And the most successful Idea People make this escape for the same reason that kids play or that other

grown-ups read novels or go to the movies—for the sheer joy of the journey, for the fun of it. All the rewards simply follow.

Creation assumes reality to be plastic and transformable, and generates ideas for new and, we hope, better ways that this reality can bend. The next step involves the process of finding out if reality will.

ACTION

If you don't act on your idea, it will pop out of your head and into the head of your competition.

—Steven Spielberg, film director

Because *action* is the step of the creative process least often associated with imagination and invention, it lends itself especially well to application of these attributes. *Action*—the phase of bringing ideas to fruition—requires great ideas to match the ideas being enacted.

Action is the stage of the creative process where innovation meets organization—meets production—meets sales—meets distribution. We need to bring innovation into every step, in order to give it a chance—if our ideas and our organizations are to thrive in this competitive world.

The creative process is global, in every sense of the word. This is not the machine age, where lockstep production and distribution could (if, indeed, it ever could) just grind out the products of the mind. More and more, every step of the way must be a product of the mind—the open mind, free to imagine, capable of passion, empowered to create.

The following chapters help you create and maintain an openness to ideas—within your organization, in your own routines, in meetings, in your home. The purpose: to help your great ideas fulfill their creator's intentions. To bring worthy ideas all the way through the cycle of physical realization from generation to fruition is, simply put, *fulfillment*.

> At IDEO, we believe that innovators focus on the verbs. They're proactive. They're energetic. Innovators set out to create, to experience, to inspire, to build on new ideas.
>
> —Tom Kelley, general manager, IDEO
> *The Ten Faces of Innovation*

C H A P T E R   1 3

Thought Capital

Evaluating New Ideas

Human history is in essence a history of ideas.
—H. G. Wells, science fiction writer

Our brain generates about ten watts of electricity, which is not enough to light a city, but enough to create the idea of a city and then build it.

Enlightened managers now recognize that the assets of their employees' minds exceed the assets of an organization's bricks and mortar. Bill Gates from Microsoft jokes about going through airport customs, and declaring nothing but having a billion dollars worth of ideas in his head. How do we weigh the economic benefits of these thoughts? The sand on a beach can be measured, but how do we calibrate the value of the idea that turned those silica grains into silicon microchips?

Ideas are the Currency of the Future

Because ideas are cumulative in nature—one leading naturally to another—they encourage us to think in terms of abundance rather than scarcity. For example, if you exchange an idea with an associate at lunch, you both walk away with two ideas. If instead you just exchanged $1 bills at lunch, you'd both walk away with $1.

Now that you know new ways to develop ideas, ideas will begin to come more easily and more spontaneously. Wonderful. Now what will you do with them? And what ideas will you have to leave behind? No one has enough time to chase every single idea out there. If ideas are truly currency, then they have a denomination associated with them.

Your new challenge is to learn how to evaluate the quality of the *many* ideas you have. Do you have a $5 idea or a $1 idea? This is part of the currency question. We need to understand the value of our ideas so that we know where to invest our thought capital. We need to think like venture capitalists, who don't throw the same amount of money and time at each idea. Instead, they want to understand the true value of what they're investing in and what yields they can expect in return.

This means you need to become adept at deciding which ones are good ideas or even great ideas, storing those that need further study or have no immediate application, and setting the wheels in motion for effective idea implementation. We must look, then, at idea evaluation.

What's So Great About It?

Everybody knows what a great idea is. A great idea is the one that worked. Everybody can look at this great idea and say, "*What a great idea!*" Or they'll say, "Look at how simple *that* is!" Or, more likely, they'll say, "Why didn't *I* think of that?" Of course, they are correct in their assessment of greatness.

They have the advantage of looking at an idea *after* someone evaluated it and determined that it was indeed a great idea, *after* someone nurtured it, *after* someone decided to run with it, *after* some people stuck their necks out, *after* the marketplace or organization or bosses or public opinion indeed got together, waved their hands in unison, and wildly agreed: "This is a great idea. We'll buy it!"

You, the lonely Idea Generator, however, don't have this advantage of 20/20 hindsight. You've just come up with an idea. Or someone else has come up with an idea. It sounds good. You like its approach, uniqueness, or other immediately apparent benefits. But is the idea really good? Idea Generators need to avoid the "Focus Group of One" trap: They think a product is a great idea, for example, simply because they would buy it. Unfortunately, this doesn't always translate into success in the marketplace.

I want to give you some quick approaches to evaluation so that you can obtain an initial "feel" concerning an idea's relative merits. You can use this quick evaluation approach to gain a sense of your own perspective or to gather information from your organization or closest colleagues. Your overall objective, of course, is to pick winners, to choose ideas worthy of your time and resources.

Gut versus Brain

According to nineteenth-century mathematician Henri Poincaré, "It is by intuition that we discover and by logic that we prove." But it is at the intuitive level that my evaluation system operates. We're not looking for the analytical evaluation, the numbers, the elaborate tests. They can all come later. What we're looking for in an initial, quick evaluation is the "gut reaction"—yours, that of your closest colleagues, or perhaps even the gut reaction of the organization at large.

Thinkers and innovators have long known the importance of this initial, often visceral reaction. Einstein, for example, sensed that he was on the right track when he felt a tingling at the tips of his fingers. A survey of top executives revealed other physical manifestations of the gut reaction:

1. *A growing excitement in the pit of the stomach.*

2. *A feeling of total harmony.*

3. *A total sense of commitment.*

4. *A burst of enthusiasm and energy.*

Sigmund Freud came up with a unique way to test out his gut feeling on a problem. He would flip a coin. First he would assign heads and tails to a yes/no decision. Then he'd flip. If the coin said yes and his gut said, "Let's go two out of three. I'm not comfortable with that decision!" then his intuitive reaction had just revealed itself.

Tuning In

You undoubtedly have your own set of feelings that you call your gut reaction. This intuition, this feeling, should serve as the very first evaluation you make of your ideas or of the direction in which you're heading in your search for ideas. To help you tune in to these reactions you already have, I've prepared a Great Idea Action Sheet at the end of this chapter for you to complete. Doing so will aid you in describing what a "good idea" and a "bad idea" feel like.

"Blink" Response

In the best-seller *Blink: The Power of Thinking without Thinking,* author Malcolm Gladwell explores decisions we make in the blink of an eye. Gladwell believes that great decision makers aren't those who just collect the most information or spend the most time deliberating, but those who have developed the ability to instantly filter relevant from irrelevant information. The term *blink response* is now heard in meeting rooms around the world to describe our gut reaction based on the brain's instant separation of the few facts that matter from the overwhelming piles of possibilities.

To improve and trust my blink response, I took a class in improvisational theater at the world-renowned Banff Centre in Canada. Improv requires making very sophisticated decisions on the spur of the moment, without any script. What is so terrifying about improv is that it appears to be utterly random. You just get up onstage and make everything up.

But improv isn't as haphazard as it looks; in fact, it's a much-rehearsed art form governed by a series of rules. My favorite rule is that to continue the dialogue, the response to any question is "Yes, and . . ." When you need to stop the scene, your response is "Yes, but . . . ," followed by an excuse for abruptly ending the dialogue. This relates to the strategies we discussed for defusing Killer Phrases in chapter 5. It is also great practice for group brainstorming, since, to achieve a great idea-generation session, every participant's first response to a new idea needs to be "Yes, and . . . ," rather than "Yes, but . . ."

Brain Check

Keep in mind that evaluation is not just a touchy-feely process devoid of analytical thinking. Quite the contrary. Any evaluation necessarily depends on a mental process of isolating objectives (What do I want the idea to accomplish?), identifying the relevant criteria that determine the relative worth of an idea (What standards do I apply in assessing success or failure?), and allocating some sort of weight to those standards (How do I apply the standards?). Gathering this initial information requires analytical thinking. The best starting point, of course, is learning to ask the right questions.

Ask the Right Questions

In the creativity software IdeaFisher, you'll find thousands of questions enabling you to decipher and think about particular problems in need of creative solutions. I offer here several types of questions that can help you begin the evaluation process. I've divided them into the following categories:

Success

Future

Failure

Personal

Mission

Timing

Ask about Success:

What criteria will you use to determine success?

Who is essential to the outcome? Who do you need to involve or influence? What can you do to win this person's support?

What activity or event must occur before your idea can be realized?

What can you do to make your idea even better?

What can you get rid of without spoiling your success?

Ask about the Future:

Will your idea be obsolete in a year or two because of evolving technologies?

When will obsolescence occur?

How quickly and effectively can you respond?

If your idea is a product or service, what effect will it have on people's quality of life? Physical health? Mental health? Safety? Standards of living? Self-fulfillment?

How will your idea affect the quality of human and animal life fifty years from now?

If a patent is important, can you get one?

What is the longevity for your idea?

If the idea catches on suddenly, can you keep up with the demand?

Which of the following changed circumstances might affect your idea? How?

Overseas competition

Corporate takeover

Change of management

Availability of materials

Cost of materials

Changing trends

Boycott

Political unrest

Societal change

Number of foreign visitors

Foreign investments in this country

Any others?

Ask about Failure:

If you failed completely, what would happen?

If you failed partially, what would happen?

Are these risks and possible losses acceptable?

Can the risks and possible losses be avoided or reduced?

If you fail, what can you salvage?

If your idea is a product that fails, can you sell it as something else?

Should you throw everything out and start over?

What are the advantages and disadvantages of starting over?

Ask Personal Questions:

If it were your *money, what would you do? Don't ask others to make an investment when you're not willing to make one yourself.*

Are you changing merely for the sake of change? If so, is that wise?

How strong is your commitment to the project?

How strong is your desire to reach the goal?

How willing are you to invest the necessary time and energy?

Should you challenge any of your assumptions?

What are you taking for granted?

What are you assuming is impossible?

What do you assume are the givens?

What steps or procedures should you question?

What ideas should you question?

What facts should you question?

What if you were to ignore the problem? Would it solve itself?

Ask about Your Mission:

Do you know exactly where this idea fits into the big picture?

Does it promote your mission?

Does it complement your other products and services?

Does it represent a step forward?

Have you been looking at this idea from all points of view or just your own?

Ask about Timing:

Is the idea timely?

Is it too late, at the end of a trend?

Is it too early, too much ahead of its time?

If it is too early, should you postpone your plans?

Vital/Fatal Ratio

After answering some of the above questions, I have our brainstorming teams fill out a Vital/Fatal Ratio on the generated ideas. This assigns numbers to the gut feelings and allows participants to sort, compare, and, best of all, rank the generated ideas.

Recently I worked with leaders in a city in Virginia to brainstorm educational opportunities for children in a time of reduced budgets and No Child Left Behind (NCLB) testing. The Vital/Fatal Ratio depicted in Figure 13-1 represents the first-round voting on one idea we came up with—allowing advertising on school buses (inside and out). The ad revenue would go toward creating a safe learning environment on the buses for the schoolchildren. This environment would include seat belts for all riders, free wi-fi Internet access, healthy snacks in the morning and afternoon, and a graduate student on each bus to tutor the children. A committee of community volunteers from the marketing, legal, and law enforcement fields—along with some students and teachers—would regulate the advertising. Arizona is the first state allowing advertising on school buses and several others are now starting up.

Vital/Fatal Ratio

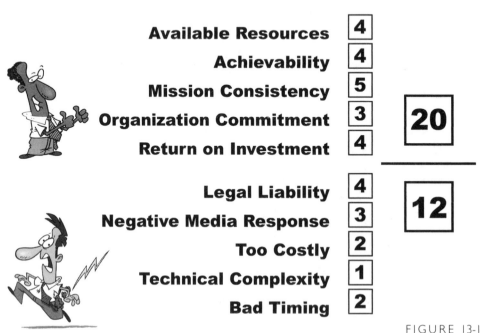

Available Resources	4
Achievability	4
Mission Consistency	5
Organization Commitment	3
Return on Investment	4

20

Legal Liability	4
Negative Media Response	3
Too Costly	2
Technical Complexity	1
Bad Timing	2

12

FIGURE 13-1

In evaluating the idea to place advertising on school buses, we completed a Vital/Fatal Ratio analysis. Then, using a scale of 1 (low) to 5 (high), we assigned numeric values for each of the parameters in the top half of Figure 13-1 to determine the likelihood of the idea's success:

Are there available resources? We scored (4).

Is the idea achievable? We scored (4).

Is the idea consistent with the school's mission? We scored (5).

Can we generate organizational commitment? We scored (3).

What will be the return on investment for the idea? We scored (4).

Next, we assigned numeric values for the following fatal questions—parameters specified at the bottom half of Figure 13-1—that could spell our idea's demise:

Is there legal liability? We scored (4).

Will the media's response to the idea be negative? We scored (3).

Will it be too costly for our budget? We scored (2).

Will the idea require a level of technical sophistication beyond our capabilities? We scored (1).

Is the timing off? We scored (2).

The total of the vital responses was twenty and the fatal responses totaled twelve. This idea would be achievable, as the city already has ads on its buses. The ROI would be undisputable: Children would receive healthy meals, a start on their homework, and a free tutor. The potential legal liability and negative media response to "advertising on public school property," as well as the potential motorist distraction, would call for tough questions of our legal, law enforcement, and marketing board members. As a rule of thumb, I like to see a 2:1 Vital/Fatal ratio before taking an idea to the next phase of development, so this idea still needs some refining. However, this is creativity and rules are meant to be broken—especially if I see a very high vital score.

Creeping Elegance

My favorite intellectual property attorney, Rob Frohwein, has coined a great term: *creeping elegance*. This refers to an initially great idea—one that seems utterly "perfect." Over time, however, you learn this or that and suddenly the idea doesn't seem perfect anymore. The layers of perfection slowly start peeling off and, before you know it, the idea has lost its luster. Unfortunately, Idea Generators often still pursue the idea, despite its drawbacks, because they have invested so much time and energy in it that they can't see that it isn't a good idea anymore. They allow the idea, in its imperfect state, to gain *creeping elegance*—that is, to approach the level of perfection in their mind that the original, untested idea enjoyed. Such blindness to the reality of your idea's success can have a deleterious effect on your organization's bottom line—not to mention on the career of the Idea Generator.

Ask the Right People

With high school graduation rates at 68 percent nationwide—and only 50 percent in urban areas—how can the United States transform education using the technologies that have transformed every other industry in the twenty-first century? That was the charge given to my colleague Susan Patrick, director of the Office of Educational Technology at the U.S. Department of Education.

Patrick became curious, and started asking a number of key questions: What did the access to technology mean to students as they entered classrooms that looked similar to the classrooms of past generations? Did access to twenty-first-century technologies influence student engagement in studies? How did students use technology inside and outside of school? How do today's students use technology and how does that make them different from other generations? Are they different or the same as other generations—baby boomers, generation X?

To answer these questions, she contacted the education researchers—the experts in the field of education—to ask if they had data on today's students. The educational researchers shrugged their shoulders and shook their heads—they had no demographic data on students or their uses of technology for learning.

The people who really had the data on the nation's students were the market researchers—the for-profit research firms hired by companies to learn about demographics driving consumer markets. And, yes, did they ever have data on today's kids! Knowing that the market researchers' data and information gave them a competitive advantage in the marketplace—and was probably proprietary—Patrick suspected that they would be reluctant to share much of it with federal government officials. However, when she called them, their response was overwhelmingly positive, even enthusiastic. "Sharing data on today's youth for the purpose of developing public policy and an education plan for Congress? Why, of course, we'd be happy to share all our information on students with you. We would love to get involved. It's just that no one in education has ever asked."

Then Patrick decided to ask the students. She developed an online survey to reach students in their "own space"—online. She expected 5,000 to 10,000 students would go online and take the survey to provide feedback for the National Education Technology Plan. Her organization called it Speak Up Day 2003—and, surprisingly, 210,000 students in fifty states contributed their ideas to the federal government to help shape national policy.

During the arduous federal review process of the National Education Technology Plan, the biggest single issue raised by federal officials reviewing the plan concerned the pages quoting the student feedback. On a marked draft of the Plan, Patrick has in writing: "Are you sure these comments are from students? They are too sophisticated."

This is exactly the point she was trying to make. Students today are far more sophisticated than we give them credit for. Schools follow a factory model from the Industrial Age, based on time and motion studies (grade levels, desks lined up in rows, bell schedules). This factory model of education, with students marching in lockstep, was designed to send 25 percent of kids to college and the rest into industrial or agricultural jobs. Well, today 68 percent of kids graduate from high school and 26 percent make it through two years of college. So we designed the system to do exactly what it is doing.

But when do we start engaging today's students in their own education? How often do we involve students in decision making? In solving budget problems? In finding ways to provide new models of next-generation education? Why don't we ask students how we can design our schools to send a higher percentage of students to college?

Patrick's conclusion is that we need solutions that are student-centered, that connect to kids in their world—next-generation education powered by online learning. We need to listen to the most creative, innovative, ambitious, technology-savvy generation ever to enter our schools. We need to solicit their thoughts and involve them in solving the challenges facing today's schools.

Similarly, in looking to create a new product or solve an existing problem, you need to ask the right people for insight. Are you in direct touch with your end user? Are you talking to the folks on the shop floor? Remember the closing comments of the GE manager in chapter 9 to his factory employees: "You blew management away with your great presentations. We've known that you have the answers to help us. We just didn't know how to listen for them."

Are you reading the same magazines and watching the same TV shows as your customer? If not, you might find yourself saying, "Are you sure these comments are from our employees or our customers? They sound too sophisticated."

Beware of the Standard Evaluation Form

Evaluation is a written or mental practice, used to assess the quality of a new idea, suggestion, or procedure. Most evaluation forms ask for positives and negatives and force you to "weigh" these factors. Then you make some final tally and come up with a score, perhaps on a scale of one to ten, so that you can look at your idea and call it an "eight."

Some standard evaluation forms, with their emphasis on negatives, might force you to fling a host of Killer Phrases at yourself, killing off your idea before it has any chance of proving its worth. Also, the traditional forms tend to look at ideas from only two perspectives: goodness and badness, positives and negatives. The proverbial thumb points only up or down. Any "in-betweenness" shows up only in flat, or average, scores—say, a five on a scale of one to ten.

But in-betweenness might be the attractiveness or strength of an idea. This in-betweenness I like to call the "interest factor." For example, perhaps you think an idea is a bad one or a so-so one when evaluating it by your articulated standards. But maybe it has an "interesting" attribute. Maybe there's something about it that is fresh or "edgy," or that grabs the attention of the group—even if it doesn't seem quite feasible in its current incarnation. This attribute, this "interest factor," might prompt you to sit on the idea for a few days, to let it simmer, rather than dismiss it outright. This in-betweenness or interest factor might be the distinguishing characteristic of a truly great idea. Yet many evaluation forms are blind to this potential.

To cure what I perceive to be a defect in traditional evaluation, I've devised a quick five-minute quality check you can use to help you form an initial reaction to an idea, whether it's your idea or that of someone else.

The Quick Five-Minute Quality Check

The initial evaluation should closely resemble the idea-generation process itself. The attempt should be to identify as many positive factors, as many negative factors, and as many interesting factors as you possibly can. Just listing these qualities will give you some notion of what your idea has going for it and against it. And forcing yourself to identify the *interesting* attributes of an idea can lead you to new ways of thinking about it, ways to refine it so that it does indeed mature into one of those great ideas we all seek.

The following chart, based on the Great Idea Action Sheet at the end of this chapter, can be printed on 4" x 6" note cards and filed in your Idea Bank.

Describe the idea: File by:
                               Date:
                               Ranking:
                               Action Date:

Qualities of the idea:

Positive	Interesting	Negative
1.	1.	1.
2.	2.	2.
3.	3.	3.
4.	4.	4.
5.	5.	5.

Creating an Innovation Challenge

The purpose of the THINC club at the Garvin School of International Management at Thunderbird University was to generate new ideas for companies like Microsoft, ExxonMobil, UPS, and others. Companies posed their real-world business challenges to students, and the club would deliver a report of the best ideas resulting from structured brainstorming sessions.

The students enjoyed the experience so much they asked themselves, "What if we could share the experience with students everywhere?" A grand vision of running a worldwide idea competition arose. MBA student teams would compete for the title of "Most Innovative MBA Team in the World."

In 2003, the Innovation Challenge was launched. In its first year, the competition received an overwhelming response, with 154 teams from fifty-two universities in six countries participating. It immediately became the largest MBA competition of its kind, with the winning team being awarded a $20,000 cash prize. The second year it grew to 251 teams from eighty-one universities in seventeen countries, and the third year it attracted 321 teams and sponsor companies such as Hilton, the U.S. Postal Service, IBM, and American Express. In 2006 the Innovation Challenge moved to the Darden Business School at the University of Virginia.

Here's how the competition works: First a business challenge is posed to all entering MBA teams. The teams electronically submit their innovation plans and a virtual team of judges then narrows the field down to ten team finalists. These top-ten teams are given a new business challenge and flown to Darden for a live presentation to a new panel of judges. All through the process the judges use the excellent judging scorecard found at the end of this chapter.

As a result of the competition's success, Anil Rathi, the founder of the original THINC club has turned the successful innovation challenge into a company called IdeaCrossing. There he combines the concepts of ideation and gaming, and provides internal idea competitions within client enterprises (open to employees only) and external competitions open to the public and sponsored by corporations seeking new ideas from loyal customers.

Why not stage an innovation challenge for your team the next time you need to create a new product, solve a budget challenge, or come up with a new PR campaign?

The "Bull's-Eye"

After evaluating numerous ideas, how do you find time in your busy schedule to bring these ideas to fruition? Here's one way.

Break the idea down into doable weekly action chunks. Organizing on a weekly basis provides much greater balance and leeway for completion than the typical daily planning does. In daily planning, crises always seem to take priority and push to-do's from one day to the next.

Therefore, try to rank your daily activities by fitting them into a priority "bulls-eye" like the one below. The "Nice to do" ring describes things that are important yet that have a low impact on your productivity or the outcomes you want to achieve. The "Ought to do" ring is for items that involve pressure from peers and society. The all-important "Must do" bulls-eye is the place that deserves your attention even when your plate is overflowing with activities and responsibilities.

Reality Check

Evaluation and decision making are sciences in and of themselves. I don't pretend that this chapter has treated these complex processes with any significant degree of scientific or practical detail. Yet evaluation relies on the gut and on the brain. The true innovators, indeed the true leaders, can feel inside whether or not they're on the right track. But these highly creative people also know how to use their intellect and evaluate their ideas before committing time, money, and people to any given innovative scheme.

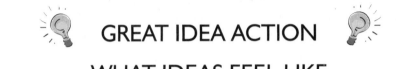

GREAT IDEA ACTION

WHAT IDEAS FEEL LIKE

Learn to recognize the qualities of your response to ideas by Idea Mapping both your positive and negative reactions.

Step 1 Idea Map your physical and mental reactions to ideas.

In the center of a blank sheet of paper place the Trigger Phrase, "Good one, go with it!" On another sheet of paper write "No, don't do it!"

In five minutes, write down as many words as you can describing your mental and physical reactions to these gut messages. Work on both maps simultaneously as words occur to you. Draw arrows from one word to another, connecting your key thoughts. Add more words as necessary.

Step 2 Look for the main concepts and patterns in your Idea Maps.

Assign geometric symbols to your main concepts and "cluster" your words by putting the respective symbol around each related word.

Step 3 Create an Idea Outline.

Now transcribe your Idea Maps into either "clusters" or a Roman-numeral outline.

Step 4 Record your feelings.

Write down four characteristics of your gut feeling that can help you in the process of evaluating new ideas.

"Good one, go with it!"		*"No, don't do it!"*
1.		1.
2.		2.
3.		3.
4.		4.

GREAT IDEA ACTION

FIVE-MINUTE QUALITY CHECK

Write a brief description of the idea. Review the list of "considerations" at the bottom of this page and add any further considerations relevant to your idea. Then identify and write down as many Positive Qualities, Negative Qualities, and Interesting Qualities as you can think of. Just listing these qualities will give you some notion of what your idea has going for it and against it.

DESCRIBE THE IDEA:

QUALITIES OF THE IDEA:

Positive	Interesting	Negative
1.	1.	1.
2.	2.	2.
3.	3.	3.
4.	4.	4.
5.	5.	5.
6.	6.	6.
7.	7.	7.
8.	8.	8.
9.	9.	9.
10.	10.	10.

CONSIDERATIONS:

Cost Savings	Improved Performance	Improved Service
Start-up Cost	Measurable Effectiveness	Public Relations Value
Distribution	Existing People/Materials	Test Marketability

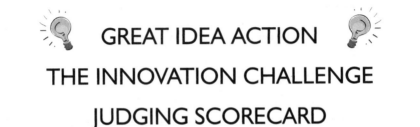

GREAT IDEA ACTION
THE INNOVATION CHALLENGE
JUDGING SCORECARD

Judging Directions: Imagine you are a consultant for one of the sponsoring companies and your job is to evaluate new concept plans proposed by MBA student teams. For each question, place a check mark in one of the six boxes that best describes how you feel about the concept plan. Your scores will be entered into our scoring database and various weights will be assigned to each question to come up with a final score.

1. Concept Originality How bold and fresh is the concept?

Ordinary ⟨1⟩ ⟨2⟩ ⟨3⟩ ⟨4⟩ ⟨5⟩ ⟨6⟩ *Unique*

Seems old and familiar, not too creative, and maybe a repackage of old concepts as new and improved.

Unique. New concept, evoking a "wow" response. May be a unique combination of old ideas.

2. Concept Presentation How persuasive and coherent is concept?

Crude ⟨1⟩ ⟨2⟩ ⟨3⟩ ⟨4⟩ ⟨5⟩ ⟨6⟩ *Well Crafted*

Not persuasive. Seems incomplete and not presented in an understandable manner.

Clear, compelling, and refined to its highest possible level.

3. Value Proposition How does concept meet/create customer need?

Low Value ⟨1⟩ ⟨2⟩ ⟨3⟩ ⟨4⟩ ⟨5⟩ ⟨6⟩ *High Value*

Disconnected from customer reality and doesn't add much value.

Meets spoken or unspoken need, anchored in customer experience.

4. Bottom-Line Results How compelling are the concept's quantitative and qualitative benefits?

Low Benefits ⟦1⟧ ⟦2⟧ ⟦3⟧ ⟦4⟧ ⟦5⟧ ⟦6⟧ *High Benefits*

Insubstantial or inadequate demonstration of quantitative and qualitative results.

Significant and credible demonstration of quantitative and qualitative results.

5. Competitive Advantage How does the concept provide a unique competitive advantage?

No Advantage ⟦1⟧ ⟦2⟧ ⟦3⟧ ⟦4⟧ ⟦5⟧ ⟦6⟧ *Big Advantage*

Does not provide significant competitive advantage for the company.

Competitive advantage is unique and difficult to mimic.

6. Feasibility How easily can the concept be implemented and are risks addressed?

Low Feasibility ⟦1⟧ ⟦2⟧ ⟦3⟧ ⟦4⟧ ⟦5⟧ ⟦6⟧ *High Feasibility*

Does not seem feasible. Poor risk assessment.

Seems feasible and risks are properly addressed.

C H A P T E R   1 4

Visible Ideas

Selling Your Ideas

All things are created twice. There's a mental or first
creation, and a physical or second creation of all things.
—*Stephen Covey,* The 7 Habits of Highly Effective People

So you've got great ideas. Now it's time to figure out how to convince others in your organization (or in your marketplace) that the ideas are indeed great and worthy of their investment of time, money, or other resources. To do that, to sell your ideas to others, you must first analyze your organization's receptiveness to new ideas. Is your organization eager for the new and the different? Or does it tend to cling to the old ways of doing things?

I believe that you can think about the openness of an organization to new ideas by considering the following formula:

$$\text{Openness} = \frac{\text{\# Ideas x (\# Implemented + Fast Failures) x Shared Vision}}{\text{Penalty for Failure}}$$

If you remember your high school algebra, you will see from the equation above that you can increase the degree of openness in an organization by increasing the fraction's numerator or by decreasing the denominator. Thus, to increase the numerator (thereby increasing openness), you should seek to increase the quantity of ideas generated, increase the fast failures, and create a common and agreed-on vision. Simultaneously, to decrease the denominator (thereby increasing openness) you should seek to reduce the penalty for failure.

Reducing the Penalty for Failure

Here's the cardinal rule of thumb for fostering an openness to new ideas in any organization or in any individual: Make sure that the penalty for failure is not greater than the penalty for doing nothing. According to Soichiro Honda, founder of Honda Motors:

> *Many people dream of success. To me, success can only be achieved through repeated failure and introspection. In fact, success represents the 1 percent of your work, which results only from the 99 percent that is called failure.*

An organization that is open to creativity accepts failure. Indeed, the organization that is open to creativity expects failure. It wants failure. For without failure, there's no innovation going on. At first, "expecting failure" might sound counterintuitive. After all, failure means a loss of money (your money), self-esteem (your self-esteem), and status (your status). You might wonder, "But I've spent my career learning how to succeed, not figuring out how to fail."

Perhaps a new image of *failure* is needed. Soichiro Honda referred to the "99 percent [of work] that is called failure." What we call failure might merely be stark evidence of the creative process at work. Perhaps we should look at failure as our best teacher, much like that memorable teacher we all had in school, the one who said, "No, that's not the right answer. Have you considered this?" Perhaps we should look at failure as a learning process, as a course. Small failures characterize the course; great ideas stand waiting as the diploma.

When Bill Gore, inventor of Gore-Tex®, explained to me that he wanted a new use for Gore-Tex® every week, he also set the guidelines for risk taking. He would say, "You can try anything, as long as it's above the waterline. If you want to drill holes below the waterline, you need to check with your sponsor [boss]." Thus, anything goes. We expect failure. Do anything but jeopardize the overall health of the organization.

Increasing "Fast Failures"

Paul MacCready, the aerodynamics whiz who invented the human-powered *Gossamer Condor,* credits his success to crude, fast, and inexpensive experimentation. That is, fast failure. "You need to test it easily, be able to run along with it, and catch it. If a tube breaks [on the airplane], you can crudely fix it with a broom handle."

If your idea is going to fail, the innovator wants it to fail fast so that time and money are not unnecessarily wasted. To speed up the failures, the successful innovator will initiate small-scale tests of new ideas, conduct personal surveys to determine the effectiveness of ideas, and always remain open to critical feedback. To get started on the path of increasing fast failures, consider replacing the word *failure* with *glitch, false start, course correction,* or more positively, *new insight.*

In my video company, we tried to be the first to produce videos on current health topics, such as AIDS, herpes, drug use, and steroids. The *Wall Street Journal* even called us, humorously, "ambulance-chasing cartoonists," because we were always the first to market, and schools would call us up with suggestions for videos on new health topics. Because we were first, many of our video distributors would say that our new video would never sell. To prove them wrong, my company would send out our own direct-mail advertising to school systems.

However, before committing to a large direct-mail effort, costing thousands of dollars, we always tried to engineer a "fast failure." I followed the advice of a major advertising executive who urged me to refrain from printing a hundred thousand pieces of a four-color print run for a new video. Instead, he counseled, print only five hundred in black and white, mail them to yourself and your sales force, to your office staff and your spouse, and to a small sampling of your customers. Then call them and find out whether the promotional effort was a success or a "fast failure."

Achieving a Shared Vision

Think back to a time when you were totally absorbed by an activity, so absorbed that you completely forgot to eat. Was it structuring a new deal, learning a new computer program, designing a new system, or playing with your child?

These hyperproductive experiences, called *flow states* by psychologist Mihaly Csikszentmihalyi, are times of intensely focused consciousness.

When we experience such a state, we feel that we are living more fully than usual.

When a task is challenging and we have the necessary skill level to do it, we will likely experience a flow state. This flow state is magnified by an increase in the level of challenge and the development or possession of the skills needed to meet the challenge. If an imbalance between the challenge and needed skills occurs, then the flow state disappears. Anxiety sets in when the challenge exceeds our skill level; boredom overwhelms us when our skill level exceeds the challenge.

The forces producing a flow state, which in turn leads to vision, are depicted in Figure 14-1.

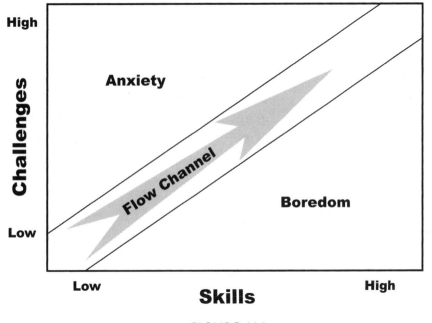

FIGURE 14-1

This simple model is an excellent way to show that we move in and out of the flow state throughout the day. As more work is piled on or as we attain new skills, we have to recognize that we will experience moments of anxiety and moments of boredom.

According to Csikszentmihalyi, the visionary leader is a person with a high level of skills who constantly seeks new challenges through "What if . . ." games. Vision results at the high end of flow-state experiences. Thus, one way to achieve the desired vision is to maximize your time in the visionary flow state. Csikszentmihalyi, in his book *Flow: The Psychology of Optimal Experience,* provides some concrete suggestions:

1. Reduce the number of unnecessary meetings in your organization.

2. Set aside office time just for thinking.

3. Don't be so worried about winning the game that you're too distracted to sink the shot.

4. Reduce the time devoted to "putting out fires."

The best measure of creativity is your enjoyment of the flow state of ideas. This is the source of satisfaction for the innovator, and the source of excellent results on behalf of consumers, clients, and organizations.

Your vision, the one you seek to cultivate in your organization, is a combination of your acquired knowledge, your instincts, and your dreams. When shared and accepted by your organization, your vision will serve as a great engine for innovation. When everyone knows the vision and heads in the same direction, successful innovation follows. Such a vision acts as a bridge to the future. To bear the heavy load of change, that *vision bridge* needs to be:

1. Directed toward the future.

2. Usable today.

3. Firmly grounded in past successes.

4. Stable yet able to respond to changing environments.

5. Easily understood.

6. Well promoted.

We'll focus on that last point—promoting your vision to your colleagues, your superiors, your subordinates, your customers, and the rest of the world—throughout this chapter.

Making Your Vision Visible

Geniuses make their thoughts visible. The explosion of creativity in the Renaissance was accompanied by the recording of this vast knowledge in drawings, graphs, and diagrams by visionaries like da Vinci and Galileo.

Now think of your company's vision statement. Is your vision alive and well? Have you moved your vision statement off the walls and into the corridors, reaching every employee, every customer, and every supplier you have? A vision engages our hearts and our spirits while it resonates with our core concerns and needs.

Could another company adopt your vision statement as it is? If so, make your vision more specific by asking, "What is the promise of our vision?" Here are some questions your vision statement should answer:

> "The key to creativity is to begin with the end in mind, with a vision and a blueprint of the desired result."
>
> —Stephen Covey

1. What is unique about us?

2. What values are true priorities for us?

3. What would commit my mind and heart to this vision over the next five years?

4. What does the world really need that we can provide?

The executives at e-Commerce leader QVC wanted to be certain that everyone understood how important innovation was to the company's continued success. One of QVC's operating values is "Pioneering Spirit." The tagline that accompanies it is this: "Initiating and embracing new ideas with enthusiasm." This tribute to creativity is sandblasted into the concrete as you enter QVC's world headquarters.

Promoting Your Vision

To promote your vision, and to make sure it is truly "shared," here are some suggestions you might consider for your organization.

1. Hang pictures of your vision.

What I said earlier about designing your own office also applies to the larger office environment. For example, while Grumman Aerospace engineers were working on the NASA moon mission, pictures of the moon were displayed all over their design and manufacturing workspaces.

2. Give feeling to your vision.

Before filming *Ordinary People,* Robert Redford, the Academy Award–winning director, gathered his cinematographers together to listen to a recording of Pachelbel's Canon in D Major. He then asked them to create an opening suburban scene that related to the music. You, too, can draw from music, art, dance, film, or other art forms to give voice and shape to your vision.

3. Rename places and things to fit the vision.

As previously mentioned, Apple Computer named its meeting rooms "Dorothy" and "Toto" to stress that there is a wizard dwelling in everyone. Du Pont calls its innovation team the "Oz" group; the members wear colorful, logo-emblazoned T-shirts at training meetings.

4. Put a vision conversation piece on your desk.

Applying another idea from the earlier suggestions for your own office, have everyone in your organization purchase—at company expense—a desk ornament that conveys the meaning of the shared vision. Sometimes the meaning will be personal and not immediately obvious to others, but if it resonates with the employee himself, that's what matters.

5. Help your people let go of the old vision.

For many people, a new vision is accompanied by a feeling of loss. A common reaction to change is this: "We liked the way things were before." To help employees let go of these feelings, consider the following:

> *What rituals have changed?*

> *Has the meaning of work changed?*

Is the perceived future going to be different?

Will any employees feel incompetent working toward the new vision?

Is control shifting to a new person or department?

By understanding and addressing these concerns, you can help employees to accept and even embrace a new vision.

6. Recognize that your organization will go through a "neutral zone"— that is, a period of uneasiness—between the old reality and a new one.

As the new vision is being ushered in, work will have a surreal sense about it and productivity is likely to suffer, as people say things like this: "I just don't understand what the name of the game is anymore." Your "vision" quickly becomes clear to your more intuitive employees. A clearly outlined plan of action and cost/benefit projections may be necessary to get your more analytical employees onboard.

7. Celebrate new beginnings as they develop into new competencies and new relationships.

It will take time for new policies, procedures, and plans for the future to become second nature to everyone in the organization. To accelerate the process, celebrate even the small successes that produce visible results along the path to the shared vision. For instance, the first time an employee or a team's suggestion is adopted, reward that team in some way—by naming its members Employees of the Month, giving them a gift certificate to a favorite restaurant, or citing them in the company newsletter. This kind of recognition goes far toward encouraging reluctant employees to embrace the new vision.

Selling in the Organization

To help foster receptiveness to your new idea, you need to communicate your vision to others, to sell them on the idea, to enlist their support and resources, and, indeed, to obtain their approval.

Do What Everybody Else Does

Selling your idea requires communicating it. So look around. How does everybody else communicate ideas or push for their adoption? They send e-mails, write memos and reports, hold meetings, launch pilot projects, and conduct surveys. They do a host of things, all involving the written or spoken word.

And what should you do when you try to sell your idea? Simple. Do what everybody else does. Then what?

Do What Everybody Else Doesn't Do

When selling your ideas, your task is to be different, not for the sake of being different, but for the sake of successfully promoting your own great idea. If people in your target audience get another report, another memo, another study, they will simply think it's just another idea. If yours is truly a great idea, then it deserves a special promotional package. Ask yourself, how would Disney or Sony or Apple sell this idea? Try the "Roll the Dice" exercise on page 167 for inspiration.

In, Up, Down, and Out

Before we get to some concrete selling suggestions, let's consider the directions such selling might take. As we mentioned in chapter 5, there are four basic directions in which you will need to sell your idea: First you must sell *in* or *inside*. That is, you must sell yourself on the quality of your own idea. Once you're truly convinced of the quality of your idea, you then must begin to sell *up* in the organization, *down* in the organization, and ultimately *outside* the organization. These are *directions* your selling efforts can go, and the direction often determines the selling strategies you should adopt.

To see the direction I must follow to sell my new idea, I complete a Force Field Analysis. Using a chart like the one in Figure 14-2, I list the forces supporting and resisting my idea. The forces may be individuals, budget constraints, inertia, organizational climate, economic conditions, and many others.

Forces Supporting   **Status Quo**   **Forces Resisting**

FIGURE 14-2

Then I break down my strategy to see what I can do to encourage the supporting forces and neutralize or diminish the resisting forces. After developing broad strategies, I look to see the four directions my promotional efforts should take: in, up, down, and out.

Selling with Political Savvy

To successfully sell your ideas up/down the food chain you will need to invoke the skill of *political savvy*. In the words of Steve Van Valin at QVC, you need to be fully aware of the various players who will decide on whether to pursue your idea, and be willing to take steps to build a coalition of support.

For example, if there is a meeting in which you'll be presenting your idea for approval, you should be able to look around the table at the start of the meeting and be certain that at least 50 percent of the decision-making power in the room already knows about your idea, and will give a "thumbs-up" on the issue of whether to take the next step toward making it a reality. Remember, this is even before you open your mouth to pitch the idea!

If that's not the case, then you need to increase your odds by contacting the individual players ahead of time to test the waters for support. If that is unlikely because of hierarchy issues, then you need to tap into your existing base of support to determine if you have champions who can influence the other decision makers.

Applying political savvy is not some manipulative technique. This is about you increasing your odds of success so that you will add value first and foremost. Oh, by the way, you will also build your reputation as a savvy player who makes things happen.

POLITICAL LANDSCAPE ANALYSIS

Steve Van Valin shared with me the following action sheet to ascertain your current political landscape.

Use the columns below to map out the "selling" status of your idea.

1. List all the players involved in the decision making and implementation of your idea.

2. Place their names in the appropriate column, depending on whether they already **support** your idea, have an **unknown opinion** on your idea, or will **likely oppose** your idea.

3. Assign a number between 1 and 10 (1 = lowest; 10 = highest) regarding their decision-making power with regard to the idea.

4. Once completed, add each column to get a Total Power Number at the bottom.

Note: If your total in the support column does not represent at least 50 percent of the grand Total Power Number, then you should consider additional legwork to build a coalition of support before presenting the idea for approval.

Name of idea: _____

(+) Will Support	Power #	(0) Unknown Opinion	Power #	(—) Likely to Oppose	Power #
Total =		Total =		Total=	

Total Power Number = _____

Selling In

Before you can possibly convince anyone else of the merits of your great idea, you must first sell yourself. In the last chapter we discussed how to evaluate your idea to be sure of its merit. You must now gain your own absolute, unbending commitment to the quality of the idea. Put differently, you must fall in love with it. You must live your idea, follow it, use it, show it off to others—well before you begin to hype it inside and outside the organization.

After falling in love with your idea, you must also be prepared to fall out of love with it. Perhaps your idea has already been tried and improved on by someone else. If so, you should be ready to learn from the results of that venture and adapt. Overall, you should be aware that Idea Generators are notoriously optimistic. They are often blinded by their love for their own ideas and must learn to wake up to reality.

Russell Linden, in his book *From Vision to Reality: Strategies of Successful Innovators in Government,* notes that the seven innovators he studied all had a love affair with their visions. He described this common trait shared by the successful innovators this way:

> *Their personalities were similar in one respect: these seven individuals are clearly driven people. They approached their work and especially their initiatives with a tremendous focus, an energy level far beyond the norm. For some . . . this energy radiated outward in a very contagious way. Others . . . focused their energies more internally. Whether extravert or introvert, each of these innovators maintained a presence and a sense of drive that inevitably affected and infected those around them.*

Once you've developed and nurtured the necessary love, drive, and commitment to your idea, it's time to "radiate" this energy to others.

Selling Up

In all organizations, there is a need to sell up. But how far up must you go? As a rule, you should try to sell two levels above yourself, that is, to your boss's boss. If you're the director of purchasing, then your boss might be the vice president for manufacturing. Your boss's boss? The chief executive officer. If you own your own business, then your boss is your customer. Two levels up is the bank.

I am not suggesting that you do an end run around your boss. Instead, I'm talking about perspective—the perspective of your boss's boss. Try to imagine how your boss's boss will react to your proposal. Thinking in this way will help you create a proposal that will "fly" up your organization.

Selling Down

Selling down requires selling two levels below your position. For once you've given your idea wings, it must be supported from below. Ideas foisted on workers from management up above often provoke cynicism because people below can't quite see your vision (or nobody's bothered to make that vision clear to them). To obtain the necessary "buy-in," consider some unique approaches:

- Open your idea up for employee suggestions. Publish it in a newsletter and request reactions. Listen to how others think your idea will affect them. Then modify the idea if necessary.

- Make your idea part of the work environment. Visually portray your idea in photos or posters. Hang them on the walls of your office and meeting rooms.

- Encourage employee participation. Assign implementation responsibilities to key staffers.

Selling Out

Some ideas are strictly internal ones that will never see the light of day outside the organization. Indeed, when it comes to inventions, trade secrets, or patents, the objective is *not* to sell outward but to keep such matters strictly confidential until the organization is ready to market them.

Other ideas, of course, must be sold outside the organization. To make your selling efforts truly creative, *creative* often means *different*. And being different requires you to . . . do what everybody else doesn't.

For example, to launch an upscale shopping mall along the river in New York City, you would hold a party, of course. And who does everybody else invite to the party? Why, all the bigwigs, all the politicos, all the VIPs.

And what did a truly creative development company do when it launched a new, upscale shopping mall along the river in New York?

The company threw a party and invited thousands of New York cabbies and their spouses. Can you imagine the ensuing free publicity to thousands of tourists asking the cabbies about new and different places to visit in the Big Apple?

So check around your market. Look at your industry. Study your sector of government. See what everybody else is doing. Then you know what to do:

1. Envision the future.

2. Ask, "What's the opposite?"

3. Challenge assumptions.

4. Create a metaphor.

5. Borrow and adapt.

6. Get out your colored pens and draw some Idea Maps.

Sell the way you create—the way you created what you're selling. That way, you're always drawing energy from the source of the idea, and that energy puts a shine on anything you do. Creativity as an approach enriches every phase of life, and speeds the acceptance of the very ideas it produced in the first place.

And Finally . . . How to Kill Your Idea!

We discussed thinking in opposites earlier in the book, when we explored the creative process. This technique can be just as effective in selling your idea! One of the best ways to sum up the actions you need to take on behalf of your idea is to consider the things you can do to undercut it. Here's my list of the top ten:

1. Expect to receive all the credit.

2. Never look for a second right answer.

3. Drag your feet; lack a sense of commitment.

4. Run it through a committee.

5. Wait for market surveys and full market analysis.

6. Hold lengthy meetings to explore its merit.

7. Boost cost estimates, just to be safe.

8. Set unrealistic deadlines.

9. Don't get views from other stakeholders.

10. Make sure it's the only idea you ever have.

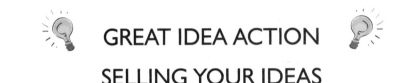

GREAT IDEA ACTION

SELLING YOUR IDEAS

Once you determine who is supporting and resisting your idea, you will develop a sales strategy for communication in, up, down, and outside your organization.

Step 1 Describe your idea.

Step 2 Complete a Force Field Analysis.
List on the arrows the forces supporting and resisting your idea. For example, stakeholder support or opposition, budget constraints, inertia, organizational climate, economic conditions, and so on.

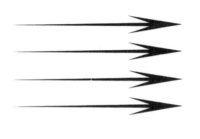

Forces Supporting   **Status Quo**   **Forces Resisting**

Step 3 Develop a broad sales strategy.
What can you do to encourage the supporting forces?

What can you do to neutralize or diminish the resisting forces?

Step 4 Develop sales efforts in, up, down, and outside your organization.

What Everybody Does   *What Everybody Doesn't Do*

What other actions must you take to sell yourself completely on this idea?

1.   1.

2.   2.

3.   3.

What actions must you take to sell this idea to those two levels above you?

1.   1.

2.   2.

3.   3.

What actions must you take to sell this idea to those two levels below you?

1.   1.

2.   2.

3.   3.

What actions must you take to sell this idea to those outside your organization?

1.   1.

2.   2.

3.   3.

CHAPTER 15

Invisible Ideas

Managing Your Ideas

As you generate ideas, you need to find ways to manage them effectively. Ironically, many people don't know what to *do* with their ideas. I emphasize the word *do* because I want you to start thinking about ideas as *things*.

Most people unconsciously recognize this tangible nature of ideas. After all, what do you do when you get an idea? You write it down on a legal pad, or a napkin, or—in a real emergency—on the inside of your wrist. The idea becomes an object, an entity, a thing, a product.

And what do most people then *do* with their ideas? They make them *invisible*. They stuff them in a hip pocket or purse. Drop them in a top drawer. Wash them off their wrist by mistake. Or the neat and organized types will "file them *away*." Most people, it's plain to see, don't treat their own great ideas with very much respect.

Instead of considering your ideas as interesting throwaways, start thinking of them as diamonds in the rough—precious gems to be cherished, worth investing your time and effort in polishing to a pristine luster. As Dr. NakaMats points out at the beginning of this book, there are even "invisible inventions"— "a new way of teaching something, a new way to spark creativity in others." Just think how empowered our teachers would feel if they realized that they were creating "invisible inventions" every time they developed a new curriculum or lesson plan.

In fact, you should view your ideas as *tangible assets,* and you should treat them as such. Therefore, you should develop a system for storing and accessing your ideas.

Discovering Gold

In 2001, Sir Paul McCartney was being interviewed on *Larry King Live.*

KING: You can't read or write music.

McCARTNEY: No.

KING: So when you think of something, someone has to write it down.

McCARTNEY: Or I've got to remember it. When we first started, it was before anything like tape cassettes. So John and I would say, "What if we forget it?" Well, if we forget it, it can't be much good.

KING/McCARTNEY: [*Laughter*]

When I heard this interview, my immediate thought was, what if a "forgotten" set of Beatles lyrics were discovered today? How much would it sell for on eBay? Do you now see why I believe that *your* ideas are the currency of *your* future?

I'm sure you have seen the old American Express TV commercial stating, "Every ten seconds someone traveling in America loses their cash." My question then is this: How many ideas are lost in corporate America every ten seconds? How many ideas will be lost when you retire?

Managing Ideas at Google

Google believes it can make every bit of information available to anyone, anytime, anywhere. The declared mission of cofounders Larry E. Page and Sergey Brin is to "organize the world's information."

To achieve this, there's a belief that good ideas should come from anyone, anytime, anywhere. All engineers at Google are encouraged to spend one day a week working on their own projects. This leads to an enviable challenge: how to manage all the new ideas and make sure the really great ideas get the attention they deserve.

According to a *BusinessWeek* article, "Managing Google's Idea Factory" (October 3, 2005), this is the job of Marissa Mayer:

> *Her workday starts at 9 a.m. and doesn't end until about midnight. Her glass-walled office is intentionally situated across from the engineering snack area, where programmers grab evening coffee or munchies. Often on these late nights, engineers will bend her ear as they take a breather from their work, bringing her up-to-date on the countless ideas percolating through the ranks. "I keep my ears open. I work at building a reputation for being receptive," she says.*

One lesson we can learn from Google is to ask the powerful question, "Is my office located at the intersection of new ideas in my organization?" If not, move your office, or, if that's not possible, create a brand-new "idea conversation area" next to your location.

The Great Idea Inventory Control System

You've got an idea. Or you've borrowed an idea. Or someone has brought an idea to your attention. You've given it a quality check. It "has a lot going for it." So what do you *do* with it?

Your objective, of course, is to implement the great ideas and to have bad ideas fail, and fail fast. The entire decision-making process, of course, will take time. Also, many ideas might just be "little ideas," a quick brainstorm you have driving to work that you "must remember to look into when time permits." So while the wheels turn to decide on the big ideas or while you do other things and come up with even more big or little ideas, you need to keep track of all your ideas in some systematic way. You should have some method of recording your ideas, storing them, and retrieving them quickly and efficiently.

Think about your organization. You want to check your inventory of copy paper. You go to the supply closet, see the inventory is low, and order some more. Do you have a systematic way to check on the inventory of your ideas?

If you do, you're to be congratulated. If you don't, it's time to start a Great Idea Inventory Control System. When you have it up and running, then you'll be able to treat your ideas with respect, to review your inventory of ideas at any time, to retrieve an idea on any subject matter, to look after and pamper your precious mental assets.

File It *Away?*

Many people have an Idea File. In advertising, people call it a "Swipe File." In public relations, it's called a "Clip File." In these various files, people stuff little slips of paper, or interesting brochures, or interesting newspaper articles. They file ideas *away*. Ideas don't want to be filed *away*. To act as great ideas or potentially great ideas, they should be readily available, easily retrievable, and preferably *visible*.

Think about your own Idea File. When was the last time you put something in it? More important, when was the last time you took something *out* of it?

Let's look at ways of improving your filing.

Keep an Inventor's Notebook

An inventor's notebook is a journal, of sorts, to record ideas as they arise. It is intended to serve as proof that you came up with an idea on a particular date. Therefore, it's important that the book is actually bound and arranged chronologically. If you could simply put in or take out pages, then it would be difficult to prove that an idea actually occurred on a particular day. If you came up with a great idea and recorded it in your journal between an entry dated October 26, 2006, and another dated November 25, 2006, then there's a probability you could prove that you came up with the idea between those two dates. Use something like the old "Mead" bound notebooks we all had as kids. Never use a loose-leaf binder or spiral notebook.

Make sure that in your notebook your idea is adequately fleshed out—rather than just scribbling a few ideas down on a piece of paper. Try your best to put as much detail as possible on one or two pages. Remember, there's more to an idea than just the so-called *high-level concept*. Equally important are the ways in which you'd implement it, unique features of the idea, and other ways to accomplish the same objective.

Some of the key points that should be contained in the journal entry for each idea are the following:

1. Date of idea conception

2. High-level description of the idea

3. Detailed description, including the structure and operation of your idea

4. Objective of the idea (What problem are you trying to solve?)

5. Other people involved in coming up with the idea

6. Work you have done on the idea to date (It's important that you show diligence)

7. Signature of a witness to verify your claims and the date

You can actually order an inventor's notebook at various sites, including www.bookfactory.com.

Fill out the Great Idea Control Sheet

To preserve your idea, you've got to commit it to paper or input it into your computer using words, numbers, or pictures. (Scan in the napkin you jotted it down on, so that you remember the birthplace of your creative thoughts.) To help you along, I've prepared a suggested Great Idea Control Sheet at the end of this chapter.

Voice Mail It!

One promising new composer I know always comes up with lyrics and music when he's not in his studio. What does he do to remember his work? He just calls up his voice mail and starts recording. The same can work for you.

Frame It!

Take your truly great ideas—those that you want to turn into goals or dreams—and *frame them!* Find a photograph or a statement or draw a picture or write a line that expresses your idea or vision, frame it, and hang it prominently in your office or throughout your organization.

File It! (But Creatively)

Kurt Ling, VP of Innovation and Knowledge at Simmons, has a folder on his computer desktop called Cool Ideas. As he explains:

> *It's stuff I cut and paste from the Internet and from stuff people send me. Do you know how much stuff I can keep? Lots and lots of junk! But when I am just curious I read through it. When I am in a slump, I look through it. It is messy. Not neatly organized. I forget what's in there. That's part of the beauty of it.*

Jim Gilmore, author of *The Experience Economy* and a true professional observer, devours the *New York Times,* the *Wall Street Journal,* and the *Cleveland Plain Dealer* every day. Over dinner one evening, Gilmore referred to a magazine stand as his "intellectual candy store." He files his clippings in pure chronological order, rather than by preconceived subject titles, as a way to simulate serendipity in his research.

Stick It on the Refrigerator Door

The refrigerator door is the most creative place in most people's home, displaying children's artwork, funny notes, and other flashes of creativity. Where's the "refrigerator door" at your office? Create a place where you will display your ideas so they'll be constantly visible.

Give It Away

What if you come up with a great idea and know that you just won't do anything with it? Give it away. Intellectual property attorney Rob Frohwein says, "I'd rather see someone benefit from the idea even if I don't get a penny out of it. From my perspective, as the Delta commercial goes, 'Good goes around.' I almost think of ideas in a boomerang sense—if I can come up with a good one for someone else, I give it to them and, invariably, something good comes out of it for me too."

Idea Management Software

Idea management company Imaginatik offers an excellent Web-based application called Idea Central. It is designed to help organizations maximize the benefits from the creativity, expertise, and knowledge of their employees, customers, suppliers, and trusted third parties.

Overall, it covers the creative process from the moment an idea is generated until a decision is made on its implementation. One of my favorite features is the IdeaMinder. It allows people to track idea threads so that they get updated when new comments or peer reviews are posted. This encourages further interaction for idea development and also speeds up the rate of interaction among participants.

Protect It?

So you have a terrific idea but you're worried about all those prying eyes stealing your great idea? Well, thanks to the government, we have laws that protect your ideas. And not only your ideas, but also your product names, slogans, symbols, writings, and the Billboard® Top 10 hit you just composed.

To simplify the intellectual property rights process, I've asked Rob Frohwein, author of the *Idiot's Guide to Patents, Trademarks and Copyrights,* to teach us the basics, in his own words:

You only need to know the basics to ensure that someone else doesn't claim your creativity as his or her own. Leave the technical details to your lawyer (yes, you may need one of those). That's what they're there for.

Here's a quick definition for you of intellectual property: a product of the intellect that has commercial value and is legally protected (and therefore owned). Once you break intellectual property into its two words, it's much easier to grasp. Lots of people run around with the great new name they came up with for their terrific new product idea and follow with "This is my intellectual property." Well, guess what. It's not. That doesn't happen until you make sure it's protected. So here's a road map on how to (1) figure out what kind of protection you need, and (2) understand a little bit about the process of getting that protection.

Ideas: Ideas are capable of protection through the patent system of the United States and foreign countries. Some things to remember:

1. Patents can protect ideas involving mechanical devices, software systems, business methods, pharmaceuticals, and most other "ideas" you come up with.

2. To obtain a patent you need only have the idea and know how you would build or develop it if you had the time, money, and resources. Some people think you need an actual working prototype—this is *not* true. So make sure you go for protection as early in the process as possible.

3. Patents can be expensive to obtain because you really should use a lawyer to make sure it's being done right. Make sure you ask your attorney specific questions about the costs of patenting your idea. It may also be a good idea to have a search conducted to ensure that no one has already patented your idea.

4. Patents take a long time to obtain—sometimes as long as four or more years! However, once you file your application, you can refer to your concept as "patent pending." After the patent is issued, you can indicate the patented status by referencing, for example, U.S. Patent No. 1,234,567.

Names, symbols, or slogans: What companies do you think of when you hear "Just do it" or "What can brown do for you?" Nike and UPS, of course. That is because these companies came up with slogans that they wanted you to associate with them. In fact, the names *Nike, UPS,* and *Coke* are also protected by the U.S. Patent and Trademark Office. If you want to learn more about trademarks and service marks, you can visit the trademark section of the United States Patent and Trademark Office Web Site at www.uspto.gov. Keep the following thoughts in mind:

1. Trademarks help your customers determine the source of the origin of goods. If you pick a name that is too similar to someone else's product name or service, then you may not be able to protect that name (and the owner of the other trademark may be able to stop you from using that name).

2. If you do have to change your name, don't get upset about it—it happens all the time. It's much easier to change a name now than it is later.

3. Since trademarks are not nearly as expensive to obtain as patents are, you should strongly consider using an attorney. While it seems relatively easy to file a trademark application yourself, there are many strategies in applying and arguing for your mark that a good trademark attorney has made hundreds, if not thousands, of times before.

4. Registered trademarks take about a year or so to obtain. You can apply for a mark before you even fully start your business, but it will not become "official" until you utilize it "in commerce"—meaning you start selling your products or services.

5. You can indicate your rights in a pending trademark with the superscripts ™ (for a product) and ℠ (for a service). Once the mark is registered, you can indicate your ownership rights with the superscript ®.

Books, articles, music, and videos: Congratulations! If you've just written a book, your writing is automatically protected via federal copyright law. You are not required to register your copyright. But registration has its benefits. Unlike patents, copyrights do not protect ideas, but rather the "expression" of your ideas. Therefore, you and I can come up with a great idea for a story about how to register a copyright. That's our idea. We can then go off and write that story with each of us owning a different copyright in the particular way each of us wrote the story—that's the expression of the idea. A few points to consider:

1. Copyrights are not expensive to protect. Generally speaking (and there are exceptions), it costs $30 to register a copyright. The Copyright Office's Web site is a fabulous resource to learn more about copyrights and can be found at www.copyright.gov.

2. Your copyright is infringed if you can prove:
   • a substantial similarity between your copyrighted work and the alleged infringed copyrights, and

   • the offender had access to your work.

3. After you file for your registration, you should hear back from the Copyright Office in approximately three months. If you haven't heard from the office within five to six months, be sure to follow up with the Copyright Office. They are also very efficient in responding to e-mail inquiries.

4. You can indicate your ownership in a copyright by using the following line:

© 2006 Your Company, Inc. All rights reserved.

To wrap it up, obtaining a patent, trademark, or copyright protecting the products of your intellect is a critical step in ensuring that your great ideas benefit your business.

Retrieval as Inspiration

Because your ideas are your tangible products, and can lead to the betterment of your life and the lives of others, it only makes sense to keep your ideas visible. Thus you don't exile them to files or bins that you'll only consult the next time you're cleaning out your office. You find ways to keep them right in front of you, and to protect and manage them, because they're guiding stars in your own constellation.

GREAT IDEA ACTION
GREAT IDEA CONTROL SHEET

Use a format like the following to record basic information about each of your ideas for future reference and retrieval.

Control #:_____   Keyword: _____

Idea Generator: Telephone:

Idea Name:

Idea Description:

What impact will the idea have on:

    1. Mission/Shared Vision:

    2. Customer Satisfaction:

    3. Service:

    4. Speed of Operations:

    5. Simplicity of Operations:

    6. Employee Self-Confidence:

    7. Morale:

    8. Profit:

What successful ideas are similar:

    1.

    2.

    3.

What areas need to be explored:

1.

2.

3.

What the idea has going for it:

1.

2.

3.

What the idea has going against it:

1.

2.

3.

Who are the interested stakeholders?:

1.

2.

3.

Do they have a different point of view?:

1.

2.

3.

How we'll know if idea is succeeding:

1.

2.

3.

How we'll know if idea is failing:

1.

2.

3.

C H A P T E R   1 6

Show Business

Idea Meetings that Work

In moving your ideas from conception to action, you'll likely be expected to share and evaluate these ideas in a familiar setting: the meeting room. Most of us have no real training in designing, participating in, or running an effective meeting. Yet we as a nation have more than eleven million meetings every single workday, and as a planet more than seventy million meetings each day. Ask yourself this question: "Have I ever held a meeting where little or nothing was accomplished?" Most of us would have to admit that we have held or, at the very least, attended such meetings.

Most people take a rather dim view of meetings. If they are correct in their low evaluation of meetings (and I think they are), then I must conclude that most executives come up short in their ability to run a meeting. To paraphrase management maven Peter Drucker, "We either work or we meet. We can't do both."

That's probably true for the vast majority of meetings held throughout the world. But I believe that with a little creative thinking, and the techniques we've learned in this book, we can make meetings work.

Meetings and Collaboration

Why do we have meetings?

Experts say that we should hold meetings for specific reasons, such as:

1. To give or exchange information.

2. To create or develop ideas.

3. To decide on goals or issues.

4. To delegate work or authority.

5. To share work or responsibility.

6. To persuade, involve, or inspire.

7. To establish or maintain relations.

Each of these reasons to hold a meeting has its own set of dynamics, its own requirements for success, and its own mix of participants. To be successful, experts say that you should never mix a "develop new ideas" meeting with a "share your work" meeting. Instead, you should call two separate meetings, perhaps with two different groups of people.

However, according to Michael Schrage, in his book *Shared Minds: The New Technologies of Collaboration,* traditional meetings and other attempts at communication frustrate people partly because those running the meetings are generally advancing their own ideas or agendas, and other meeting participants are reacting—all too often with boredom or cynicism. He describes the traditional meeting as "a linear montage of speeches, soliloquies, conversations, arguments, interjections, visual displays, gestures, and grunts all presented within a certain time frame within the same room." But true collaboration, Schrage says, is not just the sum of individual actions; it's the generation of "shared understandings" that the individuals "couldn't possibly have achieved on their own."

As explained by John Dykstra, leader of the special-effects team for the *Star Wars* films, ordinary communication is trying "to tell someone something you know"; in collaboration, "you're both trying to create something you *don't* know."

So what's the goal of a successful meeting? According to Schrage:

So you try to get a communal mind going; you want to get people's minds to interact as components of a larger mind—one person's logical sense, one person's visual sense, another person's acoustic sense. You get a communal brain. What matters is not just the individual talents but the ability to integrate them. . . . The key is to create an environment that shifts attention away from the individual participant and toward community expression.

Let's explore how an Idea Map can help us design a successful meeting that encourages collaboration and community expression.

Mapping the Meeting

Let's reframe our concept of a meeting by creating a simile.

A meeting is like . . . a performance.

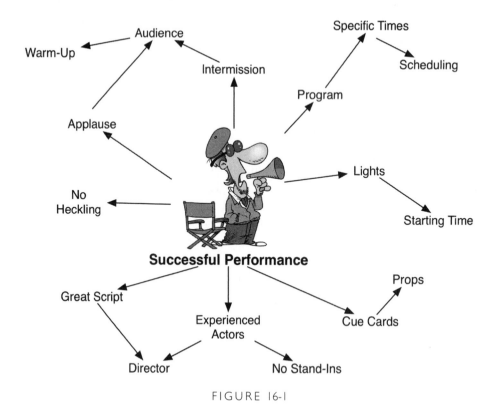

FIGURE 16-1

Our Idea Map with *Successful Performance* as the Trigger Word, as seen in Figure 16-1, yields the following elements:

great script	*no stand-ins*
specified times for acts	*audience*
experienced actors	*no heckling*
starting airtime	*cue cards*
director	*applause*
intermission	*lights*
warm-up	*program*
props	*scheduling*

The Basics

Evaluating the list produced by our Idea Map gives us the following eight basic elements of a successful meeting:

1. Great Script

A great script that both actors and director follow is analogous to a written meeting agenda received at least two days before the meeting. I always use Idea Mapping to generate my initial agenda items and then transcribe them as a linear outline for distribution. I've also found that putting the amount of time allocated next to each agenda item serves the same function as breaking a play into Act I, Act II, and so on.

2. Scheduling

Timing can be crucial to the success of a meeting. According to a survey by Accountemps, Inc., Tuesday is the day when people are most productive and motivated to learn. When asked "What is the best day for holding a training program?" personnel directors responded:

Tuesday	59%
Wednesday	9%
Thursday	6%
Friday	2%
Monday	0%

The rest thought that the day of the week made no difference.

3. Warm-up

In a rock concert or a standup comedy show, lesser-known bands or comedians warm up the crowd before the main attraction performs. How can we warm up our meeting participants? The best way I know is to bring in a prop, which can be a simple box of baking soda or a box of Crayola crayons. Challenge your group to come up with thirty uses for the baking soda, as discussed in chapter 2, or encourage them to use the crayons for creative Idea Mapping.

You'll find that warming up your crowd will pay handsome dividends throughout the rest of the meeting. To get you started with the all-important warm-up exercises, I've prepared some Great Idea Action Sheets, which you'll find at the end of this chapter.

4. No Stand-ins

Nothing's worse than showing up for a play only to find that the lead actor has been replaced by an understudy. Great meetings start *on time* with all participants present and ready.

5. Cue Cards

The notion of *cue cards* triggers for me the idea of writing key issues on flip charts or marker boards, or on large poster boards on the walls of the meeting room.

6. No Heckling

Killer Phrases aren't allowed. Levy fines or punish offenders with hurled paper wads. I also recommend putting up a list of potential Killer Phrases.

7. Applause

Audiences like to give feedback. Use large marker boards or put poster paper on one wall and have your meeting members Idea Map their problems right there in the meeting. Provide plenty of colorful markers, preferably the nontoxic ones that smell like various types of fruit.

8. Intermission

We all know how important a well-placed intermission is. Remember the three B's: brain, bladder, and butt. Each can only go sixty to ninety minutes without a break.

A Command Performance— Brainstorming Meetings

I think the best environment for brainstorming is in an informal meeting. To make sure that you achieve a relaxed and open brainstorming dialogue, the boss or team leader should not run this part of the meeting. Instead, rotate the responsibility of Brainstorm Facilitator among the staff. Otherwise, the boss might be dangerously inclined to squelch the views of others. The only views that ought to be squelched are personal verbal attacks. Thus the one ground rule should be "no holds barred *except fouls.*"

This Great Idea Meeting is more like improvisational theater, so you need someone with quick and legible writing or superior typing skills to act as an Idea Recorder. It's usually best to use Idea Maps on large flip charts, marker boards, or paper taped to the walls. Capturing ideas electronically is great if the screen can be projected for all to see.

When the Curtain Goes Up

At the beginning of the meeting, orient participants with a short introduction that covers the following:

1. The goals of the meeting.

2. The agenda.

3. If it's a problem-solving meeting:

    - The problem and its history.

    - Its likely consequences if not solved.

    - The benefits when the problem is solved.

4. The appointment of the Idea Recorder, who captures all ideas and thoughts without any personal editing. The editing comes later as the recorder writes up the notes from the session.

5. The appointment of the Brainstorm Facilitator, who most importantly acts as a verbal catalyst by using the "Yes, and . . ." statements we learned in the chapters on being curious first. The Brainstorm Facilitator's other duties include enforcing the start and end times for the session, as well as much-needed break times, and letting the group know how well they are accomplishing the goals of the session.

The Cast of Characters

If you want to institutionalize the Great Idea Meeting in your organization, you might want to consider creating small, focused innovation teams to meet specific, recognized needs. Large organizations are beginning to see the advantages of the small-team approach to idea making. They had to, when statistics showed that more than two-thirds of all inventions were created by individuals on their own time or by small organizations. That was indeed hard data to swallow: The big organizations were spending roughly 85 percent of all research-and-development money—and getting beaten at their own game. In 2004 the top R&D spender was Ford Motor Company. Yet, also that same year, Ford had its bond ratings downgraded to below investment grade. Booz Allen Hamilton's 2005 Study on Worldwide R&D Spending states, "It's the process, not the pocketbook. Superior results seem to be a function of the quality of an organization's innovation process—the bets it makes and how it pursues them—rather than either the absolute or relative magnitude of its innovation spending."

Although it might sound simple—Quick: Appoint a team!—we are seldom taught how to form such a team or how to make it function as a group.

In staffing such a team, recall that creativity as a process involves different types of people. As noted in chapter 2, from the beginning of an idea to its ultimate fruition, people with varying abilities and traits must play vital roles: the Idea Generator, the Idea Promoter, the Idea Systems Designer, the Idea Implementer, and the Idea Evaluator. Although you can assign these roles to members of the innovation team, it's often effective to try to find people who exhibit these traits to begin with, appoint them to the team, provide them the necessary wherewithal and support, and watch them work. The traits they might exhibit look like this:

The Idea Generators

They are typically the people whose main focus is on ideas themselves, not on organizational advancement or status. Their main drive in life is to deal with ideas and concepts. Sometimes Idea Generators choose not to develop other skills, including social skills, because their focus is so concentrated on concepts and ideas. Their strengths include their brilliance, insights, dedication, and consuming passion for discovery. On the downside, these strengths—if paired with eccentric behavior—can often repress the camaraderie of the idea team and result in a lack of implementation of the great idea.

Idea Generators are the inventors, the tinkerers, the discoverers. You'll find them all over the place. They populate R&D departments, product development units, government research labs, government departments of policy analysis and research, and the faculties of colleges and universities throughout the world.

The Idea Promoters

The Idea Promoters often take the idea of the Idea Generator, recognize its application and potential, and begin to put the wheels in motion for implementation. On the upside, the Idea Promoters are enthusiastic, resourceful, charismatic, and positive. They refuse to succumb to defeat. If something doesn't work, they'll try something else. They willingly take risks, whether it's the risk of their own or someone else's fortunes. At the end of the line, they always picture success, a world where all their sunny predictions come true.

On the downside, the Idea Promoters can be so single-minded and driven that they fail to recognize reality. Often they won't listen to an opposing, negative view and won't hesitate to break institutional rules in pursuit of their dreams. Their enthusiasm can be overwhelming and often exhausting to other people.

The Idea Systems Designers

Idea Systems Designers, who get the idea from the Idea Generator and its application and vision from the Idea Promoter, envision how to assemble the financial, human resources, manufacturing, or other systems necessary to make the idea work. These are the planners and designers—the ones who picture what's needed to accomplish a desired end. They paint the broad strokes. By creating the organizational chart and mapping out the work that needs to be done, they predict and plan each step needed along the way toward realization of the idea.

The Idea Implementers

The Idea Implementers relish making things work according to the design set up by the Idea Designer. They would rather "go by the book" than question the way things are. They want to know what the rules are, what the policy is, what the required procedures are. Given those rules, policies, and procedures, they will meticulously follow all necessary steps toward the idea's realization. The downside, of course, is that they can be so focused on established procedures that they emphasize only limits and obstacles, in effect, offering up Killer Phrases based on established routine. When attuned to a new idea, however, they become the greatest allies of its success.

The Idea Evaluators

The Idea Evaluators have an opinion about everything. They're supposed to. That's what they do. They look at the way things work or don't work and reach an unshakable opinion about why they work or don't work. They have their standards, whether dictated to them by the organization or created by them according to their own opinions.

Whatever the source of these standards, they will apply them uniformly and consistently. They rarely accept things the way they are, always assuming that a flaw is just around the corner, waiting to be spotted by their discerning eye. This works both for and against the new idea, depending on whether the Idea Evaluator is careful and inquisitive, or just negative and critical. Of course, by applying techniques for defusing Killer Phrases and for selling within the organization, you can convert an Idea Evaluator who's ready to slap down your idea into one whose clear vision and fair assessment of the idea enhance the concept and execution.

Once these Idea People are assembled or identified, they should then be *appointed* to serve on the Innovation Team or encouraged to *volunteer* for membership on the team. The policies and procedures guiding their respective duties and efforts might look like this:

APPOINTED TEAM	VOLUNTARY TEAM
Given issues	Self-generated issues
Meets during work hours	Meets after hours
Four to seven participants	Four to seven participants
Elects responsibilities	Elects responsibilities
Staff assistance	No staff assistance
Reports every three months	Reports every three months or less
Needs to know funding limits	Needs to know funding limits
6–12 month commitment	Commitment determined by team

When the Innovation Team meets, it should follow the procedures already discussed for holding successful Great Idea Meetings. As it begins to work its magic, it can keep score to see whether its performance will receive the sought-after "rave reviews." A suggested "scorecard" follows in the Great Idea Action Sheet at the end of the chapter.

When the Curtain Goes Down

On the following Great Idea Action Sheets, I've provided a variety of exercises to help you get warmed up and loosened up creatively in your next Great Idea Meeting. At the end of the meeting, whether it's a meeting of your Innovation Team or of your office staff, you should make sure that you answer two key questions:

1. What now? and

2. Who needs to do what?

Every meeting must inspire the group to commit to the task at hand. The participants must know what they need to do as a group and as individuals. As they conclude their work, they should get some notion that something worthwhile has been accomplished. They should get a feeling of reaching "The End." At least for now.

Otherwise you'll just have to call another meeting to find out why the first one didn't work.

GREAT IDEA ACTION

INNOVATION TEAM SCORECARD

Check the actions or attitudes of the following members of an Innovation Team.

Idea Generator

- ❑ Generated a lot of ideas.
- ❑ Sought out new alternatives, new responses, new ways.
- ❑ Stressed achieving results over conforming to rules and procedures.
- ❑ Focused almost solely on ideas and concepts.
- ❑ Asked, "What if . . . ?"; didn't say "Here's why we can't . . ."

Idea Promoter

- ❑ Visualized the end result.
- ❑ Maintained optimism.
- ❑ Saw potential applications and impacts of new ideas.
- ❑ Refused to allow setbacks to derail enthusiasm.
- ❑ Communicated team purpose in a way that generated momentum.
- ❑ Promoted ideas to the organization.

Idea Systems Designer

- ❑ Encouraged atmosphere of openness.
- ❑ Buffered team from outside limiting forces.
- ❑ Saw the big picture to identify resources needed to complete the project.
- ❑ Created step-by-step procedures necessary for success.
- ❑ Defined performance standards.
- ❑ Provided structure and guidance.

Idea Implementer

- ❑ Saw to the details needed for overall team success.
- ❑ Filled in the blanks left by the Idea Generator and the Idea Promoter.
- ❑ Played by the book.

Idea Evaluator

- ❏ Displayed concern when deadlines were missed or policies were ignored.
- ❏ Provided feedback on team performance, based on the specified rules and guidelines.
- ❏ Made clear-cut decisions, when required.
- ❏ Ensured that resources were used productively.
- ❏ Made sure that projects were guided by clear plans and budgets.
- ❏ Insisted that performance standards were maintained.

Idea Recorder

- ❏ Accurately captured ideas and main discussion points.
- ❏ Did not edit ideas (other than to abbreviate or add explanations necessary for clear communication of the ideas).

Brainstorm Facilitator

- ❏ Managed the meeting-room logistics, provided an agenda, and explained the meeting's ground rules.
- ❏ Encouraged "Yes, and . . ." dialogue while defusing "Yes, but . . ." Killer Phrases.
- ❏ Established the meeting's start and stop times and monitored breaks.
- ❏ Discouraged unproductive side conversations.

GREAT IDEA ACTION
THE PAPER CLIP WARM-UP

This exercise is similar to the baking soda exercise from chapter 2, when you used it to open to your mind to new ideas. It's also a great way to encourage creativity at your next staff or Innovation Team meeting.

Take three minutes to write down as many uses as you can for a wire paper clip. Let your mind blast away in divergent directions. Think bizarre!

1.

2.

3.

4.

5.

6.

7.

8.

9.

10.

11.

12.

13.

14.

15.

16.

17.

18.

19.

20.

21.

22.

23.

24.

25.   43.

26.   44.

27.   45.

28.   46.

29.   47.

30.   48.

31.   49.

32.   50.

33.   51.

34.   52.

35.   53.

36.   54.

37.   55.

38.   56.

39.   57.

40.   58.

41.   59.

42.   60.

LIFE OF A BOOKWORM EXERCISE

This exercise challenges your problem-solving style. Are you analytical, spatial, or can you apply both modes when necessary?

Each of the four volumes depicted below has the same number of pages and the width from the first to the last page of each volume is two inches (5cm). Each volume has two covers and each cover is one-sixth of an inch (4mm) thick.

Our microscopic bookworm was born on page one of volume one. During his life he ate a straight hole across the bottom of the volumes. He ate all the way to the last page of volume four. The bookworm ate in a straight line, without zigzagging. The volumes are in English and are right side up on a bookcase shelf.

Challenge: How many inches (cm) did the bookworm travel during his life?

Your Answer: _____

 **GREAT IDEA ACTION**

THE NINE DOTS REVISITED

This exercise challenges your assumptions about the problem you are trying to solve. Are you willing to let go of your assumptions to find the solution?

Challenge: Connect these nine dots with four straight lines. (Once you start drawing the first line you cannot lift your writing implement off the paper. You can cross over another line, but you cannot retrace the same line.)

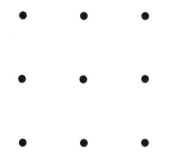

Now try it with two straight lines.   **Finally, try it with only one line.**

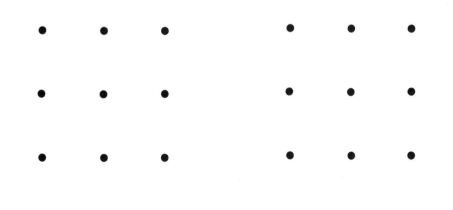

GREAT IDEA ACTION

MAKING THE STRANGE FAMILIAR

Acts of creativity usually can be reduced to small, common steps of discovery. Many of these involve turning seemingly unrelated, strange occurrences into sudden flashes of discovery.

Challenge: Decode the following groups of words and lines into common phrases.

For example, the translation of number 1 is *thermal underwear.*

Wear **thermal**	**me quit**
0 **B.S.** **M.A.** **Ph.D.**	**knee** **light**
r/e/a/d/i/n/g	**ecnalg**
t **o** **u** **c** **h**	**w** **o** **r** **h** **t**
moth **cry** **cry**	**iiii** **O O**

Then answer the following questions:

1. Did you feel a sense of discovery when you solved one of the puzzles?

2. If you saw each grouping again, would you also see the common phrase?

3. Did recognizing a pattern help you decode the puzzle?

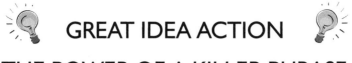

GREAT IDEA ACTION

THE POWER OF A KILLER PHRASE

This exercise shows the power of the Killer Phrase and the need for challenging it in everyday activities.

The historic conquest of North America progressed from east to west, following the New World's discovery in 1492. What if Christopher Columbus had given in to the Killer Phrase of the day—"Everyone knows the earth is flat"—and never set sail? Then, what if, years later, a courageous explorer sailing east from Asia had discovered the New World on the West Coast, thus leading to settlement from west to east?

Challenge: How would the United States be different in language, politics, religion, wars, food, sports, and holidays?

1. Language:

2. Politics:

3. Religion:

4. Wars:

5. Food:

6. Sports:

7. Holidays:

How would you have defused the Killer Phrase "Everybody knows the earth is flat"?

What Killer Phrases in years past have courageous individuals and organizations overcome?

Answers to Action Sheet Exercises

Answer to Life of a Bookworm Exercise

If you said nine inches (23cm), you attempted to solve this problem with a straight numerical approach. To get the correct answer you need to think first from a spatial point of view. The correct answer is five inches (12.7cm), because the first page of each book is on the right side of the volume. The last page is on the left side. Pull out four books, put them on a shelf, pretend you're the worm, and see that, indeed, your trip covers just five inches (12.7cm).

Three solutions to the Nine Dots Revisited exercise

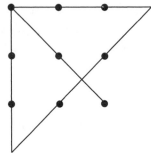

Typical Assumption	**Creative Action**
With four lines:	
Keep lines inside of box formed by dots.	Allow lines to go outside of the box.
With two lines:	
Use a standard pencil.	Use a wide marker that touches two dots.
With one line:	
Keep paper flat.	Accordion-fold paper between dots.

Answers to Making the Strange Familiar exercise

thermal underwear	quit following me
three degrees below zero	neon light
reading between the lines	backwards glance
touchdown	throw up
mothballs	circles under the eyes

Conclusion

Even though it may appear to involve a blizzard of details and analysis— and certainly control sheets, quality checks, and force fields strengthen that impression—*action* is a product of creativity and a field for the application of great ideas, just like every other step we've covered.

In our world, creativity isn't fully creative until we bring it into physical reality. As we saw in the third step, *creation*, your ideas won't make it into reality unless you see reality as something you can change. In *action*, creativity works on communication with the other people and organizations whose help you need to bring ideas to fruition. *Action* also involves a creative approach to your own internal order of communication and organization— your ways of evaluating, accessing, and using your ideas.

Having re-created reality by formulating ideas, we need to reorganize reality in order to make ideas work. This means we must do much more than simply exercise creativity in our own minds. We must see creativity as something we bring to our meeting with other minds. We may need to acknowledge that the most satisfying *action* of all could be the experience of working anew, with others, in creative concert.

CHAPTER 17

Ideas for Life

The Home of Creativity

As Yoshiro NakaMats suggests at the beginning of this book, creativity is no longer only 1 percent inspiration, 99 percent perspiration. Inspiration is now the critical creative force. Truly creative people derive inspiration from all facets of their lives—their work, their thoughts, their play, their family, their friends, and their home. Thus the creative process doesn't start and stop. It continues as an ongoing process.

If you don't already, you should take creativity home with you. You can cultivate a creative outlook in every member of your family, first and foremost, by defusing that Killer Phrase "I'm not creative" you hear so often uttered by those you love.

Here's a four-part process to spark your creativity at home.

Part 1: The Dinner Table

Listen to your family's dinner-table conversation, including your own, and see if you recognize any Killer Phrases or other stifling actions. Then ask everyone when and where they tend to have their best ideas and most significant feelings. Ask if they bounce these ideas off other members of the family. You'll probably find that we

don't make ample time to listen to the ideas of others, especially children and teenagers.

See if you can establish dinnertime as a "safe" place for new ideas, a time when anyone can bring up ideas that spring to mind. Then explain what Killer Phrases are. Confess which ones *you* tend to utter at home. Ask if there are any others your family has heard you say. Be prepared. You'll be surprised at the number of Killer Phrases you yourself use at home!

On another evening, after the dishes are cleared, pull out a large piece of white paper and show your family what Idea Mapping is all about. Start off by putting the Trigger Word *weekend* in the center and give everyone a pencil, pen, or crayon, and have them write down keywords describing what they want to do that weekend.

After a few minutes, have everyone step back to look at the big picture. Have one person draw arrows connecting similar ideas about new, more creative weekend activities. Another evening, do the same thing with the Trigger Word *vacation*. Or before a child's birthday, have her Idea Map the ideal gift.

After mapping the ideal gift, teach your family my favorite creativity technique: the power of opposite thinking. Have them Idea Map "What I would *never* want for my birthday." Then compare the maps and see if you can turn an opposite into a never-thought-of great idea.

Then, down the line, you can show your children how to use opposite thinking, metaphorical thinking, assumption challenging, and all the other creativity devices we've used in this book. Show them how many of these mental approaches can and do apply directly to their schoolwork. Have your child use an Idea Map as a preliminary outline for a book report or paper.

Part 2: Go to Your Room

Remember when "Go to your room" was the ulti-mate Killer Phrase, the ultimate punishment? These days, with many teenagers' rooms equipped with video games, access to the Internet, Instant Messenger, TV, and a host of other thought-provoking stimuli, "Go to your room" should become an invitation to creativity. (With this new stimuli also comes the

parental responsibility to monitor these creative interactions to prevent our children from saying, posting, or videotaping anything inappropriate or dangerous.)

A teenager's room should be equipped with a large marker board or butcher paper on the walls. Encourage your children to use Idea Mapping for their homework assignments. You'll be amazed how much easier it will be to remember the causes of the American Civil War if you Idea Map them with your children. Then leave the Idea Map on the wall until test time and watch their grades improve. A roll of butcher paper works great on the wall, because you can roll it up and refer to it later.

Many educators are now advocating background music during study time. I'm not referring to hard rock or rap, but rather to largo classical movements, those with beats slower than the normal heartbeat. As mentioned earlier in the interview with Dr. NakaMats, such music has been found to produce a sense of balance and to improve concentration.

Part 3: The Bedroom

If you think this section is about creative bedroom activities, you're right. Sex has been shown to increase creativity, by providing a break mentally and physically. Interestingly, abstinence also increases creativity, by providing for focused concentration. But other things happen in the bedroom, too. Sleep. And dreams.

A great deal of research has been done on the relationship between dreaming and creativity. A dream is our moment of pure creativity. It's like five hundred ideas all Scotch-taped together. In your dreams, which normally comprise 20 percent of your sleep time, you are the producer, the director, the actor, the cast of characters, and the cameraperson in your own epic.

Noteworthy Dreamers

Throughout our history, great thinkers have used and relied on their dreams as guides to the creative process. We've mentioned Friedrich von Kekule, the chemistry professor who in 1890 dreamed the solution to the structure of the benzene molecule and revolutionized organic chemistry. There have, of course, been many others.

In the 1850s, Elias Howe couldn't get his newly developed lock-stitch sewing machine to work properly. In a nightmare about being boiled alive, he noticed that the cannibals' spears all had holes in the tips. Howe awoke with the ingenious idea of threading a needle at the tip rather than at the middle, like conventional sewing machine needles, and solved his problem then and there.

General George Patton's personal secretary was frequently called on in the middle of the night to take dictation after Patton had been startled awake with a fully formed battle plan.

Alan Huang, the former head of AT&T Bell Laboratories' Optical Computing Research Department, used a recurring dream to make what *Success* magazine called "the greatest breakthrough in computer science since the microchip." In Huang's dream, two opposing armies of sorcerer's apprentices carried pails of data toward each other but stopped short of colliding. Then, one night, the armies passed through each other. To Huang, they were like "light passing through light."

For years Huang had been trying to solve the problem of creating an optical computer, using laser beams. The dream revealed to him that because laser beams would pass through each other, unlike electric currents, they each didn't need their own pathways. "Then I knew," Huang says, "there was a way." Huang went on to create the first working optical computer, transmitting data with tiny laser beams passing through prisms and fiber-optic threads.

Huang's message is to listen to the unconscious. "Too often," he says, "we are shamed into not going with our instincts." An inventor, he says, must be willing to look foolish; unique ideas can be lost through self-censorship: "Oh, that's ridiculous" or "It's just a dream" or "No one will understand." I think I understand Huang, because, like me, he's always struggled with dyslexia and so never felt comfortable with words and equations. But, "Early in childhood, he 'saw' mathematical equations as having shapes and colors" (Jason Forsythe, "The Dream Machine," *Success*, October 1990).

As the world's pace of change accelerates, left-brained "words and equations" analysis is often too slow to be effective. Many times it is the right-brained "shapes and colors" that defy logic—or it's the "blink" flash of insight that reveals the best solution.

Recording Your "Dreamed-Up" Ideas

I have found it very beneficial to record my dreams. For the record, we all dream and we all dream in color. If what springs to mind is the Killer Phrase, "I never dream" or "I can't remember my dreams," allow your mind to be open and read on.

Here are some steps to successfully remember, record, and interpret your dreams.

1. As you are falling asleep, state that you want to remember your dreams.

2. On awakening, do not open your eyes for at least one minute. Think back to any dreams that you had and play them back in your mind.

3. Record the dream immediately on paper using an Idea Map, and look for any metaphors that may symbolize a real-life problem.

4. Give the dream a title and file it for further reference.

Tomorrow Morning's Assignment

Use an Idea Map to explore one dream that you've had. If you can't remember one, try again tonight.

Record Your Semiconscious Ideas

Just as you are falling asleep and just as you are waking up are key times of free association. One music historian observed that Johann Sebastian Bach did most of his composing while lying in bed after a nap. (Reputedly, he also had nineteen children!)

Keep a pad of paper and a pen in front of your alarm clock so that the display provides some light. Be prepared to write down ideas or images you have right before falling asleep or immediately on waking up. Do not be discouraged if some of your thoughts do not make any sense. Remember, you're after large quantities of ideas. Just throw the bad ones away.

Part 4: The Bathroom

Remember the top ten idea-friendly times? Numbers 1 and 3 occur in the bathroom. Here they are again:

10. While performing manual labor.

9. While listening to a sermon.

8. After waking up in the middle of the night.

7. While exercising.

6. During leisure reading.

5. During a boring meeting.

4. While falling asleep or waking up.

3. While sitting on the toilet!

2. While commuting to work.

1. While showering or taking a bath.

The Greek scientist Archimedes was taking a bath when he realized that water displacement could be used to determine the composition of different metals in the king's crown. Ecstatic and quite naked, he ran to tell the king about his discovery, shouting, "Eureka, Eureka! (I have found it!)" If only Archimedes had had a pad of our Great Idea Notes, he might have saved himself considerable embarrassment.

So along with *Reader's Digest* and an adequate supply of Charmin, keep pads of paper and pens at hand in the bathroom. Right there in the middle of a shave, a brush, or a flush, you might come up with great ideas.

No End, No Limit

Some people think that our civilization is in decline, that we've lost our spark, that culture as we know it is crumbling. I believe that, to the contrary, what these observers are seeing is merely the evidence of profound, powerful change—change that demonstrates our growth and vitality. The most fundamental change I see occurring is the breaking down of barriers to the human spirit.

The creative human spirit has given notice that it cannot and will not be contained. Now we live in a time when it *must* be free, in order for us to find a way to live in harmony with our home, the earth. Because necessity is the mother of invention, and the necessity for change is so compelling, you can be sure that we're in store for some great innovations. And we can see everywhere that the human mind and spirit are rising to the task.

The spark that sustains our creativity could simply be called love, for I believe that the great thinkers, inventors, and artists of this world are those who love life and who feel free to give to it what they receive from it. In order for that spark to burn, we need to be free, within and without, as Yoshiro NakaMats says at the beginning of this book.

That's the precondition for creativity—and that's the wave we now see moving over our planet:

Freedom. What a great idea.

AFTERWORD

Become
Immortal

*A person who views the world at fifty the same as they did
at twenty has wasted thirty years of their life.*

—Muhammad Ali

According to Einstein, in a world without change, each day is the last day of your life. It is not the strongest of the species that survive, nor the most intelligent, but the one most responsive to change. Therefore, if the rate of change inside your organization becomes slower than the rate of change outside, the end is in sight. The only question is when.

So open your arms to change, but don't let go of your values. Forget your job title. You are now competing globally based on your knowledge and creativity, so what do you know and what do you create?

1. What makes you unique?

2. Are you a catalyst for ideas?

3. Are you curious first?

4. What do you do that adds measurable, distinctive value?

5. What do you do that you are most proud of?

6. Are you harnessing your creative energies?

Plato said that as humans we all strive for immortality. He showed us three ways to achieve this—by having children, by planting trees, and by creating an idea and making it happen.

Purposeful creativity seems to come when we are faced with a challenge that causes us to question things deeply, act deeply, and most of all, love deeply. My greatest idea came in the last year of my father's life, in 1991. I was trying to think what could I buy my parents for Christmas and all they kept saying was "Nothing. Just come home." My brother suggested that the family go on a cruise, but my mother killed the idea (apparently they didn't travel because "Dad gets constipated"). Under pressure, my mother said that she could use a new meat thermometer—hardly the meaningful gift I was hoping for.

Out of love, I used the opposite technique and asked my mother what she would "never" want for Christmas. She immediately said a bikini. We all laughed so hard that tears came to our eyes. Then she said a computer and then a new car and then . . . she was on a roll.

When my brother heard her say *computer,* he "flipped" the never into all of the things an eighty-two-year-old could do with a computer. When my mother heard about e-mail and genealogy software, she was intrigued. We got them the computer, but the computer wasn't the best part of the idea. It was all the neighborhood kids who started coming over to my parents' home to play with the computer and to teach my parents computer skills. My parents' language changed, their stimuli changed: Eight-year-olds were teaching eighty-year-olds.

Upon my father's death, we had to move my mother into an assisted living facility. What do you think she wanted in her little living room? The computer and the kids to help her with her online shopping.

Go forth, become immortal.

And, along the way, pass notes, write on walls, and stare at ceilings.

Your Creative Action Plan

1. State the challenge.

2. Then start with the end in mind.

- What is the result that you want to see, feel, and hear? Be specific.

- Why do you want to achieve this result? Be passionate.

3. What is your "blink" solution?

- Do some initial brainstorming of possible solutions to clear your mind of preconceptions.

4. Be curious first . . .

- What do you have to be more open-minded about to see new possibilities? Identify potential Killer Phrases that would stifle your creativity.

- What is unique about the challenge that you have not seen in another situation? Identifying its unique features can help you see the root cause of the problem or the seed of the solution that you need to grow.

5. Break out of old thought patterns by using creative stimuli and by reframing your challenge.

- What is similar to the challenge? What analogy can give you insight and strategies to benchmark? Think in terms of nature or music.

- How would another industry respond to this challenge? Think like Disney, Ritz-Carlton, Starbucks, NASCAR, or another country.

- Play the game of opposites. List the characteristics, variables, or ingredients of your challenge. Then ask: What if we reduced the first characteristic by 50 percent? What possibilities did we create? What if we doubled that characteristic? What possibilities did we create?

6. Visualize the opposite.

- Create an IdeaMap of ideas you would "never" suggest as possibilities. Fill up the map with as many "never's" as you can think of; don't challenge these "never's" until you fill up the paper.

- Then ask, What if we actually did this "never" idea? Could there be a breakthrough idea here? Write down your ideas.

7. Evaluate your ideas.

- Finally create an Idea Board. Take your ideas and put them on the wall or lay them out on a table. Rearrange them, combine them, and add to them. Be careful not to group ideas that, when combined, hide the unique value of the individual ideas.

- Use the Vital/Fatal Ratio on page 200 to rank your ideas.

8. Renovate while you innovate.

As you are creating ideas to implement, it is vital for you to identify unsuccessful or inhibiting ideas, programs, and policies to abandon. Four questions to ask are:

- What should we start doing?

- What should we stop doing?

- What should we do differently?

- What should we continue to do?

The energy released from abandoning unsuccessful programs will help drive your innovation efforts.

9. Present your ideas with passion.

Most people only think of one way to present their idea. This approach tends to limit the possibilities radiating out from the idea. Create at least two presentations for your favorite idea and see what you can learn from the divergence of approaches.

A few suggested presentation formats:

- The one-minute elevator speech

- The golf-cart strategy—selling the idea during eighteen holes of golf

- A one-page paper

- A commercial or magazine ad

- A highway billboard

A Final Thought: Be curious, be passionate, and be bold.

SUGGESTED FURTHER READING

Creativity

Cameron, Julia. *The Artist's Way: A Spiritual Path to Higher Creativity*. New York: Jeremy P. Tarcher/Putnam, 2002.

Csikszentmihalyi, Mihaly. *Creativity: Flow and the Psychology of Discovery and Invention*. New York: Harper Perennial, 1997.

Denning, Stephen. *The Leader's Guide to Storytelling: Mastering the Art and Discipline of Business Narrative*. San Francisco, Calif.: Jossey-Bass, 2005.

Gelb, Michael. *How to Think Like Leonardo da Vinci: Seven Steps to Genius Every Day*. New York: Dell, 2000.

Katz, Lawrence C., and Manning, Rubin. *Keep Your Brain Alive: 83 Neurobic Exercises*. New York: Workman Publishing Co., 1999.

MacKenzie, Gordon. *Orbiting the Giant Hairball: A Corporate Fool's Guide to Surviving with Grace*. New York: Viking Penguin, 1998.

Michalko, Michael. *Cracking Creativity: The Secrets of Creative Genius*. Berkeley, Calif.: Ten Speed Press, 2001.

Norins, Hanley. *The Young & Rubicam Traveling Creative Workshop*. Englewood Cliffs, NJ: Prentice Hall, 1990.

Pink, Daniel H. *A Whole New Mind: Moving from the Information Age to the Conceptual Age*. New York: Riverhead, 2005.

Sawyer, R. Keith. *Explaining Creativity: The Science of Human Innovation*. New York: Oxford University Press, 2006.

von Oech, Roger. *A Whack on the Side of the Head: How You Can Be More Creative*. Third ed. New York: Warner Books, 1998.

Wycoff, Joyce. *Mindmappinng: Your Personal Guide to Exploring Creativity and Problem Solving*. New York: Berkeley Books, 1991.

Zander, Rosamund, and Benjamin Zander. *The Art of Possibility: Transforming Professional and Personal Life*. Boston, Mass.: Harvard Business School Press, 2000.

Innovation

Christensen, Clayton. *The Innovator's Dilemma: The Revolutionary National Bestseller that Changed the Way We Do Business*. New York: HarperBusiness, 2001.

Christensen, Clayton. *The Innovator's Solution: Creating and Sustaining Successful Growth*. Boston, Mass.: Harvard Business School Press, 2003.

Drucker, Peter F. *Innovation and Entrepreneurship: Practice and Principles*. New York: Harper & Row, 1985.

Foster, Richard, and Sarah Kaplan. *Creative Destruction: Why Companies That Are Built to Last Underperform in the Market*. New York: Currency/Doubleday, 2001.

Hamel, Gary. *Leading the Revolution: How to Thrive in Turbulent Times by Making Innovation a Way of Life*. New York: Plume Books, 2002.

Johansson, Frans. *The Medici Effect: Breakthrough Insights at the Intersection of Ideas, Concepts and Cultures*. Boston, Mass.: Harvard Business School Press, 2004.

Kelley, Tom. *The Art of Innovation: Lessons in Creativity from IDEO, America's Leading Design Firm*. New York: Currency/Doubleday, 2001.

———. *The Ten Faces of Innovation: IDEO'S Strategy for Defeating the Devil's Advocate and Driving Creativity Throughout Your Organization*. New York: Currency/Doubleday, 2005.

Kim, W. Chan, and Renée Mauborgne. *Blue Ocean Strategy: How to Make the Competition Irrelevant*. Boston, Mass.: Harvard Business School Press, 2005.

Linden, Russell. *From Vision to Reality: Strategies of Successful Innovators in Government*. Charlottesville, VA: LEL Enterprises, 1990.

Moore, Geoffrey A. *Dealing with Darwin: How Great Companies Innovate at Every Phase of Their Evolution*. New York: Portfolio, 2005.

Robinson, Alan G. *Ideas Are Free: How the Idea Revolution Is Liberating People and Transforming Organizations*. San Francisco, Calif.: Berrett-Koehler, 2004.

Sutton, Robert I. *Weird Ideas That Work: 11 1/2 Practices for Promoting, Managing, and Sustaining Innovation*. New York: Free Press, 2002.

Thought Stimulators

Alexander, Shoshana. *Women's Ventures, Women's Visions: 29 Inspiring Stories from Women Who Started Their Own Business*. Freedom, Calif.: Crossing Press, 1997.

Carroll, Kevin. *Rules of the Red Rubber Ball: Find and Sustain Your Life's Work*, ESPN Books, 2005.

Collins, James C. *Good to Great: Why Some Companies Make the Leap—And Others Don't*. New York: HarperBusiness, 2001.

De Pree, Max. *Leadership Jazz*. New York; Currency/Doubleday, 1992.

Florida, Richard. *The Rise of the Creative Class: And How It's Transforming Work, Leisure, Community and Everyday Life*. New York: Basic Books, 2004.

Friedman, Thomas L. *The World Is Flat: A Brief History of the Twenty-first Century*. New York: Farrar, Straus and Giroux, 2006.

Gerstner, Louis V. *Who Says Elephants Can't Dance?: Inside IBM's Historic Turnaround*. New York: HarperBusiness, 2002.

Gladwell, Malcolm. *Blink: The Power of Thinking without Thinking*. New York: Little, Brown and Co., 2005.

Gleick, James. *Chaos: Making a New Science*. New York: Penguin Group, 1988.

Handy, Charles B. *The Age of Paradox*. Boston, Mass.: Harvard Business School Press, 1994.

Helgesen, Sally. *The Female Advantage: Women's Ways of Leadership*. New York: Currency/Doubleday, 1990.

Kohn, Alfie. *Punished by Rewards: The Trouble with Gold Stars, Incentive Plans, A's, Praise, and Other Bribes*. Boston, Mass.: Houghton Mifflin Co., 1993.

Land, George Ainsworth. *Grow or Die: The Unifying Principle of Transformation*. New York: Random House, 1973.

Lundin, Steven C., Harry Paul, and John Christensen. *Fish! A Remarkable Way to Boost Morale and Improve Results*. New York: Hyperion, 2000.

McDonough, William. *Cradle to Cradle: Remaking the Way We Make Things*. New York: North Point Press, 2002.

McGraw, Phillip C. *Self Matters: Creating Your Life from the Inside Out*. New York: Simon & Schuster Source, 2001.

McMoneagle, Joseph. *Mind Trek: Exploring Consciousness, Time and Space Through Remote Viewing*. Norfork, VA; Hamptons Roads Pub., 1993.

Packard, David. *The HP Way: How Bill Hewlett and I Built Our Company*. New York: HarperBusiness, 1995.

Peters, Thomas J. *Thriving on Chaos: A Handbook for a Management Revolution*. New York: Knopf, 1987.

Pine, Joseph B., and James H. Gilmore. *The Experience Economy: Work Is Theatre and Every Business Is a Stage*. Boston, Mass.: Harvard Business School Press, 1999.

Rotella, Robert. *Golf Is Not a Game of Perfect*. New York: Simon & Schuster, 1995.

Schwartz, Petter. *The Art of the Long View*. New York: Currency/Doubleday, 1991.

Scrage, Michael. *Shared Minds: The New Technologies of Collaboration*. New York: Random House, 1990.

Senge, Peter M. *The Fifth Discipline: The Art and Practice of the Learning Organization*. New York: Currency/Doubleday, 2006.

Yasuda, Yuzo. *40 Years, 20 Million Ideas: The Toyota Suggestion System*. Cambridge, Mass.: Productivity Press, 1991.

Zaltman, Gerald. *How Customers Think: Essential Insights into the Mind of the Market*. Boston, Mass.: Harvard Business School Press, 2003.

deBono, Edward. *Lateral Thinking: Creativity Step by Step*. New York: Harper & Row, 1970.

May, Rollo. *The Courage to Create*. New York: Norton, 1975.

INDEX